Felix Mitterer: A Critical Introduction

Studies in Austrian Literature, Culture, and Thought

Felix Mitterer
A Critical Introduction

Edited by

Nicholas J. Meyerhofer

and

Karl E. Webb

ARIADNE PRESS

Ariadne Press would like to express its appreciation to the Austrian Cultural Institute, New York for assistance in publishing this book.

Library of Congress Cataloging-in-Publication Data

Mitterer, Felix : a critical introduction / edited by Nicholas J. Meyerhofer and Karl E. Webb.
    p.   cm. -- (Studies in Austrian literature, culture, and thought.)
    Includes bibliographical references and index.
    ISBN 1-57241-010-8
    1. Mitterer, Felix, 1948- --Criticism and interpretation.
I. Meyerhofer, Nicholas J. II. Webb, Karl Eugene, 1938- .
III. Series.
PT2673.I79Z66   1995
832'.914--dc20
                        95-1618
                        CIP

Cover design:
Art Director & Designer: George McGinnis

Table of Contents

Foreword

Nicholas J. Meyerhofer

The metaphor that "all the world's a stage" is obviously quite ancient, but the theatre—that delightful admixture of display, ideology, social criticism, tradition and entertainment—has always been a particularly popular artifact in Austria. Even in the age of movies and television, the theatre remains in Austria a mainstay that refuses to be dislodged from the country's cultural and intellectual scene. Felix Mitterer, whose literary aspirations were jump-started in 1974 because of the tremendously successful play *Kein Platz für Idioten*, has continued his career as a dramatist, but also as a writer of scripts for television and cinema. Twenty years later, there is little doubt that Mitterer is Austria's most sought-after writer, and that he is to be numbered among the country's most important authors, as well. The fact that the plays of Mitterer—still a relatively young man in his mid-40s—have already been translated into languages and cultural settings as diverse as Hungarian, Welsh, American and Finnish is testimony to the universality of many of his themes, and there is no reason to suspect that either his amazing productivity or his international appeal will soon abate.

This introduction to Mitterer for an English readership, therefore, is really quite timely if not already overdue, and it will complement the newly published translations of this author's works by Ariadne Press. For both of us editors, this has truly been a labor of love, primarily because of Felix Mitterer himself, in whom we have discovered not only a significant and thematically fascinating writer, but also a humble, generous and ingenuous human being. On various occasions and most especially during the interview with him, Mitterer gave us his time and assistance on this project. Beyond this, he did so in unstinting fashion and with a generosity of spirit that astonished us; for these encounters, we are in his debt.

Any book such as this, of course, is the product of many collaborative efforts. My colleague Karl Webb and I wish to thank Dr. Donald Daviau of

Ariadne Press for his recognition of Mitterer's importance, and for his consistent support for this volume. We are also grateful to administrators from Northern Arizona University who extended to us financial support for travel and research, namely Dr. David Prior, Dean of the College of Arts and Sciences, and Dr. Karl Doerry, Director of the Office of International Studies. Finally and perhaps most importantly, we wish to thank Ms. Louella Holter of the university's Bilby Research Center; without her editorial virtuosity and tact, this volume could never have assumed its present form.

Nicholas J. Meyerhofer
Flagstaff, Summer 1994

An Introduction to Felix Mitterer and his Critics

Karl E. Webb

Felix Mitterer is without doubt one of the most popular playwrights in German-speaking Europe. His plays appear regularly on all of the major stages in Austria, including the *Landestheater* in Innsbruck, the *Thalia* in Graz, and the *Volkstheater* and *Burgtheater* in Vienna, and are regular program features on the stages of Munich, Bonn, Berlin, and Zurich. Small, provincial stages, particularly the one in Telfs, Tyrol and the public square in Stumm in the Zillertal, have become famous in their own right as the scene of Mitterer premiers. Despite this fact, however, Mitterer's contemporaries, Peter Turrini, Peter Handke, Elfriede Jelinek, and even the recently deceased Werner Schwab, are amassing quantities of serious scholarly attention and analysis, while Mitterer himself has been largely ignored, especially by literary scholars in Austria and Germany.

How does one account for this phenomenon, particularly given the enormous and growing popularity of his works wherever they are performed, his astonishing ability to attract world-famous actors to accept roles and famous directors to direct his plays, and the increasing number of awards and recognitions he is receiving?[1] Perhaps the following has something to do with it: Mitterer's plays, to a large extent, draw heavily upon his native Tyrol and its culture and traditions for their themes and structure. They remind us of the forms of folk art still current in Tyrol such as the *Schwank* (farce), the *Volksstück* (folk play), and the *Passionsspiel* (passion play), all forms which have tended to be ignored by historians of the theater and disregarded as being unworthy of serious analysis by literary scholars. In truth, Mitterer consciously holds to his connections with his homeland and its people and seeks to address their particular needs and concerns in his works. For this reason, he has resisted moving from Inns-

1

bruck to the theater capitals of Vienna or Munich, though he might well have been better served professionally and also in the eyes of the critics had he done so. His most important plays he has premiered on the small stage in Telfs, Tyrol as part of the annual Tyrolean Folk-Theater Festival (*Tiroler Volksschauspiele*).

Secondly, his style, which has often been described as a type of Naturalism, runs counter to the prevailing theater dramaturgy in much the same way as a "realistic" painting would have stood out in the New York of Abstract Expressionism. Mitterer rarely experiments with new structures, his characters are three dimensional and "human," and his themes come from the everyday life of the people. For post-modernist critics and scholars, it is difficult to re-orient oneself to these traditional ways and not to dismiss them on that account. The fact that Mitterer has also written for television, a "popular medium," gives further reinforcement to a basically critical stance. How could one be so successful in television and not compromise one's artistic standards, they might think.

Thirdly, there is indeed a certain naiveté and simplicity in Mitterer's person and in his works for which he has been criticized and which might have caused the scholars to ignore him. He admits to being an essentially self-taught writer and naturally draws upon his experiences in the theater of his homeland. Not all of his characters or his themes are as subtle, as oblique, or as "revolutionary" as those of other current dramatists. There are times when he clearly tries to combine too many ideas into one play, and the message gets confused. He has a tendency from time to time to preach too obviously, and in that regard some of his characters may appear too "wordy." These are all "flaws" which some of his reviewers, and some of his directors, have pointed out. On the other hand, it is just this straightforward honesty of his works and the genuineness of his characters, without the usual obscure and learned allusions or dazzling formulations, that reach out to the audience as other contemporaries are hardly able to do, and it is just these qualities which could effect the changes which Mitterer clearly has in mind with his plays. He seeks to go directly to the hearts and souls of his audience, and in that he apparently succeeds. He might indeed have found more critical resonance had he exhibited in his writing and in his person a little less directness and a great deal more cynicism, but that is foreign to his personality and to his artistic goals.

Whatever the reasons, the scholarly analyses are modest to this point, but let us consider them nevertheless. The secondary work consists of five separate articles and an interview with Mitterer himself:

1. Herbert Herzmann, "The Relevance of the Tradition: The *Volksstücke* of Felix Mitterer," *Modern Austrian Literature*, XXIV, Nos. 3/4 (1991), 173-182.
2. Deirdre McMahon, "The Resurrection of the Passion Play: Remarks on Felix Mitterer's *Stigma, Verlorene Heimat*, and *Kein schöner Land*," *Das*

zeitgenössische deutschsprachige Volksstück, Akten des internationalen Symposions University College Dublin, 28. Februar-2. März 1991, eds. Ursula Hassel and Herbert Herzmann (Tübingen: Stauffenburg Verlag, 1992), pp. 239-246.

3. Karl E. Webb, "Configuration of Power in Felix Mitterer's Works," *Modern Austrian Literature,* XXVI, Nos. 3/4 (1993), 143-152.

4. Mike Rogers, "'Nie sah ich einen dummen Jungen geistreicher dargestellt!' Zur 'Dummheit'-Problematik bei Felix Mitterer," *Das zeitgenössische deutschsprachige Volksstück,* pp. 261-269.

5. Gerlinde Ulm Sanford, "Brutalität und Zärtlichkeit in Felix Mitterers Volksstück *Die Wilde Frau,*" *Modern Austrian Literature,* XXVI, Nos. 3/4 (1993), 167-182.

6. "Felix Mitterer im Gespräch mit Ursula Hassel und Deirdre McMahon, 19. November 1988," *Modern Austrian Literature,* XXV, No. 1 (1992), 19-39. This interview was also reprinted in *Das zeitgenössische deutschsprachige Volksstück,* pp. 287-304.

The first three articles (Herzmann, McMahon, Webb) seek to place Mitterer's works within either the literary context of the *Volksstück* and the passion play, or within the cultural and historical context of the typical society of Tyrol. After a brief definition of the *Volksstück* itself, including in his opinion the typical passion play, Herzmann discusses examples from several of Mitterer's plays which appear to fit within this definition. He sees in *Stigma* a typical example of the Catholic passion play, incorporating structurally and thematically the stations of the cross, and he places *The Children of the Devil (Die Kinder des Teufels)* in that same context since its theme (but not its structure) incorporates and criticizes the Catholic folk traditions regarding probable witches and evil spirits and how they should be dealt with. *No Place for Idiots (Kein Platz für Idioten),* to his thinking, is a modernized, inverted peasant farce that includes the typical characters of the genre: the mayor, the *gendarme,* the cross wife, and of course the inevitable village idiot. The play is inverted, however, since the figure of the idiot is tragic instead of farcical as in the traditional form. *There's No Finer Country (Kein schöner Land),* which thematizes Nazi collaboration and collusion in the Tyrol of the thirties, is also built on this model, though again the theme is contemporary and deadly serious. Herzmann then compares Mitterer's *Coming Home (Heim),* a play about disaffected youth and their corrupted parents, with Karl Schönherr's *Handcart People (Karrnerleut),* one of the well-known and traditional folk plays of Tyrol. He recognizes Mitterer's use of the earlier play as a model for his own work. Finally, Herzmann comments on Mitterer's adaptation of the theme of Hofmannsthal's mystery play *Everyman* for his own play of the same name which had just been commissioned at the time of the writing of this article by the *Theater in der Josefstadt* in Vienna. Overall, Herzmann maintains that Mitterer has drawn heavily on the traditions he knew from his own theater experiences as a youth in Tyrol and that these traditions form a fundamental aspect of his works.

McMahon concentrates specifically on those Mitterer works which demonstrate aspects of the Catholic passion play: *Stigma, Lost Homeland (Verlorene Heimat),* and *There's No Finer Country.* In her discussion of *Stigma,* McMahon carefully delineates the main character's (Moid's) progression through the stations of the cross, comparing this progression with Christ's own in the New Testament. McMahon attributes to this obvious parallel the basic reason for the Church's extremely negative reaction to the play at the time of its first performance in Telfs. She herself does not view the play as blasphemous or as contrary to the passion play traditions. Rather, its theme, she believes, goes to the very heart of both in that it illustrates the need for a re-humanization of society on behalf of the poor and powerless. In *Lost Homeland,* McMahon emphasizes as typical of the passion play tradition the involvement of the entire populace of the Zillertal region of Tyrol in producing and acting in the play. She points as well to the historical topic, the expulsion of the Protestants from the Zillertal in 1837-38, as providing a close bond between the play and the *Zillertaler,* another usual feature of the Bavarian and Tyrolean passion play. The fact that Mitterer was commissioned by the residents of the Zillertal to write this play, and the fact that it can only be performed there once each decade, further illustrates the work's traditional heritage. Finally, McMahon likens *There's No Finer Country (Kein schöner Land)* to the same tradition because of its primary symbol, the cross, its stage setting in the village square (similar to *Lost Homeland*), and its obvious comparison of the main character, the Jew Stefan Adler, to the martyred Christ. It is interesting, of course, to note the differences in emphasis between Herzmann's and McMahon's analyses of the plays, but that has undoubtedly to do with some of the vagaries in the traditional forms themselves.

Webb is more interested in the social structure of the Tyrolean village in which many of Mitterer's plays take place and how this structure finds expression in his plays. He believes that the typical power relationship in the village between the farmer, the priest, and the politician, on the one hand, and the victims of this power—the children, the farm hands, the poor, the outsiders, the women, etc.—on the other, is clearly and realistically represented. In his plays, Mitterer unmistakably pleas for more understanding and concern for the disadvantaged and seeks to effect a positive change in their lives. Webb detects a further aspect to the power relationships, however, which has even more impact on all of Tyrolean society, the power holders as well as their victims. This is the invasion of destructive economic, political, and cultural forces from outside, such as the foreign tourists, modern industry, and modern pop culture. Mitterer is even more explicit in his criticism of these forces and sees in them the potential total dissolution of the society, both good and bad, of his homeland. The tensions within the traditional social and political world of the village, and between this world and the threatening external environment, form, in Webb's view, the fundamental social framework of Mitterer's Tyrolean works.

The other two articles (Rogers and Sanford) address specific thematic and linguistic aspects in some of Mitterer's works. Rogers is concerned with various problems of communication and with language, as demonstrated in two of Mitterer's plays, and how this affects the relationship between the characters themselves and between the stage and the audience. In making his analysis, Rogers concentrates on examples from the plays *No Place for Idiots* (*Kein Platz für Idioten*) and *Visiting Hours* (*Besuchszeit*). He demonstrates how Wastl, the mentally handicapped youth in *No Place for Idiots*, is able to fully communicate his true feelings directly to the other characters and to the audience by a simple, straightforward means of expression, unconstrained by the demands of polite society. The other figures in the play, however, speak a more refined language but communicate little and deceive a lot. Even Wastl's silence, for example in the pub scene where everyone speaks except he, is pregnant with meaning. Rogers claims that these forms of communication, real and feigned, between outsiders and those inside, represent the actual meaning of the play and not the specific plight of a mentally retarded person. Rogers compares Mitterer's use of this feature with similar attempts by earlier *Volksstück* authors such as Nestroy and Horváth, and he compares how each author illustrated the communication problem with a specific audience in mind. Mitterer's audience, in comparison to the others, is presumed to be less sophisticated but more susceptible to the condition of the disadvantaged and the outcast. In Mitterer's *Visiting Hours*, it is the outsiders—the old men and the imprisoned wife—who have the remarkable ability to express themselves truthfully and meaningfully while the insiders—the daughter, the husband, etc.— find real communication almost impossible. In this case, it is the outsiders' distance from society and its norms which provides the communication facility. Again, the constraints of polite society form the barriers to genuine expression for all the others.

Sanford undertakes an analysis of the play *The Wild Woman (Die Wilde Frau)* in terms of its contrasting expressions of brutality and tenderness, especially vis-à-vis the silent, mystical figure of the wild woman. While each of the five male figures, with the exception of the 17-year-old Wendl, expresses himself in a more or less primitive fashion indicative of his simple background, each, depending on age and station in life, is capable of not only extremely brutal and crude expressions and actions, but also of a kind of tenderness towards the woman that isn't so obvious at first. Some of this has to do with the puzzling qualities of the woman herself, who is both the helpless female sex object and the erotic, supernatural siren, well known from the legends of rural Tyrol. Sanford gives a careful analysis of both the brutality and the tenderness demonstrated and expressed by each of the characters and compares them one to another. At the conclusion of the play, Sanford believes, when brutality obviously gains control as the men graphically kill one another, the real meaning of the play becomes apparent: uncontrolled passions and brutality, however they might be justified, lead inevitably to self-destruction. The male figures, again with the exception of Wendl, illustrate that principle in utmost clarity.

The interview with Mitterer, conducted by Ursula Hassel and Deirdre McMahon, contains several interesting and important facts about Mitterer's background, his orientation, and his concerns both as a person and as an author. Mitterer, as usual, is very forthcoming. He explains his feelings in general, he talks about his humble background where he had little opportunity to get to know the traditions of world or German literature, and he discusses the influence he feels on his writing from the folk theaters of Tyrol. He seeks to write for all of the people, not just for a small group of intellectuals, and that is the reason why he is also so interested in writing for television, where he has the potential of reaching an audience of many thousands more. His object in writing is to cause us to think and to reflect on our previous assumptions about life. He is proud of his continuing close connections with the traditions and the people of his homeland, and he believes that he has finally gained their trust and that they know now that, for all the earlier controversy, he is not going to betray them with what he writes. He speaks of his serious interest in history and how he tends to over-research the historical topics from which he has taken his plays. He acknowledges the importance of strong women characters in his plays but contends that his purpose for writing such roles has more to do with his personal admiration for women and his desire that there be a true partnership between males and females than that he espouses any specific feminist objectives. He explores his relationship with the Bible and with traditional religion in Tyrol and admits that his real attraction is based primarily on the religious customs and not on the doctrines themselves. When asked, he speaks of his dismay that the Tyrol he knew as a child, despite all of its flaws, is being unalterably changed for the worse by the effects of the tourist industry and the technical advances of the outside world. Finally, he speaks of his future plans as a writer which include more work for children, more work for television, and a number of projects based on historical or current events, primarily as they have occurred in Tyrol.

In contrast to the sparsity of scholarly analyses, Mitterer's works have been considered in literally hundreds of newspaper reviews and articles over the years. These reviews are to be taken seriously because, unlike so many American reviews, their authors are usually well versed in literary matters and make a point of being informed on the traditions and current events in the theater in general. Of course, they have their own biases as well which must be taken into consideration when analyzing their comments. Still, these reviewers as a whole have contributed more than any other group to a general understanding of Mitterer's artistic production and to the specific strengths and weaknesses of his *oeuvre*. For that reason, they will be given a prominent place here. First, we shall undertake a general critical summary based on the reviews of the plays.

Newspaper interest in Mitterer's works began very tentatively with the first reviews of the Innsbruck performances of *No Place for Idiots* in 1977. As the play succeeded in gaining prominence on other Tyrolean stages (with Mitterer himself playing the role of Wastl), a wider group of newspapers editors took note. Finally, as *No Place for Idiots* was engaged by more prominent theaters in Salzburg, Linz and Vienna, Mitterer came to be recognized by some of the newspaper readers of these larger cities as well. The real breakthrough in newspaper attention came with the premier of Mitterer's second play *Stigma*, which was first performed in 1982 in Telfs at the Tyrolean *Volksschauspiele*. This play, with its controversial topic involving the stigmatization of Moid, a farm maid, caused so much stir among the conservatives and the Catholics in Tyrol that, as we have noted earlier, it was boycotted by the Catholic Church, the theater and the author himself received bomb threats, the mayor of the town in which it was originally to be performed condemned the whole enterprise, and a large security force had to be called out to ensure public order at the time of its first performance. All of this scandal drew the attention of the press, and Mitterer and the play were featured in extended articles in all of the major German-speaking newspapers, including *Die Zeit* in Hamburg, *Die Frankfurter Allgemeine* in Frankfurt, and the *Süddeutsche Zeitung* in Munich.

From that time forth, each premier of a Mitterer play gained increasing attention, even more so as prominent directors such as Ruth Drexel and Franz Xaver Kroetz became involved, well-known actors such as Fritz Muliar accepted parts, and theater directors as prominent as Claus Peymann sought to secure performance rights for his plays. Mitterer became a household name in Munich and in Vienna, and he received commissions from some of the most prominent theaters in both cities for new works. Naturally enough, these events and the subsequent performances received additional attention in the newspapers. At this point, each new Mitterer work can expect to be reviewed substantially in all of the well known periodicals in Austria, Germany and Switzerland.

Overall the reviews are very mixed, depending on the quality of the performance itself, whether the reviewer liked the play or not, and also what the general orientation of the reviewer is. *No Place for Idiots* has been generally very well received, beginning with its premier at the *Volksbühne Blaas* in Innsbruck and continuing throughout its long life of over 1500 performances to date. The reviewers in general clearly recognize it as representative of a Tyrolean folk play, and are therefore justified in overlooking some of its lack of subtleties in plot and characterization. Mitterer himself elicits positive evaluations for his earlier performances in the main role. The critics are generally moved by the topic itself, and except for their occasional dislike of the black-and-white quality of the text, they acknowledge this first work as the tremendous beginning of a promising career. The play has been performed all over Central Europe and has been successfully rewritten into several German dialects, including the North German *Platt*, in order to give it local currency.

The real divergence in reviews began with *Stigma*. The initial reviews essentially concerned themselves with the controversial nature of the play, particularly at its premier in Tyrol. Is it indeed blasphemous? Was the Mayor of Hall justified in disallowing the play's performance in his town? Will bombs actually be thrown at the premier? Even the German-speaking international newspapers ran long articles about these events. They conducted extensive interviews with the author and found him humble and approachable and surprised by the outcry. They detected, to their occasional disappointment, that he seemed not to enjoy upsetting his fellow Tyroleans and that this was not a media trick on his part to gain attention. When the premier took place despite all of the outcry, and all of the bomb threats against the play and against the author failed to materialize, the reviewers seemed disappointed. The play itself was anti-climatic and received less favorable reviews than it might otherwise have gotten. Some of the critics detected in the play a lack of plot coordination, an oversimplified set of characters, without depth, who had more to say than was necessary, and a gratuitous series of scenes such as Moid's gynecological examination on stage and her exorcism, both of which elicited unpleasant or even embarrassed reactions in the audience. When the play was premiered in Germany at the *Residenztheater* in Munich (1987), the reviewers generally praised the director, Franz Xaver Kroetz, himself a well-known folk play author, and his drastic changes to the plot and the characters in the play. Above all, they praised Kroetz for having eliminated substantial portions of the text and thereby increasing the tension and dramatics of the work. Some of the reviewers went so far as to name Kroetz the second author of the play. Other critics complained again about the explicit and for them embarrassing scenes involving Moid's exorcism and gynecology. This Munich performance of the play continues to be mentioned in later reviews of Mitterer's other works, and it is interesting to note that the reviews have become increasingly positive as time elapses. The play has become a kind of standard against which Mitterer's later works seem always to be compared. Like *No Place for Idiots*, it continues to find itself on the program of many theaters throughout Austria, Germany and Switzerland.

Visiting Hours, a series of four one-act plays, was first performed during the 1985 Vienna Festival at the *Theater Die Tribüne*. It has since become one of the most oft performed works by Mitterer, including a well-received performance in New York City in 1990. Like *No Place for Idiots*, it has been rewritten in other dialects, and it seems to have found real resonance with both the critics and the audience. It has the advantage of requiring little stage scenery and at most two characters per act. Although some of the critics complain that the work has little new to say to a contemporary audience, most others reflect what a Berlin reviewer, Andrea Hilgenstock, said of the performance at the *Statthaus Böcklerpark* in Berlin: "Even if you have already heard all of this before, you cannot hear it often enough until you finally learn something from it" (*Volksblatt Berlin*, November 29, 1987).

Dragon Thirst or the Rusty Knight or Black and White, Money and Bread, the Living and the Dead (Drachendurst oder der rostige Ritter oder Schwarz und Weiß, Geld und Brot, Leben und Tod) was premiered at the *Volksschauspiele* in Telfs in 1986 to generally enthusiastic audiences and reviews. There is debate about whether it truly is a children's play or whether it is a fairy tale for adults, but most of the reviewers found its fantasy world enjoyable. This was also true of the performance at the *Theater der Jugend* in Vienna a year later and at the *Wolfgang-Borchert-Theater* in the North German city of Münster in 1990. Because of its specialized topic, the play has not appeared as regularly as some of the other Mitterer works.

The Wild Woman also premiered in Tyrol in 1986 in the tiny *Bierstindl Theater* in Innsbruck and was reviewed at first essentially by local critics. It was later picked up for the season by the *Marstalltheater* in Munich where it gained a great deal more attention. The reviews are very mixed, ranging from accusations of "kitsch from the Alps" (*Münchner Theater Zeitung*, March, 1988) to "an old story which has nothing new to tell us about the relationships between men and women" (*Frankfurter Rundschau*, February 16, 1988) to "Mitterer ... has written here a piece about the peculiar sexually neurotic damage done in our society" (*Münchner Merkur*, February, 1988). It has regularly been compared with *Stigma* and has been either praised in that regard or has been found wanting. With the ensuing years, this work has gradually been more positively received and will eventually no doubt be considered one of Mitterer's most pivotal works.

Lost Homeland, the play Mitterer wrote by commission for the inhabitants of the Zillertal region of Tyrol, was performed in 1987 in the town square of Stumm, the only village in the Zillertal which still has all of the historical and visual requisites in place for the stage setting. Because its theme deals with the expulsion of the Protestants in 1837-38, the play had particular meaning for the local people, and more than 150 of them took part in the performance as either actors or stage hands and technicians. Like other passion plays in the region, *Lost Homeland* was performed throughout the summer of 1987 and will be performed again in ten years. The play received a great deal of attention by the large newspapers, but most of the reviews dealt exclusively with the historical event itself and with the difficulties of utilizing lay people in such a production. Generally, the reviewers were impressed by the abilities of the lay actors and the professionalism of the entire enterprise. They admired the fervor and the respect paid to the subject by the entire population and the restraint they exercised in prohibiting the event from becoming just one more tourist attraction for the summer.

There's No Finer Country premiered in 1987 in the *Landestheater* in Innsbruck. It was later performed in the famous *Volkstheater* in Vienna and then in the *Stadttheater* in Ingolstadt. Because of the relevancy of and the controversy surrounding the topic—the rise of the Nazi party in Tyrol in the years prior to and following the *Anschluß*—the play received much attention before its premier. Many critics were happy to see the topic finally being treated and looked forward to a full airing of the subject as a result of the play's performance. Since Mitterer's works increasingly found their source in historical events, the reviewers were careful to take note of the details of the life of the Tyrolean Jew, Rudolf Gomperz, upon whose story the play was based. After the long build-up, many of these same critics were a bit disappointed with the play itself and said so in their critiques. They criticized some elements of style, such as the play not being current enough in its dramaturgy, or incorporating too many sub-plots, or that the characters are given too much to say, diluting the dramatic tension, or that the original ending is too sentimental, etc. Other reviewers were much more positive, and in fact saw in this play one of the foremost documentations of Nazi collusion in Austria. Further, they comment on the immense relevancy of the topic since at the time of its premier, the Kurt Waldheim scandal was prominently featured in the news throughout the world. They even point to the final speech of the Mayor in the play as being reminiscent of Waldheim's own repeated attempts at dismissing his Nazi past.

Coming Home, which was premiered at the *Kammerspiele* in Linz in 1987, is about a young man who tries to return home to Tyrol after having fled northward years earlier and after having lived as a biker in Berlin and elsewhere in the meantime. He finds it impossible, of course, to come back, just as his alcoholic father and Fascist grandfather find it impossible to accept him for what he now is. The audience was apparently very receptive to the piece, but the reviewers essentially were not. It was perceived by the local critics as lacking real characterization and having a plot that seemed forced and unnatural. One reviewer even characterized the plot as a "Western in the wilds of Tyrol" (*Neues Volksblatt,* September 28, 1987). The play has not proved too popular since its premier, though there is apparently increasing interest in it since the *Schauspielhaus* in Zurich performed it in March of 1994.

The Children of the Devil is the first Mitterer play to have premiered outside of Austria. It was commissioned by the *Theater der Jugend* in Munich and was performed there in 1989. Because it again is based on a true historical event, an inquisition in Salzburg in 1675-1681 in which over 200 beggar children were put to death, the details of the historical facts got substantial emphasis in the reviews. Much was made of the fact that Mitterer found actual characters and passages from the historical documents to use in the play, especially the most sensational ones. Again, a few critics have concerned themselves with matters of form and structure and worry that the play is too long or too talkative. Some of these critics, for contemporary times, are surprisingly reactive to the crude and overtly sexual expressions of the beggar children. Mitterer claims to have taken these passages directly from the documents, however, and to have used them in order to substantiate the brutality of the times. Most of the critics have been very positively disposed toward the play, though, including Helmut Schödel in a long article in *Die Zeit* (April 21, 1989) and Christine Dössel in an extraordinarily positive review in the *Süddeutsche Zeitung* (April 11, 1989). These reviewers are impressed particularly with Mitterer's use of "antiquated" dramatic forms which, they believe, are just the ones to capture the drama of these events; they are also moved by the theme itself and by the ability of the playwright to create compelling characters from among these disadvantaged and rejected figures in society.

With *Siberia (Sibirien)*, a play about an old man who gradually wastes away in a rest home, Mitterer reached the pinnacle of his renown. He returned to the *Volksschauspiele* in Telfs for the premier (1989), which was judged by essentially all of the critics to have been a resounding and heart-rending success. The play was then engaged by the *Werkstattbühne* in Bonn where the reviews were mixed, primarily because of the production and the actor. Finally, it arrived at the *Burgtheater* (actually its affiliate the *Akademietheater*) in Vienna for an unusually emotional response by the audience to the actor, Fritz Muliar, to the director, Franz Morak, and, of course, to the playwright himself. For an Austrian author, there is no greater recognition than this. Martin Schweighofer (*Wochenpresse*, October 25, 1990) describes the scene as follows: "Susi Nicoletti [a famous *Burgtheater* actress] was the first who could not hold herself in her seat. Demonstratively, she sprang up, demonstratively, she held her hands high above her head, demonstratively she applauded those up on the stage. Not only Fritz Muliar, the celebrated soloist of the evening, understood this sign of approval (and bowed thankfully in the direction of his esteemed colleague ...). Following Nicoletti's example, the rest of the guests at the premier soon rose as well, row upon row, and demonstrated for their part what a standing ovation really is. Fritz Muliar, his friend and director Franz Morak, the author Felix Mitterer and the set-designer Herbert Kapplmüller were brought back on stage again and again by the continuing enthusiasm and the calls of 'Bravo' and were given the opportunity to indicate their obviously heartfelt gratitude at so much appreciation." To have an actor with the obvious talents of Fritz Muliar play the single role in this play helped immensely to make it a success, of course, but for the first time, there is very little criticism on the part of the critics about the play itself. After Vienna, the work was performed in a variety of theaters in Austria and in Berlin, and in 1993 it premiered in Sweden (in Swedish) and Los Angeles (in English). The production at the *Burgtheater* completed 100 successful performances and was broadcast over television by the Austrian Television Network. The critics have predicted that most of the older male actors in the German-speaking world will seek to secure this role for themselves at the first opportunity. They have also commented repeatedly on the highly personal and emotional impact the fate of the old man had on them and on the audience, and how this work contributes to an understanding of how Western society has so badly treated its elderly citizens.

In contrast, the following play, *Everyman (Ein Jedermann)*, which was commissioned by the *Theater in der Josefstadt* in Vienna, received almost universally negative critiques when it premiered in 1991. Even those like Ulrich Weinzierl (*Frankfurter Allgemeine Zeitung*, January 12, 1991), who truly dislike the classic mystery play by Hugo von Hofmannsthal upon which Mitterer's work was based, and upon which it to some degree serves as a parody, have judged the piece as boring, garrulous and ineffective. Those in the audience at the *Theater in der Josefstadt* who applauded and appreciated the production, he maintains, "will, as punishment, be forced to appear next summer in Salzburg at the Cathedral Square in order to submit themselves to an entire performance of the Hofmannsthal play. It's the least penance they should have to pay." Mitterer's modernization of the play, setting it as he does in the high rise office of a contemporary capitalist, is criticized as being too close to pop culture, bordering on kitsch, and overstepping the capabilities of its author. In the words of Helmut Butterweck (*Stuttgarter Zeitung*, January 18, 1991) the premier performance was simply "ein Flop." Interestingly enough, the production went on to have a highly successful run of over 70 sold-out performances. It later was picked up by the *Kammerspiele* in Linz where the production was judged to be a success by the local critics (*Oberösterreichische Nachrichten*, April 20, 1991).

Munde, a play about politics in the workplace and uncontrolled personal ambition, was written to be performed at the summit of the *Hohe Munde* (August, 1990), the peak which borders on the Tyrolean village of Telfs where so many of Mitterer's other plays have first been performed. The reviews, though fairly extensive, concentrate essentially on the unusual "happening" of such a performance and all the arrangements that had to be made, including those by the intrepid audience who had to scale the mountain, pack on back, to attend the premier. There is very little written about the play itself except for comments about the fact that it was hard to hear for all the wind up there, or that it didn't last very long for all that effort, or that Mitterer when asked why he wrote such a play said: "Once in your life you just have to do something like this" (*Der Standard*, August 6, 1990). The local papers, as one might expect, were full of letters to the editor from outraged citizens who could not understand how even a figure as prominent as Mitterer could get permission to abuse the mountain in this fashion. The play has been performed one additional time in Klagenfurt with modest success.

The television work of Felix Mitterer has had an enormous impact on his fame as a writer. His four-part series, *The Piefka Saga* ("Pfiefka" is the Austrian pejorative to describe the obnoxious German tourist from the North who invades Austria each summer), was seen by approximately 30 percent of the viewing audience in Austria. The two-part series *Homeland, Sold Out (Verkaufte Heimat)*, about the plight of the South Tyroleans during World War II, was a great success as well. The third part already contracted for was halted by the untimely death of Karin Brandauer, the director, but is again in the process of completion. As mentioned above, both Brandauer and Mitterer received a "Romy," the Austrian equivalent of an Oscar, for their work. Neither television series has received serious critical discussion in the same way as the plays have, but in the eyes of the public, and in Mitterer's own view, these works represent some of his most important work.

The most recent plays, *Amazing Fate (Das wunderbare Schicksal)*, 1992, and *Abraham*, 1993, have had too little time to receive much attention to this point. It remains to be seen what their ultimate impact will be.

Having gotten an overall glimpse of the critical reaction in newspapers to Mitterer's several plays, it is important now to consider in more depth some of the specific motifs that have appeared throughout the reviews. Let us begin with the negative critiques, in which several of the reviewers continue to dwell on certain stylistic deficiencies that they detect in the plays. They write that Mitterer includes too many disparate themes or perspectives that cannot be integrated into a unified work and that his plays are disjointed and confused. On occasion they use the word *montage* to describe his style. Renate Schostack, for example, in writing about the play *The Wild Woman (Frankfurter Allgemeine*, Feb. 5, 1988), says: "An antiquated obsession with witchcraft, which seeks to make the woman the cause of all evil, is combined here with a type of contemporary feminism that sees in the witch a kind of woman who is wise and who possesses a special understanding that is unavailable to the men in the play. Does progressive emancipation present such confused images? What kind of obsessive masculinity is working itself out in this play? This is truly a cloudy broth that Felix Mitterer stirs here." Gert Gliewe writes the following about *There's No Finer Country* in *Theater Heute* (June, 1987): "This technically solid piece nevertheless gets carried away at the end in a 'too-much-at-the-same-time' perspective and suffers throughout from the wordy desire of the characters to explain everything ..."

Also with regard to style, some of the reviewers criticize what they see as the black-and-white structure of his themes and characters, along with the cliché-ridden sentiments expressed. In the *Neue Zürcher Zeitung* (April

19, 20, 1987) a review of *There's No Finer Country* states that "Sometimes, of course, you realize that the extreme certainty of the views expressed are all too cliché-ridden." Eva-Elisabeth Fischer in the *Süddeutsche Zeitung* (April 27, 1980) describes the performance of Enzi Fuchs as the evil mother in *No Place for Idiots*: "In an admirable way, Enzi Fuchs tries to conjure up at least a few gray tones in her role as a raven-black cliché of a witch." And further on: "What is one to do as director with such a black and white piece of folkloric ... schmaltz?" Other critics support her view in calling the plays too sentimental, superficial, and kitschy. In his review of *The Wild Woman*, Hans Krieger states that "it is clear that what we have here is only a curdled variation of kitsch from the Alps. So far so silly. And so boring" (*Münchner Theater Zeitung*, March, 1988). Overall, this type of review leaves the impression that Mitterer may never have gained control of his material, that it is presented in a confused manner and that it lacks real substance and depth.

In recognizing that much of Mitterer's work originates in historical events or specific contemporary episodes, several of the negative critics believe that the author relies too heavily and too strictly on this material and that he acts more like a journalist than a playwright. They perceive that he includes too much detail in his "Doku-Drama" style and that his works display too little dramatic development and refinement as a result. Because of this "lack of artistic refinement" and "journalistic reporting," one reviewer uses pejoratively the term *Kolpertage* (cheap sensationalism) to describe Mitterer's works (Gert Gliewe, *Theater Heute*, June, 1987). Otto Hochreiter, in *Die Presse* (Vienna, April 18, 1985), writes the following about *Visiting Hours*: "It does not suffice just to be dissatisfied with the conditions of the world and to put that dissatisfaction into the mouths of one's preferred characters and to depend for the rest on a kind of similarity to reality. To call to mutual memory life's misery has very little to do with drama. Mitterer creates his figures mostly as modest narrators or as even more modest lead writers. When they occasionally really do react comically or tragically, in a dramatic sense, they are written so distanced that only the blindness of tears arises in the audience and no comprehension ... Mitterer's well-meant criticism of society is turned then in effect to an affirmation of the existing evil." About the play *The Children of the Devil*, H. Lehmann writes (*Tiroler Tageszeitung*, April 14, 1989): "No drama in the real sense. Only the same account again and again of an inhumane trial of children who have been taught by society that they must adapt at all costs. Since every connection to us of the historical period has been excluded, not explained or motivated or interpreted, only denounced from a contemporary point of view, one has to wonder what the purpose of recounting this horror really is."

Some of the critical reviewers also accuse Mitterer of pandering to popular taste and of incorporating strong elements of sensationalism in his works in order to attract public attention and increase attendance at the performances. These critics have detected what they believe to be an unholy alliance of pop culture and traditional folk clichés, as for example the fourth part of the television series *The Pfiefka Saga*. "A series of gags which in sum present a not always planned parody of James Bond, Terminator, Mad Max and other films of the fiction genre" (*Die Presse*, January 29, 1993). Others comment on the unsatisfactory "hodgepodge" of science fiction and Tyrolean sentimentality, for example in the play *Everyman*: "In awkward, exaggerated ways ... elements of science fiction are coupled with a sentimental garrulousness" (*Neue Zürcher Zeitung*, February 1, 1991). One critic, Margaret Czerni, has even compared the play *Coming Home* to a Tyrolean Western: "In this fashion, the play turns into an anachronistic Western there in Tyrol,... but the Wild West is not as wild as it used to be" (*Neues Volksblatt*, September 28, 1987). The most "sensational" theatrical endeavor in this vein, as per the critics, is the premier performance of the play *Munde* on the summit of the *Hohe Munde*. Norbert Cziep writes that "The genuine friend of nature, usually a loner, would find the spectacle [of the performance and its preparations] very disturbing because what took place in the play would have been just as 'average' in a traditional theater as it was at the summit ... The theme containing highly current conflicts was chosen by Felix Mitterer with his infallible sense of what is 'in'" (*Die Presse*, August 6, 1990).

Not all of the reviews by any means are negative, however. Among the positive critics, there are certain motifs which appear again and again as well. These reviewers admire Mitterer's honesty, his lack of affectation (despite the great amount of attention he receives), and his desire above all to communicate important social messages directly and straightforwardly to his audiences. Brigitte Ehrich (*Hamburger Abendblatt*, September 30, 1986) writes about *No Place for Idiots*: "A play about a mentally retarded boy? Is such a thing possible without making the audience feel uneasy? It's possible! Felix Mitterer, having grown up himself in a poverty-stricken village atmosphere, knows first hand the milieu that he describes. And it's not only pertinent for the Tyrolean Alps, it can apply just as much to the Lüneburger Heide ... An emotionally stirring performance which utilizes deep feelings to cause one to be impacted for a considerable period of time afterward. With such a topic this is both permissible and effective." Also writing about *No Place for Idiots*, Jutta Höpfel states that "His [Mitterer's] message is so valuable ... that it deserves to be performed in many theaters. It is a didactic piece, but without the pointed finger of a lecture; it is modern literature without exhibitionist errors in taste, a play just as we need it in theaters today" (*Kultur*, September 17, 1977). The same sentiments appear in reviews of Mitterer's much later and most famous play *Siberia*. Grete Müller writes that "Felix Mitterer ... is a moralist, a fighter against injustice and indifference among people. [He directs his attention] toward those uncomfortable figures at the edge of society who are exiled from it. In this play, it is the old people, those who have become useless, those whom we euphemistically call 'senior citizens' and deport to institutions ... To demonstrate clearly, or more exactly, to cry out about this injustice is Mitterer's only concern, and the dramatic form only the means to an end" (*Südkurier Konstanz*, November, 1990). Michael Cerha, while recognizing certain deficiencies in Mitterer's literary techniques, states (about *Siberia*) that "Mitterer's strength lies in his ability to have his characters present all the arguments which the people on the street are incapable of presenting. In his powerful moments he is a philosopher of the naive in the best sense" (*Der Standard*, August, 4, 1989).

Mitterer is positively recognized, by implication above, and explicitly in several analyses below, as a natural talent who is unaffected by and uninterested in the theatrical traditions and trends going on around him. Peter Kraft calls him "a great auto-didactic talent" (*Salzburger Nachrichten*, June 29, 1981). Duglore Pizzini says about his purposes and style that "As always, the author is not concerned about the finely crafted brilliance of his text, but rather with an evocation of sympathy for his characters. One could even consider it an appeal on his part ... to the conscience of society. He is concerned with a message, therefore, which in fact then materializes on the stage, although its translation does not attain the higher literary plateaus ..." (*Die Presse*, October 22, 1990). Heinz Sichrovsky writes about *Visiting Hours* that Mitterer has particular, natural talents for recreating realistic dialogues from the simple people, which lead irrevocably to the audience's own experiencing of their fate. "The exactness with which Mitterer observes simple people is timelessly new. His dialogues have an impact because they are real. Without any current, special dramaturgical devices or any tricks of alienation he is able to get the audience interested and then to bring them to the point where they experience it themselves. This is because he touches all our fears as well as our bad consciences" (*Arbeiter Zeitung*, April 18, 1985). Some of the critics are especially delighted with Mitterer's sense of imagination, which is particularly on display in his fairy tale play *Dragon Thirst or the Rusty Knight*. Typical are Elisabeth Moorwessel's comments in the *Frankfurter Rundschau* (April 19, 1990): "Mitterer uses without hesitation all of the overflowing sources of imaginary figures and constructs with them a fanciful and incredible fairy tale plot. Of course, there is a beautiful virgin ... who is captured by the bloodthirsty dragon. Naturally, there is a mild and loving fairy queen who makes everything good at the end. And sometime or other, as expected, a brave and yet somewhat naive dragon slayer appears, burning with love and constantly exasperated by a bothersome imp ... An anarchic and wild and in part primitive story by Felix Mitterer—written in *Knittelverse*—which gives the wild goings-on an additional appeal ... a wonderful theater evening, an unusual success."

The critics also praise and are astonished at Mitterer's choice of themes because of their social immediacy and relevance, and they project that his plays will thus exercise a genuine and positive impact upon the audience. (This view, interestingly enough, stands in stark contrast to some of the negative critics' opinions that there is little in the plays that speaks to a contemporary audience.) The positive critics, for example, point to the relevancy for modern society of the theme of *Siberia*. They mention in that connection the incredible coincidence of the play's appearance at the *Burgtheater* just days after it was revealed that a group of nurses at the Lainz rest home outside Vienna had been caught murdering some of their more bothersome inhabitants by lethal injection. Mitterer's *No Place for Idiots* was performed extensively during the "Year Commemorating the Mentally Handicapped," serving as a dramatic vehicle for illustrating society's failures in this regard. The pertinence of *There's No Finer Country* to the Waldheim affair has been mentioned above. In general, however, whether there is a specific temporal appropriateness or not, the plays are viewed as having illustrated vital and basic problems that need to be faced in modern society, such as the plight of the poor, the gender biases against women and their overall role in society, and the need for Austrians to confront their political past. Mitterer is praised for having given expression to these issues in a manner that exercizes a positive and even profound influence.

Finally, these positive critics believe that part of the reason for the enormous impact that Mitterer's plays have had on their audience is the genuineness and the ring of reality that particularly the interpersonal relationships exude. Lona Chernel (*Wiener Zeitung*, April 18, 1985) writes the following about *Visiting Hours*: "Mitterer relates his vignettes with a real sense for people. And he attempts absolutely not to draw in black and white or to attribute total blame to anyone. He describes situations, he describes reactions ... it is not completely harmless to illustrate such problems without pointing to possible solutions. But it is also essential to have such discussions because without them no change or new way of doing things is possible." Following the performance of *Stigma* in Linz, the *Landestheater* organized a lecture by Dr. Erwin Ringel, a local, well-known Freudian psychologist, to address the extent to which the characters in the play had psychological validity. Professor Ringel described the plot as "highly realistic." He also described the clinical hysteria, the typical neuroses, and the other psychological illnesses exhibited in the work. He believed, particularly, that the maid, Moid, displayed typical and specific sexual neuroses in her apparent stigmatization. As reported in the paper, the theater hall was absolutely full for both the performance and the lecture. The theater reviewer assumed that the impact would be enormous upon those who attended (*Oberösterreichisches Tagblatt*, June 5, 1985). Helmut Schödel (*Die Zeit*, April 21, 1989), in writing about Mitterer's *The Children of the Devil*, finds just the opposite of "real" conversations or relationships. He anticipates, nevertheless, no lack of impact upon the audience. He sees in this play a kind of occult reality which is no less potent and effective: "This Mitterer piece is also gloomy, stifling, and puritanical (and completely uninterested in modern dramaturgy) ... *The Children of the Devil* demonstrates that he [Mitterer] has no need of such modernizations. You go through this "out-moded" play as through a broken soul ... Mitterer is no "enlightener," but rather an exorcist. In these times of horrible plagues, black masses and the Ayatollahs, he actually appears pretty modern ... Felix Mitterer is still chronically undervalued as an author."

While additional reviews could be cited, the above evaluations, both positive and negative, represent the scope of what has been written about Mitterer's plays. These and the scholarly articles discussed earlier provide, of course, much additional material to help in the understanding of the playwright and his works, but even the casual observer will recognize that much more remains to be done. Perhaps given Mitterer's young age and continuing productivity, we can expect the situation to change in the future. Perhaps as his works also become better known outside the German-speaking world there will be more recognition of his importance by scholars and critics. The editors of this volume and of the recent volume of Mitterer's plays in English[2] have in part that purpose in mind. If that is the result, we will be sincerely gratified.

Notes

1. The Peter-Altenberg-Prize in 1984. The Peter-Rosegger Prize of the State of Steiermark in 1987. The Tyrolean State Prize for Art in 1988. The Decoration of Honor for Service to the Republic of Austria in 1991 (refused). The "Romy" (the Austrian equivalent of an Oscar) for his television play *Homeland, Sold Out (Verkaufte Heimat*).

2. Felix Mitterer, *Siberia and Other Plays* (Riverside, CA: Ariadne Press, 1994).

Felix Mitterer Interview

Translated by Nicholas J. Meyerhofer

Conducted at Mitterer's home in Innsbruck on 14 March 1994
with Karl E. Webb and Nicholas J. Meyerhofer

KEW: Felix, the English-speaking public that will be reading the book in which this interview will appear really knows very little about you and your biographical background. Perhaps we could begin from this standpoint and then get more specific with respect to our questions.

NJM: This will no doubt mean giving information that you may feel you've given many times before, but it's important for our English readers to have this glimpse of where you came from, how you got from there to here.

KEW: I'd suggest starting with the Tyrol, of course, since this is where you are from and since this is so fundamental to so many of your works.

NJM: And perhaps how you came to be a writer in the first place, too.

FM: Well, these of course are matters that I have discussed on many occasions with interviewers in the past, but I'll try to give you both a short version of the biographical introduction that you are asking about, and if I overlook something that you consider essential, then you can supplement what I am saying with the information contained in volume two of my collected works.

Well, first came reading—reading came before writing— and reading was, for me as a child, a kind of flight from reality. As

19

is indicated in my published biography, I grew up as the adopted child of farm laborers in Tyrol, where life was not easy and where flight from reality via daydreams and reading was desirable. At first it was difficult to get something to read, since there wasn't much reading material of this sort in the country in the early 50s—this was seen as a waste of time. But I somehow managed to get hold of serialized novels, westerns and science fiction—things of this sort—also a few comics now and then, along with peasants' calendars, which were always meant to tell a story, of course. These latter didn't satisfy me much, however, since they told stories about precisely the milieu from which I wanted to flee.

And then a bit later we had summer guests on the farm from Vienna, a woman teacher with her daughter; she brought me the first real books. I can't remember most of the titles anymore, but I do recall that Edgar Rice Burroughs'*Tarzan* was among these books and that this fascinated me. Now *here* was a completely new world for me! Also among these books were the collected works of Mark Twain, and I really enjoyed these, as well.

As for writing, well, I discovered I had a certain talent for writing when I began to do essays for my lessons in grade school. Most of the time, of course, I ignored the assigned topic and just began writing about what interested me—the same thing is happening to my daughter now in school. But my teachers noticed I had a certain talent anyway, and ...

NJM: If I could interrupt for a second, Felix: does your daughter Anna have the same inclination to become a writer?

FM: Yes she does. Actually we started doing a book together some time ago, and the fact that it still isn't finished is entirely my fault. It is an interesting story actually.

NJM: What's it about?

FM: It's called *Madame Marie, The Opera Cat, or The Quest for High C*. It takes place in Venice and also has to do with the fact that my Anna wants to become an opera singer some day. Anyway, the story begins in the eighteenth century, at the time of Casanova, and concerns a Venetian countess, an opera singer, who is thrown into prison and who, as she expires, sings a beautiful high C. This high C is captured and placed into a marble casket by her captor, who keeps it hidden from his servants. He is finally killed because he keeps on beheading his servants and such. Time passes until, at the beginning of this century, there is a search for this high C, you know, with different groups after it, including the Mafia etc.

Anna has these artistic tendencies not only from me, but

she also has her interest in graphic design from my wife Chryseldis; Anna has been drawing ever since she was old enough to hold a pencil. But back to my life. I then started writing down my own stories outside of school whenever I got the chance. These were also stories that had absolutely nothing to do with the world in which I lived—some even took place in Arizona! Yes, they were really violent stories from the Wild West, with guns and whips and so on. And then there were also gangster stories from Chicago, Soho and London, along with trying my hand at science fict—strange stuff. Unfortunately all of these early attempts are buried and lost forever. That's because my mother had a small house on swampy ground next to a river, and every time there was a serious storm, everything in the cellar would get flooded—the rations of butter and detergent and food specials that had been stored—and my childhood manuscripts were also down there and were finally left when the house was abandoned.

One day my grade school teacher asked me what I wanted to be when I grew up—I was about 10 at the time—and I answered, a writer. I kind of whispered the response since I felt that this was a pretty absurd answer to his question. I didn't really say 'writer' as such but rather 'journalist', and he answered that this wasn't much of a profession, I'd have a tough time making a living this way and so on. And sure enough, a bit later on we had as a guest on the farm an actual journalist from the *Tiroler Tasgezeitung*, a man named Zetser, and I told him about my plans. He went to my parents and told them that whatever happened, I shouldn't be allowed to pursue journalism, since it was a profession that was only good for going hungry, and that I should study something sensible instead. Apparently he didn't have much use for his colleagues in the journalistic profession. A little later my teacher came back to me and said I really had two choices in terms of a profession, either to become a priest or a teacher. Of course, studying to become a priest would have meant basically a free education—studying in a Catholic seminary and so forth—but I didn't want to become a priest. So I promised I'd attempt to become a teacher, and for his part, my own teacher promised to try to get scholarships for me to help me out, since my parents were quite poor. But when I turned 14, there was suddenly no longer a need for servants and hired farmer laborers—it seems we jumped from the nineteenth to the twentieth century all at once, what with the onset of modern machinery—and my parents were both out of work. So my mother began working as a cleaning woman in small hotels in the area, and my father started working as a road sweeper in Kitzbühel, a job he held until he died.

NJM: What was the name of this teacher, and is he still alive?

FM: Yes, he's alive and lives in Kirchberg, where I went to grade school for seven years. His name is Herbert Sojer; he's very much alive and helped me out a great deal.

NJM: Are you still in contact with each other?

FM: Yes, we're still in contact, unfortunately not so often any more, but we're still in contact once in a while. He is the one who drove me to Innsbruck at the end of June, 1962, where I was to begin my course of studies at a teachers' training school. I took my immatriculation exams and passed them—but with only an average grade in German, a situation which greatly disturbed Mr. Sojer, who didn't understand how the student who had been writing such wonderful essays could get such a middling grade in German, of all things!

In the fall I started my studies in Innsbruck. I had lodging in a Catholic boarding house and, in general, was extremely happy to be away from home. Most of my classmates who came from the Tyrolean countryside had horrible homesickness, but not me. I didn't miss the extreme poverty I had left behind—not a poverty which led to starvation, but a poverty that was bone-grinding in that it demanded, in the case of my mother, that one work like a dog in order to make ends meet—which she did until her death. It ruined her health and her nerves, and for this reason she also treated my very very badly. This of course pained her a great deal later on.

At any rate, I was very happy to be away from home, and for me Innsbruck was a metropolis—I had never been in a city before. There I discovered the movies; I had only been to a movie twice before in my life, once in Kitzbühel—maybe around 1954, or was it 1956—and then once with my father, when I saw *The 10 Commandments*, starring Charlton Heston. This was the very first time my father had been inside a movie theatre and he was quite old by then. He found it so disturbing that he never went back to another movie for the rest of his life, simply because this wasn't a "reality" that he could come to grips with, the parting of the Red Sea, the Egyptians whipping the Israelites and all that. So he resolved never to go to another movie, whereas the entire experience fascinated me completely. And then of course I saw *Ben Hur* shortly afterwards; it was terrific, too.

At any rate, I went to school in Innsbruck and was very happy there indeed. The money that I spent on movies was of course spending money that was supposed to be used for school supplies, but I always came up with excuses and white lies about what I was using this money for—which of course led in turn to a bad conscience, but this was certainly a big influence on me at the time. The second major influence was the school's library, which contained the masterpieces of world literature in German, and I devoured everything there was from French and British and American authors, to the extent that I began to neglect my school work. Complicating this situation was the fact that I was shy, and my teachers for the most part seemed to express themselves with a kind of cynicism that was unfamiliar to me. I was used to being mistreated physically, but cynicism was something that I couldn't deal with adequately, simply because I was too naive to understand how to deal with it. I frequently embarrassed myself and felt inadequate. Math and Latin were difficult for me, and they became progressively more difficult.

During my vacations I always worked in a bakery and a grocery store in Kirchberg. I also mentioned this is my published autobiography, the fact that this bakery was a particular delight for me, such that I stopped visiting my poor mother who only lived half an hour away. And at this time I also continued writing fictional pieces, short "Who Dunnits" and stories, things that were popular at the time because of illustrated magazines that featured such works, not just by German-speaking authors but also pieces by people like Alfred Hitchcock. So I imitated these short stories in my pieces. And then at this time I read an ad in a newspaper that promised to get such pieces into print, so I sent in some handwritten work I had done. Nothing ever came of this youthful attempt—thank God.

Back at school things continued to go downhill, and I had a very bad conscience vis-à-vis my teacher Mr. Sojer, since I was doing so badly in Math and Latin. I felt indebted to him and began going out of my way to avoid him. No doubt this bothered him, especially after he had done so much to get me into the school, secure a scholarship for me, etc. And I suffered horrible pangs of conscience and was totally ashamed.

At the age of 16 I decided to emigrate to England and get away from everything. In Rotterdam the police caught up with me and sent me back home. I told my parents that I didn't want to go to school any longer, that I wanted to become a writer instead. They said fine, if you don't want to go to school, then you can find a real job and learn what work is. My problem with their suggestion was that to that point I had only been a student and didn't know a thing about practical matters or working as such. But later I did have an acquaintance who worked in the customs office, and he mentioned to me that they had a position opening up and asked if I was interested. I said sure, I'd like to take the job, and I took up this post in Innsbruck—not at the border as such, but rather at a desk filling out customs declarations.

And I liked this job quite a bit, actually, since it gave me the chance to have some time to myself and get my bearings again. Of course, I was a horrible customs official, constantly coming late to work and having no real interest in the job. I had shoulder-length hair, and my colleagues were not pre-disposed to like me, which I can very easily understand. At any rate, this was 1966, and I was 18 at the time; I didn't earn much and as a result stayed in a so-called Kolping-House, where I boarded cheaply with other apprentices. Kolping was a priest in the nineteenth century who founded these houses for people in precisely my situation, especially in the cities.

About this time I started to get interested in politics, too— 1968 was just around the corner, after all. I didn't take part directly in any political activities but did follow these events closely in the newspapers and magazines of the time: *Spiegel* in Germany, *Pardon* and *Konkret* here and so forth. And at this time I also began to come to grips with my own background, with the milieu in which I grew up and why conditions were what they were, with my mother and the way she had treated me.

NJM: I think that it's necessary to be gone from home for some time before one is capable of getting the requisite emotional distance to a parental situation such as this.

FM: Yes of course, and that's what I did. Before this it was too emotional for me, just a matter of accusations and counter-accusations and hurt feelings and what you did to me and back and forth. But finally I gained some appreciation for my mother's situation and what she had to endure, and I started going home to visit once in a while, I mean aside from the required times such as Easter and Christmas. And I got to know my adoptive parents better through these visits; not that I ever had any difficulties with my adoptive father, that wasn't the case at all. He was a fine man who helped me a lot and without whom I never would have made it.

And suddenly it was as though I could now write about the world from which I had come. Chicago and Soho were now over and done with, and I was writing about my own milieu.

NJM: If I may interrupt for a moment: your style, then, you always had from the very beginning, but your thematic nexus—

which in your case has to do with the milieu from which you came—that you arrived at later?

FM: Yes, yes that's right. And I began with stories—prose— although the very first piece published in essence comprised dialogue and was broadcast by the ORF in 1970; it was a brief monologue that I myself had narrated on tape.

My colleagues at work began noticing that I was writing things all the time, and they started to treat me not only with understanding but respect, since they decided I must be some kind of artist and, after all, artists are just a bit crazy anyway. And besides, when you work together for years, you get used to each other, regardless of whether you have long hair or not. It wasn't always easy for me to go to the office each and every day to perform this stupid job, but it afforded me the chance to do what I wanted, namely my writing. Besides, I always knew I'd be able to move on and get away from this job some day. Of course, I thought it would just take a couple of years when in fact it took me 11, but that's the way it goes.

Gradually I got things accepted in newspapers and magazines with increasing regularity and then, in 1977, my breakthrough of sorts came with my first television film and first book. And these enabled me to leave my job.

KEW: The topic you just mentioned, television and writing for it, is an interesting one. That must be a completely different kind of writing experience for you, say when compared to something like writing for the stage. Isn't that true? And just how did you get started doing this kind of writing?

FM: It got started through a contest sponsored by Radio Austria entitled "Stories from Austria." Prospective authors from each Austrian state were supposed to write something about their respective region. So I decided to submit something about my office situation and my colleagues there and myself, of course disguised with fictitious names. And this story was eventually filmed, although it was initially performed on stage. The director from Vienna had problems with adapting my script for the stage, which was to be expected. I simply had to accept his modifications.

And at this point in my life I was writing plays for the stage and scripts for television at the same time; for me the two have in common the fact that dialogue is at the heart of the matter. Film is of course much more expansive, what with 90 or even 100 different scenes. But critical for the medium of film is the question of theme—some themes are simply better suited for a television film, in my opinion. Works such as the *Piefke-Saga* or *Verkaufte Heimat*—they simply couldn't be performed on stage; there are too many characters, the requisite landscape cannot be reproduced, and it's too long.

NJM: So you wouldn't actually say that you prefer writing for one or the other medium, television or the stage?

FM: No, I wouldn't say that I prefer one over the other, and I would like to continue writing for both. For me theatre is so original, so direct—I could never let go of theatre. Theatre of course is more stylized, even if it is realistically presented; it's still more stylized that what one does for television. And t.v. offers the possibility of reaching millions of people.

NJM: One aspect of the medium of television is that you as author work so closely with a respective director on your project; who actually has control or the final say when this happens? And are there some directors with whom you work particularly well?

FM: You're right of course, to mention this difference. As an author, if things don't go well at the premiere of a play of mine, then at least I know that there will be subsequent performances at which these difficulties can be ironed out. One doesn't enjoy this luxury with television, but I must say that to date I've been pretty lucky with the directors I've worked with and have been happy with the end results.

NJM: And the question of your input on a given project, on who has the final say-so? Do you enjoy total control over aesthetic matters?

FM: No, but I do have a fair amount of input in determining how one of my films is made. You see, most of the t.v. films have taken place here in Tyrol, and often it's been me who has suggested which actor should play whom in a film. In the *Piefke-Saga* , for example, I knew the Tyrolean actors and suggested them, while the director, a German, knew the German actors and made the determinations there. So yes, I do enjoy input on these projects; after all, it's really just a question of trying to assist each other in putting something like this together. In general, I should also say, I try not to meddle in preparations, whether it's television or the stage. I do not, for example, show up for rehearsals and the dress rehearsal and offer suggestions as to how something could be improved; many directors and actors frown on this, anyway. On the other hand, many directors feel it is a compliment to them that an author shows up for a premiere. Often, this is also a question of time for me. I'm here in Innsbruck and am very busy with my writing obligations and simply cannot make it to everything that I should or would otherwise want to attend. Finally, I've also got my family to think about and don't wish to be on the road all the time.

To sum up: as far as film goes, the author is really pretty inconsequential with respect to the genesis of a film. And again, in terms of time, it can take two or three months to film a project, and I simply cannot afford this. Besides, one tends to just stand around and wait for hours, which can then culminate in shooting a scene of only 5 minutes' length. And then with weather delays and changes in location and so on: I simply have to place my faith in a given film director's competence with respect to the decisions he makes.

NJM: And do you have favorite directors, so to speak, on film and stage projects?

FM: With respect to the stage, that's difficult to answer, since there are so many directors all over who are staging my things these days. Each theatre house in Germany has its resident director, and I simply can't keep up with the various productions anymore. Film is of course different in this respect. I really enjoyed working with Karin Brandauer. Unfortunately she died recently, and it was she who was supposed to direct *Verkaufte Heimat* . I will miss her a great deal.

I also enjoy working with a director from South Tyrol by the name of Werner Masten; he's been working in Germany for many years now. And then I also have favorites, if you will, among television editors, people with whom I've enjoyed good collaboration.

KEW: As an author, would you say that you experience greater satisfaction in the successful production of a stage play over a work for television, especially in light of the fact that as a writer for television you are, in your own description of things, rather unimportant or inconsequential to the production?

FM: I would say that, as is normal for any author, I am happy when something I have written reaches an audience. For example, with the *Piefke-Saga* it happened that, when it was being shown on television, it was *the* topic of conversation all over Austria, in every village and on every ski slope. What more could any author hope for? I have cartons full of letters that I simply cannot get around to answering right now.

That means, of course, that I have an audience, and that makes me happy, since I don't want to be writing material that no one reads or that moves no one. I am a bit different from my

German-speaking colleagues—whom I do not wish at all to criticize—in this respect. Many of them write "internalized literature," that is they are subjective and thematically quite self-focused. They frequently, for example, write about the problems they have with writing; that's not what interests me. I want to reach a viewing audience, and television allows me to accomplish this.

The other matter that interests me is related to theatre and has to do with maintaining contact with what is fundamental, what is real. That's why I accept commissions from certain specific and local groups, for example the Zillertal production in 1987, which dealt with the banishment of the Protestants from this valley 150 years earlier, and in which people from the valley were exclusively involved in the acting and production of the piece. These were people who otherwise perhaps never had anything to do with the theatre, but they participated gladly since it had to do with something they knew and understood. After all, it had to do with their own ancestors and what they did—or what was done to them.

Similarly, last year I did a piece for the Tyrolean Lechthal Theatre about the so-called Geier Wallie. The Geier Wallie is in this region a legendary figure from the middle of the nineteenth century, a woman who wanted to become a painter and who did in fact become one. Her life as such was difficult, however. As a 15-year-old girl she had robbed an eagle's nest, a nest that was located in a high and dangerous area where the boys of the village had been too timid to climb. At the time all birds of prey in this region were called buzzards [Geier]—hence her name. And it happened that a woman from Munich, a popular novelist of the time, originally heard the story of this woman from Lechthal, the Geier Wallie, and she wrote about her in a work that became a best seller of the day. There was a subsequent Italian opera and then, in this century, several film versions of the story, as well, but all of these were set in the Ötz Valley and not in the Lech Valley, and it was for this reason that the locals in the Lech Valley came to me and asked me to write a play and to restore the myth of the Geier Wallie to its rightful home, namely the Lechthal. And so I did it, and it became a real event for the entire valley much like the Zillertal production I was just mentioning, with all of the locals involved in the production of the play. This kind of contact and collaboration is just as important for me as for the people it affects, and I need it.

NJM: Felix, a bit ago you mentioned the *Piefke-Saga.* Can you speak a bit more about the incredible reaction to this production, perhaps comparing the responses in Austria and Germany?

FM: Well, in general I'd say that the Austrians felt a bit parodied by this, whereas the Germans simply seemed to be amused by the entire affair. I personally would say that the German visitors to Austria in the film were presented more critically, but they took it all with good humor. I suppose they understood that there really are tourists like this on the one hand, and that, on the other hand, the story could just as well have been depicting Austrian tourists in Italy or British tourists in Spain or whatever—the dynamics are the same.

In Austria the *Piefke-Saga* gave rise to a large and very public discussion. You see, there are places in Austria where tourism has simply become too much; the people can no longer cope with the numbers, physically and psychologically. But the older generation of innkeepers, resort managers etc., those who had built up this industry after World War II, felt especially insulted by the *Piefke-Saga* . Their response was: we worked like dogs for our whole lives in order to have something, and now this Mitterer comes along and makes fun of us. But the children of this generation, they found the series to be right on the money in its portrayal, and felt it could have, in fact, been even more critical of the industry. And so it was that a truly beneficial discussion arose as a result.

The fourth part of the series was less positively received than the others, in large measure because it had so little to do with the first three and was really just science fiction. But this was my great chance, if you will, to try my hand at something completely different. I knew that I had a captive audience at this point, and so I went ahead with something that was radical. About half of the viewing audience was outraged at this fourth part, but they all watched it to the end nevertheless! But this too contributed to the general discussion surrounding the *Piefke-Saga* and, in fact, this outrageous fourth part has in the meantime become a cult film among the youth of Austria. At Carnival time in this region, the younger people are wont to dress up like the characters in this fourth part, sporting machine guns and sun glasses. Again I say: what more could an author ask for?

NJM: On to the topic of television again. Have you ever tried your own hand at directing, or is this something that doesn't interest you?

FM: No, this really doesn't interest me. You see, directing is horribly stressful, what with trying to keep everyone happy and getting things done both well and on time, and knowing the while that making a film is incredibly expensive. I wouldn't rule it out entirely, say for directing a stage piece at some point in the future, but in general an author should not, I would say, attempt to be the director for the filming of one of his works. He's too close to the original and has lost any imaginative touch in making the film version. A good director, on the other hand, brings his or her own imagination to the author's original and makes the piece into something more than it was. No, an author shouldn't direct his own works. The one exception I can think of is Kroetz, who didn't shrink from brutally modifying his original works when he set about filming them. He threw things out, he added whatever he felt was right. Most authors cannot do this.

NJM: Do you two have much contact with each other?

FM: No, not much anymore, he lives in his world and I live in mine. And then too, he hasn't written anything in quite some time now. I hope he does so soon again. On the other hand, I suppose it's understandable that he's not writing anymore—he wrote forty-some works, all pieces of social criticism, and at some point any one well simply dries up. In my case, I've always maintained a bit more thematic variety in my writing, otherwise my well would have gone dry by now too, I suppose. I've always wanted to keep growing and learning while I'm writing. At the moment, for example, I've accepted a commission for a two-act play for German Television. It's about the RAF—the terrorist Red Army Faction in Germany in the 70s. Earlier I had done something on terrorism in South Tyrol in the 60s, a piece that I researched for a full two years, and something like this is utterly fascinating for me, I mean the connections and the people one gets to know etc. At any rate, I don't think writing will ever become uninteresting for me.

KEW: Earlier you were discussing the critical response to your works. Sometimes in newspapers and reviews the response is positive, sometimes you are perceived as the purveyor of scandalous material—how do you handle it all, how do you respond to criticism?

FM: I would say in general that the critics are not too fond of me. Actually, whenever I have given rise to a scandal or pseudo-scandal, the critics seem to like me just fine. But in general I'd say I receive more negative than positive reviews, simply because I am too common and popular for the critics in Germany and Austria. My works are not "artistic" enough for them, and they hold it against me that I do work for television. T.v. for our critics belongs to the mass media and mass consumption and it has nothing to do with culture, with art. In the English-speaking world this wouldn't be held against me, but it is here.

I can live with this response. My publishers send me these reviews—some of them horribly negative—and I read them all. At first of course I am upset, but then sometimes I see that they are right in certain criticisms too, and one should never stop learning. And besides, I am not so taken with my own works that I think they are without blemish or mistakes. My God, I mean, I am constantly being invited to performances of my plays, and at times I am terribly embarrassed, not at the performances themselves, but at the mistakes I see in my works.

But in general my attitude is: read the reviews, make note if the negative ones have a valid point to make, and then forget about the rest. It would be much worse not to have an audience than to simply have to live with some bad reviews. Not having an audience would be far worse, but thank God that isn't my situation; I have an audience both for the stage and for television. For example, with *Ein Jedermann* in the *Josefstadt Theatre* (Vienna), I experienced the worst reviews of my life, and still there were 70 sold-out performances. The critics brutalized me there and I even had to ask myself, my God, what did you write here, but the audience was fascinated by the work and kept coming. So I would much prefer getting an audience to getting positive reviews all the time. And in the final analysis, negative reviews do not keep people from coming to the theatre. Sometimes, however, negative reviews can prevent one's work from being accepted for performance elsewhere.

NJM: You withdrew your second work, *Veränderungen*, from further publication. Was this because of its critical reviews, or because of your own assessment of the work?

FM: It was the latter—it was simply too awful.

NJM: What did you find bad about the work?

FM: It was only my second piece, and I was under time pressure to produce a follow-up, so to speak, to my successful first work (*Kein Platz für Idioten*), so I quickly dashed this off for performance in Vienna and then went on tour in Germany. The director kept telephoning me at various sites in Germany, telling me the piece was too long-winded etc., but I insisted that everything had to be retained because it was all important. I never saw the play on stage, but did see it on television, and was so embarrassed and upset by the piece that I withdrew it at once. There were some interesting moments in *Veränderungen*, and these I took out and wove into *Besuchszeit* later on. But otherwise, the piece was simply too didactic and wordy and I just couldn't stand it.

NJM: Would you call one of your works your "favorite," or is this impossible?

FM: No, it's not at all impossible; my favorite is certainly *Kein Platz für Idioten*, simply because it is so personal, so autobiographical. When I wrote the piece, I did not yet understand that I was actually writing about myself; I thought it was about a child who was an outsider because of his mental retardation. But when I actually played the lead role, I realized the play was about me, as well. And the old man who accepts the boy, this was my adoptive father; it's really a monument to his humanity and to the manner in which he took me into his world. It is certainly my most simple and most naive play, but it's still the one that's closest to my heart.

NJM: And, at the same time of course, it represents your artistic breakthrough.

FM: Yes, it represents my breakthrough, despite the fact that for a long time it was performed only by amateurs on provincial stages, simply because the work was considered too naive by the professionals. Recently I finished a revised film script for the work, and it will be shown in April (1994) by German Television. In conjunction with the revisions I made, I had discussions about the work with my publisher who informed me that there have been over 1,500 performances of the original, world-wide.

NJM: On how many different stages?

FM: Over 80, according to the publisher. The play remains extremely popular. It's performed in Low German in north Germany, in the local dialect in South Tyrol , in Rhaeto-Romanic in Switzerland, and so on. And it is still primarily played on amateur stages.

NJM: But despite these numbers, *Besuchszeit* is probably still your most popular play, wouldn't you agree?

FM: Yes, that's certainly true, especially since *Besuchszeit* is performed on amateur and on professional stages. It's easy for amateurs to perform, since basically it's just two people talking to each other.

NJM: How do you account for the popularity of this work?

FM: Well, I suppose it's because the problematics of the play are truly international—the play's theme is universal, in that sense. *Besuchszeit* is performed in many countries, since many countries have people who are "stuck away" in institutions because society doesn't want to deal with them. And recently, *Sibirien* is beginning to overtake *Besuchszeit* as my most popular play—it's being performed in Chile and Belgium and Australia and literally all over the world, for the same reason: every country has old folks' homes. And then too, I wrote *Sibirien* in High German and not in dialect, which meant that it became popular faster in the German-speaking world, simply because people could understand it better.

KEW: Are you continuing to write in dialect on your present projects, or is it primarily High German now?

FM: That all depends on the theme of a given work. If it's something about Austria and a definite Austrian milieu, then I write in Tyrolean dialect—which of course is changed to Viennese dialect for performance in Vienna, to Styrian dialect for performance there, and so on. *Ein Jedermann*, on the other hand, I did not write in dialect, because it's meant to portray a wealthy industrialist as he might be found in a skyscraper in Frankfurt or Tokyo or wherever.

NJM: Felix, is it appropriate or accurate to describe you as a "moralist," or would you reject this categorization?

FM: I am really rather uncomfortable talking about matters such as this. And I think if you were to categorize an American author in this fashion, he'd take you to court for hurting his sales—even if it were accurate or true!

Of course, if one considers my work in toto, one has this impression of me as a "moralist," as you say; how else can it be for one who commits himself to causes involving outsiders or society's "losers"?

NJM: For those whom we would call "underdogs" in English?

FM: Exactly, underdogs is a good term. But I must say that the motivating impetus for my involvement is not a moral cause as such, but rather, it has to do with the fact that I feel drawn to these "underdogs." It isn't that I feel morally obligated to engage myself in their causes, it's more that I identify with them and am attracted to them. If it were a moral impetus, then I'd be placing myself above them or in some sort of superior position, and this isn't the case at all. And it has nothing at all to do with pity for these "underdogs," it's rather that I prefer them to the so-called normal people. When I played the lead role in *Kein Platz für Idioten* I was truly in my element, since I identified with this miserable boy—I had suffered similarly as an outsider. And I suffered while playing this role, simply because, as an amateur actor, I wasn't able to distance myself from the role the way a professional actor can and must do. I've played this role over 200 times, and there were many moments when I felt I just couldn't do it anymore, it was too painful. It was the same with *Die Wilde Frau*—her pain was my pain, too.

NJM: So does this imply that you wouldn't admit to attempting to create in your audience a critical awareness about a particular topic or cause?

FM: Yes, of course that is my intention, but I'm not comfortable admitting this, it's almost painful talking about it. I could cite an analogous example from an American author who was asked whether his writing should be considered art. He replied: "Art, please don't use this horrible word!" Of course he was producing art, but he was uncomfortable putting himself up on such a pedestal. I mean, who's comfortable admitting that he's now about to sit down and produce some art? It was of course very rewarding to me as an author when I met with the first people who saw *Kein Platz für Idioten*, and they were moved by the play to reconsider their prejudice and attitudes about mental retardation, but to describe myself as a moralist, there's something too didactic about the term and it makes me uncomfortable.

NJM: Perhaps a question about a different kind of pain. How is it for you when you receive a commission or contract to complete a work for whomever by a given date. Have you ever experienced writer's block in your work? Have you ever arrived at the point where you told yourself, I just can't do this after all?

FM: No that's never happened to me, and I doubt that it ever will. When I work on a topic or a theme, I research it very carefully and have all of the materials and information spread out on my desk in front of me. My problem is not writer's block, it's rather coming to grips with the wealth of information and facts. My dilemma is always, how can I incorporate all of this important material into two acts of 90 minutes each? It's not at all like composing lyric poetry, where you wait for the muse to inspire you and then you write six lines on paper. When I finally sit down to begin writing after exhaustive research, I never have to worry about whether it will "flow." That doesn't mean, of course, that I do not have moments where I seem to be at an impasse with respect to how to complete a scene or whatever. When that happens, I simply take a break or put the project aside until the next day, and then I find a solution. So writing for me is work or discipline in the truest sense of the term, it's not waiting for inspiration; my inspiration comes from writing, and during writing.

NJM: Do you typically read the first drafts of your works aloud to your wife or some other friend?

FM: No, my first reader as such is always my secretary. I've never mastered typing and write everything long-hand, such that my secretary has to type up everything for me. Sometimes I dictate to her, too, if it's urgent. At any rate, she's always my first audience, and she's very good.

NJM: And you've been working together for years in this fashion?

FM: Yes. And then of course things go off to directors and editors and such, and then I get the chance to discuss my work in some critical detail, and this of course is extremely important. Any writer needs this kind of discussion with someone in order to gain distance and perspective. When I did my work on terrorism in Austria in the 60s, I actually did enough for three movie scripts but, as Brandauer pointed out, it was simply way too much material.

KEW: And will you ever do something with all of this collected material?

FM: I always have that on the back burner, but somehow never get around to it. I have an incredible amount of material, but the more time goes on, the more difficult it is to come back to this with a fresh attitude.

NJM: Felix, tell us something about your work routine. Are you one who, à la Thomas Mann, blocks out so-and-so many hours per day for writing and then rigorously sticks to this fixed plan, day in and day out? And how do you combine the demands of your work with those of family and home?

FM: Well, answering the latter question first: this was a bit more difficult when our daughter Anna was smaller. In those days my wife and I would take turns working in the study and minding Anna, but now that she's 14 this kind of attention isn't so necessary anymore. And now things have turned around; as I mentioned earlier, Anna and I are working together on a book project, and she's using me as her private secretary.

   With respect to work discipline, I'm not really so very disciplined at all. There are two reasons for this: first, I tend to put off the actual writing on a project for as long as possible, since the beginning of any piece of writing is always the most difficult. Sometimes my themes are so complicated that it is horribly daunting to think about how to begin and, as we say in German, "Every beginning is difficult." So I tend to procrastinate for as long as possible, but finally am compelled to begin by virtue of deadlines.

The second reason for delay is that I am almost fanatical about researching my projects, and I always have the feeling that I do not yet know enough about my historical topic to begin writing. It's usually a director or an editor who calls up and says: "For God's sake Felix, stop your research already and get moving on the writing, we need this!" And then it's always the case that I have to discard at least 70 percent of my research findings and information anyway.

So those are the two reasons for my typical delay in getting started writing on a given project. I must say, however, that I don't see this process as a disadvantage, since when I actually do begin writing, I have to do so in an incredibly concentrated fashion, and I write quickly and straight through. Once I have begun, the story and its characters almost write themselves. And this is more exciting to me than if I had planned everything out exactly in minute detail, well in advance.

NJM:　　What are you working on at the moment, and what gives you your greatest pleasure as an author?

FM:　　In terms of pleasure: I get to learn constantly in doing the preparations for my writing, and people pay me for it, besides. What could be better? And at the moment I'm working on a t.v. film on the RAF abduction and murder of the German industrialist Hans-Martin Schleyer in fall, 1977 in Cologne. I really wanted to do a four-part series, starting with the year 1968, but it was simply too large a project to complete in timely fashion.

NJM:　　In terms of your research, where do you conduct this, typically?

FM:　　It really depends on the topic. Of course I do work in archives and libraries, but I also spend a great deal of time interviewing people. With *Verkaufte Heimat*, for example, I spent many many hours interviewing a significant number of people who were survivors of the events described. Similarly, it's been possible for me to interview many people who, directly or indirectly, were involved with the RAF or were affected by it, in addition to reading all of the material that appeared in magazines and newspapers.

NJM:　　An additional question about your craft, if I may put it that way. Many authors feel that the creative process of writing is for them tantamount to a kind of self-development and self-discovery.

Is this the way you feel about writing, as well?

FM: Yes, I do, even when one isn't writing directly about one-self and one's own feelings and life and so on. My own experience colors everything that I write.

NJM: Even when working on something as "objective" as the RAF story?

FM: Yes, because my own perspective shades even something like this, and this despite the fact that I attempt to be as objective as possible. This is because it's my job as an author—say as the author of the RAF story—not to invent or to dig open old graves as such, but rather to add an element of excitement, of tension to the story. I of course still try to be fair and just in representing both sides of a story—the state versus the RAF members—but this element of ten-sion that I inject always involves subjectivity.

NJM: What is the title of this RAF project you're working on?

FM: It's only been given a working title until now; it's tenta-tively called *Herbstzeit*, since everything took place in the fall.

KEW: Are there other authors here in Austria to whom you feel especially close or with whom you collaborate?

FM: In general I would say that the writers here in Austria are pretty individualistic in their approach; each lives and works for and by him- or herself. And then too, I'm a bit isolated, geograph-ically speaking, since I choose to live here in Innsbruck, while almost all of the others, even those who came from the country, have moved to Vienna. There are some in Graz, too, but most of them live in Vienna. Also, I have opted to not have much to do with the business side of literature and literary circles, and this of course takes place in Vienna.

Once in a while, however, I see Peter Turrini, and I like his work, too. Now and then I see Wolfgang Bauer, whom I also like a great deal. I'm good friends with Reinhard Begruber, a Styrian author who wrote a very popular satire about Styria in the 70s and whose work is published by Residenz-Verlag. Recently I met a young author named Robert Schneider at the Bregenz-Festival; he comes from Voralberg and had a best seller last year. He's a bright young talent on our literary horizon. His story was funny but typical, in that he sent his manuscript to over 40 publishers here and no one would accept the novel. Finally a publisher in Leipzig took it on, and of course it was a best seller and met with critical acclaim.

NJM: Did you ever get to know Thomas Bernhard while he was still alive?

FM: No, I never got to know him personally, unfortunately. I say unfortunately, because I consider him an extremely important author, not to mention one of this country's greatest humorists, in my opinion. My countrymen, it seems to me, never appreciated this side of Bernhard, but he had an incredible sense of humor, not only in his writings, but also in his interviews.

NJM: Maybe just one or two more questions about other authors. Do you have any contact at all with Peter Handke?

FM: No, none. He's living in Paris and is a completely different author and human being than I. I mean, I very much appreciate his work, but he's more a demi-god and an artist and all that—and he acts the part—while I'm just a common man with more mundane concerns. I've always enjoyed reading Handke, however, especially the early Handke who was such an exact and accurate observer. He had a marvelous knack for describing details that the rest of us tended to overlook.

NJM: Felix, would you place yourself into the context of a specifically Austrian literary tradition, say as the author of *Volksstücke*, and then also, which authors do you especially like to read, contemporary or otherwise?

FM: Well, as far as reading is concerned, I have the problem that most authors have in that I find almost no time for it anymore. Which is to say, I read an awful lot, but it's material that has to do with my work. I deeply regret not having time for leisure reading, believe me. I find that I read reviews in newspapers and then buy the books in question, and then they lie on my desk for two years and are still unread. It's terrible. I really wish I had more time for reading—my wife, for instance, is a voracious reader.

As for your question about an Austrian literary tradition: people have placed me in such a tradition, say that of the *Volksstück*, but this has never corresponded to any intention on my part; it's not something I have ever striven for. I simply write the way I feel I should write. Some of my works are of course related to Austrian tradition and traditions. That has to do with thematic concerns first of all, and second, it has to do with the fact that my own earliest experiences with theatre were in village theatres here in Tyrol. *Kein Platz für Idioten*, for example, is a peasant farce (*Bauernschwank*) that has been stood on its head. The complete personae of a *Bauernschwank* are in this play: the peasant family, the village idiot, the village policeman, etc. And the Tyrolean dramatists Karl Schönherr and Franz Kranewitter also have to be seen as influences on me and my work, even though the latter is no longer known or appreciated. Schönherr was a doctor who was incredibly popular in the 1920s and was then suppressed during the Nazi time, since he wasn't chauvinistic enough for them. Since 1981 a group of us have been meeting regularly in Telfs and have been active in the staging and re-interpretation of some of these older Tyrolean *Volksstücke*. We've put on something by Schönherr each year, and we've also premiered new pieces.

But back to your question: no, I don't consciously write *Volksstücke* as such—not one of my works bears this label [editors' note: *Kein Platz für Idioten* was given this label by Mitterer's publisher]—and I don't write with any restricted or elitist audience in mind, either. I simply write the way I feel I must, and do so in order to be seen and read by as many people as possible.

NJM: You mentioned the Nazi era a minute ago. In this context, what was the reaction to your play *Kein schöner Land* here in Austria? Did critics or others respond by saying: "Please, Mr. Mitterer, would you and others like you just let go of this topic once and for all and forget about it? Why dredge this up again?"

FM: Yes, one will always get such a response to this topic. In 1986 at the premiere in Vienna, I feared that no one would attend for precisely this reason, but that was not the case. It was in fact very well attended and was also very well received by the critics, to tell the truth. This surprised me, since I thought it would be labeled as "sentimental theatre" and dismissed as such by them.

Actually, I have no interest in producing purely "intellectual theatre." If one were to live by intellect alone, one would have to say that the Nazis were right in their program of eugenics. Of what practical use are the mentally infirm and the physically handicapped, after all? It's only the heart, not the head, that understands that they have the same right to life as we, and that they can enrich our lives and make us more human. If one considers *Kein Platz für Idioten* with the intellect alone, it's a ridiculous piece, it's sentimental nonsense.

NJM: Was the response to *Kein schöner Land* stronger in Germany or in Austria?

FM: Well, the play was premiered in Vienna just before the presidential election, and for this reason it was particularly popular, as these things go, since it was thematizing precisely Austria's Nazi past. But I guess it didn't have much of an effect, did it, since

Waldheim was elected anyway.

NJM: Back to the topic of the stage for a moment, if you will. Frequently at the end of a stage performance there is a discussion of the play in question. Do you miss the opportunity to participate in such discussions?

FM: I hate these discussions! I just can't stand them—they're terrible! I'm constantly forced into these situations, of course, but that doesn't mean I have to like them. Recently, for example, this was the case at the premiere of *Abraham*. I mean, I understand why such a discussion is important and maybe even necessary, especially for a new work like this that is dealing with controversial matters such as homosexuality and all. But as the author, I have obviously thought about all these topics at great length and besides, I am now well into a new project that has different thematics. So I have to admit that participating in such a discussion is no fun for me; I guess I've done this so often, I've simply had enough of participating in such discussions. My feeling is: I've done my research, written this play, and now you can have a look at it and, if so inclined, involve yourself in a discussion about the work, but leave me in peace to continue my work.

NJM: I guess that's perfectly understandable. And for now, I would say that we have covered a fair amount of ground in this discussion. Thank you very much for sharing with us your feelings on these matters, Felix, and for offering our readers these many insights into you and your work!

KEW: I feel that this has been an interesting and, in the best sense of the term, a revealing discussion, and I know that you've helped us and our readers a lot, Felix. This conversation will appear as its own chapter in our book, and I am certain that our American audience will be very interested in the information and comments you have provided. Thank you so much for your time and patience!

FM: You're both very welcome. It's been my sincere pleasure to spend this time with you, and I am honored that you are going to these lengths to help me become better known in America. I look forward to seeing the book when it appears!

Felix Mitterer and the *Volksstück* Tradition

Herbert Herzmann

While the relationship between tradition and innovation, between that which is considered to be the norm and that which is perceived as deviating from it, determines the reception of any work of art or literature,[1] this applies particularly to the various manifestations of the *Volksstück* genre.[2] These latter include Alpine Passion Plays, the Viennese Popular Comedies of the eighteenth and nineteenth centuries (Emanuel Schikaneder, Ferdinand Raimund, Johann Nestroy), peasant farces, the kind of theater which Brecht dismissed as crude and undemanding theater ("krudes und anspruchsloses Theater"),[3] or the renewed *Volksstück*[4] of the thirties (Ödön von Horváth, Jura Soyfer) and the so-called critical *Volksstück*[5] of the sixties, seventies, eighties and the present time.

What all of these have in common is that they were and still are written for and performed in front of audiences of particular regions. In other words, they are provincial in character; their popularity is, at least initially, not a universal one.

Who Are the People?

The term 'Volk' (people) has been the topic of much discussion. The Viennese popular comedies of the eighteenth and early nineteenth centuries were written for the craftsmen, artisans, and tradesfolk of the suburbs who did not have access to the theaters of the Imperial Court. When we today define the Viennese popular comedies of that time as *Volkstheater* (popular theater), we understand the term as being in opposition to *Hoftheater* (court theater). However, while the court theater excluded the burghers of Vienna, the Volkstheater of the suburbs were attended not only by the middle and lower classes but also by the aristocracy. It is worth remembering that Mozart's and Schikaneder's *Magic Flute* was first per-

41

formed in one of Vienna's most important suburban theaters, the *Theater an der Wieden*. In other words, the popular comedies performed in the suburban theaters of Vienna were true *Volkstheater* in the sense that they were a theater for the whole population, low and high. Yet, there is no doubt from which sources the Viennese popular comedies drew their strength. Their sources of inspirations were local jokes, local ambiance, local dialect and local events. Aristocratic behavior and ambiance, idealistic and flowery language (High German), mythological and allegorical figures served mostly parodistic purposes. The mixing of a fantastic or ideal world and local (middle with lower class Viennese) ambiance was an inexhaustible source of amusement.[6]

In our time, the term Volk is not so clearly definable as the clear-cut opposition to a Court which no longer exists. The Viennese playwright Gustav Ernst defines the contemporary Volk as the underprivileged, those who have no power, no possibility of partaking in decision-making ("tie Unterprivilegierten, die jenigen, die keine Macht, keine Möglichkeit haben, sich einzumischen").[7] This appears to be a more workable definition than that of Peter Turrini who simply says that everybody is part of the Volk.[8] Whatever one may think of Turrini's definition of Volk, his *Volksstücke* clearly side with the lower classes, the outcasts of rural society, industrial workers who are made redundant and become superfluous—in short, with the underdogs of society.

From what we have said it follows that, in order to appeal to their intended audiences *Volksstücke* of any kind must use traditions (themes, plots, structures, language, stage devices etc.) which these provincial, regional, or local audiences are familiar with and fond of. An international *Volksstück* is thus a contradiction in terms, at least as long as the utopia of the global village has not become realized in cultural (and linguistic) terms.

There is, of course, an international popular culture of which certain musicals, Hollywood films, television soap operas and family sagas are proof. Yet it is not difficult to argue that these internationally popular productions (of which most are, incidentally, of Anglo-Saxon origin) derive their popularity not from the fact that they use particular local traditions but rather that they eliminate anything that smacks of regionalism. They achieve universal acceptance by not having anything whatsoever to do with the traditions of any Volk anywhere in the world.[9] They may be compared to the so-called international cuisine whose main merit consists of having eliminated any local flavor which may upset the stomach of the modern tourist who wants to visit as many countries as possible while avoiding any contact with them which is not absolutely necessary.

To demonstrate this last point one may compare the internationally popular family saga *Dallas* with the television series *Homeland, Sold Out* (*Verkaufte Heimat*, 1988/89)[10] for which Felix Mitterer wrote the script.[11] As is evident from the subtitle *Eine Südtiroler Familiensaga von 1938 bis 1945* (A

South Tyrolean Family Saga from 1938 to 1945), Mitterer does not have any qualms about making use of elements of the new international popular culture as we have described it above. But his family saga does not take place in some remote "Dallas" with which the inhabitants of the real place of that name probably cannot identify any more than a television consumer in Sicily. Mitterer's television series tells the history of South Tyrol (Alto Adige) from 1938 to 1945. It follows the lives of a few families in that Alpine region who fall victim to the historic events that have shaped Central Europe in our century: Italian occupation of the once-Austrian region after World War I, the struggle of the German speaking farmers to preserve their identity, their false hopes concerning Hitler, Hitler's 'betrayal' of the region as the natives saw it, and the new beginning in Austro-Italian relationships after the Second World War. It is more than simply a family saga; it is also a history of a region and of the sufferings of its inhabitants, some of whom are still alive today. Although it reminds the viewer of an Alpine Passion Play in so far as it is a story of persecution and suffering, it also contains some scenes that are quite comical. In highlighting the often absurd consequences of world history on life in a remote Alpine community, Mitterer does not resist the temptation to incorporate elements of the traditional peasant farce into his series. *Homeland, Sold Out* can thus be described as a fusion of a modern-day television family saga with the traditional regional genres of Passion Play and peasant farce.

The result of this fusion is an informative and at the same time entertaining television series. In spite of the good intentions of its author to contribute towards the reconciliation between the different camps in South Tyrol, not everybody agrees with the kind of information the series offers. Although *Homeland, Sold Out* was produced jointly by ORF, ZDF and RIA (Austrian, German and Italian television), it was only shown in Austria and Germany. The Italians decided not to show it in their country because they took exception, among other things, to a scene in which Italian Carabinieri (policemen) beat up German-speaking locals. In other words, Mitterer's series offended some people and not only in Italy. It is nothing unusual that critical *Volksstücke* and their counterparts in films or on television offend parts of the audience.

We have distinguished between three kinds of popularity. The kind of popularity achieved by eliminating all local traditions does not concern us any further. The traditional Passion Play and peasant farce are popular in a different way. They give the audience what it knows already, what it expects, no less and no more. In these uncritical *Volksstücke*, especially in the peasant farces, dismissed by Brecht as crude and undemanding theater, neither information nor innovation play any part. Their main purpose is to entertain. The renewed and the critical *Volksstücke*, however, mix traditional devices and innovation. By affirming and at the same time subverting tradition, critical *Volksstücke* aim at change: literary change, theatrical

change, even social change. In his foreword to *Homeland, Sold Out* Mitterer
has expressed the hope that the audience may 'learn' something from it.[12]
An effective method widely used in critical *Volksstücke* and their counterparts on television is the employment of familiar devices in a context that
makes them appear out of place or *fremd* (alien) in a Brechtian sense. At the
beginning of *Homeland, Sold Out* the camera sweeps over a typical Austrian
Alpine village while one hears children singing the Italian Fascist anthem.
Then the camera focuses on the inside of a school where we see the singers:
local children, some in Italian Fascist (Balilla) uniforms, others in traditional Austrian/Tyrolean *dirndl, lederhosen* etc. We realize immediately that
things are not as we would expect them to be, that the world is out of joint.

It has been rightly pointed out that theater in the age of television and
film has been forced to reconsider its position. Whereas the strength of television is based on the fact that it can transcend all borders and achieve true
internationality (often at the price already pointed out), its dependence on
physical proximity to the audience has forced theater to rediscover the
value of physical immediacy.[13] Regionalism, provincialism, local relevance
and dialect are part of this newly appreciated immediacy. The (formerly
Eastern) German playwright Heiner Müller has emphasized that the theater keeps on needing the local dimension ("die lokale Dimension") in order
to have an effect also outside the sphere from which it has originated
("außerhalb seines engeren Entstehungshorizontes").[14]

For or Against the People?

Any theater that takes itself seriously and wants to offer more than
cheap entertainment must offer something new. It is, however, the balance
between the two poles of tradition and innovation, between entertainment
and intellectual challenge that poses special problems to the writers of
Volksstücke. Whereas other kinds of plays can afford to be recklessly avant-
garde, to the point that nobody understands them, a *Volksstück* ceases to be
a *Volksstück* if it ignores tradition. No matter how thought-provoking and
daring it tries to be, a *Volksstück* must at the same time be entertaining to
appeal to its audience. And it can do so only if the traditions of the audience are recognized in some form. The history of the genre has, in fact,
from its very beginning been characterized by this tension between the
demand for entertainment on the one hand and for aesthetic refinement
and educational improvement on the other.[15] Whether there can be, as
Gustav Ernst has put it, a *Volkstheater* which by being critical appears to be
against the people while it really is for the people, in that it represents their
interests even if they may not be aware of it or not even like it, is the question at stake.[16] Ernst goes so far as rejecting traditional genres such as the
peasant farce because they are too laden with meanings, too worn out, as it
were, to be useful for carrying new messages.[17] Obviously it is a balancing
act that playwrights have to sort out individually. It is fair to say that the

majority of the writers of critical *Volksstücke* in Germany and Austria since the sixties have not got it right in so far as they have not succeeded in reaching the kind of audience they wish to be accepted by. Although Martin Sperr, Franz Xaver Kroetz, Peter Turrini and others have been successful as playwrights, the audience who applauded them was not the common man in the street but the academic and the intellectual.[18]

Perhaps the only playwright who has achieved the right balance is Felix Mitterer. He has on the one hand provoked a good number of public outcries, scandals and controversies which clearly prove that he does not simply give the audience what is wants; on the other hand he has over the years achieved a degree of popularity in his native Tyrol for which other playwrights can only envy him. His regional audience, noted for its traditionalism, seems to have accepted him as one of their own, as one who understands them, even if he sometimes criticizes and even shocks them. What would be highly offensive and immediately rejected out of hand if it came, for example, from the Vienna-based Peter Turrini is treated with curiosity and interest (and is thus given a chance) once the audience knows that it has been written by Felix Mitterer.[19]

Virtually all of his plays and TV films are made of local material: regional dialect, local history, Alpine legends, and Tyrolean theatrical traditions. Mitterer stresses his attachment to and (although critical) love for his region, although his biography could easily have given him plenty of cause to reject his roots. Having been brought up in dire poverty at the very fringe of society, he could have easily become one of those Austrian writers like Thomas Bernhard or Franz Innerhofer who drew strength and inspiration from hatred of their country.[20] Mitterer seems to have written himself into the society on whose fringe he grew up and not out of it as others have done.[21] All his plays are first staged in Tyrol, very often by one of the amateur groups in which the region abounds. For many years he has been associated with the *Tiroler Volksschauspiele* (Tyrolean Festival of Volksstücke) in Telfs, a village near Innsbruck where he and some friends stage an annual festival of *Volksstücke*. Some of his own best plays have first been performed there, for example *Stigma* (1982) and *Siberia* (Sibirien, 1989).

Audience Participation: The Tradition of the Passion Play

We have already mentioned the TV series *Homeland, Sold Out* as drawing on local history and playing on the audience's familiarity with the Passion Play genre. A Passion Play of sorts is also *Lost Homeland* (*Verlorene Heimat*), written for an amateur group, the Zillertaler *Volkssschauspieler*, and first performed in the summer of 1987 in the village of Stumm in the Zillertal. It is an open-air play that re-enacts the expulsion of Protestant inhabitants of the Zillertal in 1837. The play was performed on the very spot where the events had taken place one hundred and fifty years earlier. The Zillertaler *Volksschauspieler* hold the exclusive performance rights. The declared intention to perform the play every ten years in Stumm brings to mind the example of famous Passion Plays like the ones in Oberammergau in Bavaria. *Lost Homeland* is similar to *Homeland, Sold Out* in that it deals with the persecution of a whole community. What makes *Lost Homeland* special is the physical immediacy it offers, the fact that it is performed on the spot where the events of 1837 took place by the direct descendants of those who were involved in the expulsion of their Protestant fellow Tyroleans. Like in a Passion Play, the whole village becomes the stage; once again the audience, like the villagers one hundred and fifty years earlier, take part in what is happening. Like a Passion Play it can be said to have a cult function. By re-performing the sufferings and wrongdoings of the past one not only remembers them but one brings them back to life and is thus given a chance of doing penance for past wrongs. The main difference between a real Passion Play and Mitterer's contemporary versions of the genre is easy to see: everybody agrees that Christ has been put to death unjustly and that we have to atone for it. There is no such universal agreement about the events of 1837 or 1938–1945. It was thus an achievement to have *Lost Homeland* performed in front of the Catholic Church whose priest was once behind the forces who expelled the Protestants. It was equally an achievement to have Italian actors participating in the making of *Homeland, Sold Out*.[22]

It is obvious that television series pay for their wider appeal with a loss of physical intensity. *Homeland, Sold Out* and *Lost Homeland* thus represent two very different ways of dealing with a similar subject matter. And although Mitterer has on various occasions said that television is today's true *Volkstheater*,[23] it is very unlikely that he would ever be prepared to give up the physical intensity which distinguishes theater from other media. The proximity to suffering, the corporeal contact with the action, and the audience participation that characterize the true Passion Play is carried to the extreme in Mitterer's play *Munde* (1990). It was first performed on the top of the *Hohe Munde*, a mountain near Telfs in Tyrol. The plot: employees of a roofing company (the foreman, his helpers, a Turkish guest worker and the girlfriend of one of the employees) climb the *Hohe Munde* in order to stage a celebration around a bonfire. As often happens in Mitterer's plays, which frequently show how people behave in extreme situations, deep-rooted resentments and rivalries come to the fore. These lead to the death of the aging foreman and to a dramatic fight at the edge of a cliff between the Turkish worker and one of the native employees on whom the blame for the possible suicide of the foreman rests.

In order to see the play, the audience had to climb the mountain. As if this were not enough, the visitors also had to spend the night in the camp which was set up on the top of the mountain as it would have been too dangerous to descend in darkness. In the morning everybody—actors, author and audience—descended and had breakfast together. As there was not much room on the top, only seventy-five persons could see the play at any one time. One may ask: is this still *Volkstheater*? How about reaching the common man? Is this kind of limited theater not elitist? The answer depends on how one understands these terms. Mitterer was adamant that even the critics who came to review the first performance must climb the mountain. In other words, people whose physical condition did not allow them to climb the Munde were discriminated against. Yet, everybody who was fit to climb a mountain (and there is no shortage of such people in Tyrol) was welcome. No money or status could buy the privilege of being flown in. The climbing of the mountain was, as Mitterer stressed, very much part of the performance.[24] However, being a man of the twentieth century, Mitterer has not undervalued the importance of the mass media. He allowed the performance to be filmed by the ORF and the performance was duly broadcast. Later performances of the play were allowed to take place anywhere, for example on roof tops. Yet the performances on the *Hohe Munde* during the summer of 1990 were very special events. Each performance created a closely knit community. There was a sense of participation that would be hard to find at any other theatrical event. The experience of having climbed the mountain and spent the night together put everybody, regardless of social status, on equal terms. In this sense it was a truly democratic event, or as one may call it, it was *volkstümlich* (popular) in the best sense of the word.

A different kind of physical participation by the audience led to the success of the controversial play *Stigma* (1982). It bears the subtitle "Eine Passion" (A Passion) and deals, appropriately, with the Christ-like sufferings of a female farm-hand in the Tyrol of the 1840s who develops stigmata. Here Mitterer combined many of the features that have since become associated with his theater: usage of familiar theatrical traditions (Passion Play, elements of peasant farce), local (regional) subject matter, performance in a regional (local) ambiance (*Tiroler Volksschauspiele*) with local actors, and usage of local dialect. This play in particular with its seemingly blasphemous and anti-clerical as well as anti-authority stance—the heroine, Moid, who is considered a saint by the poor people is excommunicated by the Church, accused of hysteria and declared a cheat by the medical authorities and finally shot by the police—hit a raw nerve with the Tyrolean audience. Local priests attacked the play in their sermons long before it was performed, the author received bomb threats, and demonstrations were staged against the play. The *Tiroler Volksschausspiele* were banned from the town of Hall near Innsbruck and had to move to Telfs where they have been held ever since. With his local theater Mitterer achieved what he probably could have never achieved in the anonymity of the big city: a whole village was drawn into the controversy surrounding a play.[25]

The Tradition of the Peasant Farce

Apart from the Passion Play it is the traditional genre of the *Bauern-schwank* (the peasant farce) which Mitterer frequently assimilates into his theater. Up to this day Tyrol (like Bavaria) abounds in amateur groups that specialize in this harmlessly entertaining genre. They normally perform in country inns and such places. Mitterer's foster mother was very active in one of these groups.[26] In Mitterer's own words it was no coincidence that his first play, *No Place for Idiots* (*Kein Platz für Idioten*, 1977), was a kind of peasant farce with different means ("eine Art Bauernschwank mit anderen Mitteln").[27] The play is about a slightly mentally retarded boy who is marginalized and finally institutionalized by the village community. All the stock figures of the peasant farce—the teacher, the wicked mother, the village drunk, the *gendarme* and, of course, the village idiot—appear in it: "except that they are used differently by me" ("nur werden sie bei mir halt anders eingesetzt").[28] The innovation is in using this traditionally harmless (or if one likes: socially affirmative) genre in a non-harmless, critical way. In the conventional peasant farce the village idiot is an object of derision and fun, and not, as is the case in Mitterer's play, an object of pity. A conventional farce ends happily; Mitterer's play, however, does not satisfy the audience's expectation of a happy ending. He puts the old genre on its head so to speak. Something similar had been done before by Ödön von Horváth, who for example in *Stories from the Vienna Woods* (*Geschichten aus dem Wiener Wald*) used the vehicle of the kitschy Viennese clichés of women, wine and song in a highly satirical and subversive way. Mitterer, however, goes one step further in that he had his play first performed by the *Volksbühne Blaas*, an amateur group that specializes in traditional peasant farces. The audience who went to see *No Place for Idiots* expected something different from what they actually got. This is part of Mitterer's strategy by which he tries to make people interested in a kind of thought-provoking theater which they would normally stay away from.

Farce-like configurations are prominent in many of Mitterer's plays and television films even if the subject matter is deadly serious. In the play *There's No Finer Country* (*Kein schöner Land*, 1987), which tells the gruesome story of the persecution and ultimate extermination of a Tyrolean Jew during the Third Reich, we encounter farcical plot confusions connected with matters of the heart. Anna, the daughter of Stefan Adler, the play's main character, is engaged to the Nazi Erich. Their marriage plans suffer a setback when it becomes known that Adler is a Jew, but ultimately, the confusion is 'solved' in a rather grotesque fashion: in order to save his children he declares that he is not their natural father! We find all the familiar stock figures of the *Bauernschwank* in the play: teacher, priest, burghermaster, gendarme, and, of course, the village idiot. That this works well is not as surprising as it may seem at first: the play shows up the farcical aspect of big historic events. World politics are unmasked as a farce while at the same time it becomes clear that what is under normal circumstances the stuff of apparently harmless farce can lead to deadly consequences once the political context has changed. Thus Toni, the village idiot, is finally put to death by a doctor who gives him an injection while kindly smiling at him.[29]

What he used so successfully in this play was repeated on a somewhat larger scale in his television series *Homeland, Sold Out*. Mitterer does not have to exaggerate or obviously satirize what happened in South Tyrol in order to create farcical effects. The quasi-realistic treatment suffices. The attempts of the local authorities of the remote Alpine village to translate the many twists and turns of international developments and, particularly, of Italian-German relationships into village politics can be farcical indeed. *Difficile est satiram non scribere!* Once again he employs the confusions arising from love, which are characteristic of the *Bauernschwank*. He has Anna, the daughter of a family with strong German leanings, fall in love with and even get married to Ettore, an Italian Carabinieri, which leads to at the same time serious and farcical situations, for example when her brothers disguised as *Perchten* beat up Ettore very badly.[30]

Perhaps the most obvious example of a peasant farce is Mitterer's television series *Piefke Saga* (1991/1992). "Piefke" is the not very flattering nickname by which Austrians call Germans, especially northern Germans. The theme of this television farce is the erosion and destruction of traditional ways of Tyrolean life by tourism. The central figure is Mr. Sattmann, an industrialist from Berlin, who wishes to adopt his beloved Tyrol as a second home for himself and his family. As he brings in money, he is welcomed by the locals who at the same time deeply resent and despise him because he is German. There is ample room for the depiction of absurdities arising from contradictory situations. The Tyrol we encounter is like California, a breathtaking Alpine scenery cut into pieces by motorways over which rushes the traffic of a highly industrialized society. Nevertheless traditional *dirndls, lederhosen* and brass bands abound, forming a strange contrast to the high-tech surroundings. In the Tyrol of today there is no longer a need for Italian Fascists with their alien way of life contrasting with Tyrolean traditions to create a sense of alienation. The fact that *dirndls* and *lederhosen* appear to be very odd when worn by the Sattmanns who speak German with a northern (Piefke-like) accent does not mean that they look right if worn by the locals. If the northern German Sattmanns unsuccessfully try to imitate what they perceive to be the Tyrolean customs, the locals themselves try to live up to what the tourists expect. They are, in other words, imitating themselves.

The destruction of the traditional way of life by modern developments is a central theme in Mitterer's work. In *There's No Finer Country* (1987), village life is destroyed by National Socialism which, characteristically, is not simply presented as something that descends upon the villagers from the outside but rather as something that they participate in to various degrees, and bring upon themselves. In the television series *Homeland, Sold Out* South Tyrol is changed beyond recognition by the Italian Fascists and then by Hitler's interference. Again, however, not only Hitler sells the "Heimat" of the South Tyroleans to Mussolini in exchange for support of his expansionist policies but many natives are themselves keen to sell their mountain farms to southern Italians in exchange for new farms promised to them in the more fertile, newly conquered lands of Eastern Europe. In *Piefke Saga* too, the locals sell their homeland quite happily to German tourists, and beat up a journalist from Vienna who has written an article against the Piefkes. Although he has only said openly what all Tyroleans privately fully support, he has to be stopped because his articles are threatening the lucrative tourist industry. The last part of the *Piefke Saga* shows Tyrol after the turn of the millennium, a Tyrol whose Alpine meadows are of artificial grass and whose cows and even whose robust *lederhosen*-wearing natives are robots (as there no longer exist real meadows, real cows, or real *homines Alpinenses*).

Some commentators are of the opinion that in *Piefke Saga* Mitterer had gone too far in appeasing public taste and in giving in to the demands of the television gurus. Yet, it cannot be denied that this series was viewed by many people and that it was entertaining while at the same time raising serious issues. In a way, Mitterer has succeeded in doing what Gustav Ernst expects a writer of *Volksstücke* to do: he has written a (television) play that is seemingly against the people as it exposes the corruption and opportunism that prevails on all levels of society, even in the supposedly unspoiled Alpine villages, but which in truth is for the people as it defends their way of life against a falsely understood progress.

The Naturalistic Tradition

Mitterer's theater is usually considered to be in the naturalistic mode,[31] that is to say it aims at verisimilitude, at depicting situations and people that the audience is familiar with from their own real life. His characters often speak the local dialect, wear the local outfit and move in the familiar ambiance of Tyrolean village or countryside. Like the theater of the naturalists, Mitterer's plays take a socially critical stance: they aim at unmasking social injustice or brutal human behavior which in turn is shown to be the result of circumstances. The *Volksstücke* at the end of the nineteenth century, for example the plays of Ludwig Anzengruber, have many of these features in common with the naturalistic movement of the time. It is not surprising that, in turn, playwrights who are considered to be representatives of the naturalist movement, or at least close to it, have written *Volksstücke* or *Volksstück*-like plays.[32]

At the beginning of the twentieth century, the Tyrolean playwright Karl Schönherr combined the features of the naturalist drama with those of the realistic local (regional) *Volksstück*. Mitterer is certainly familiar with his work. The *Tiroler Volksschauspiele*, in whose organization Mitterer plays an active part, often does plays by Schönherr. Another Tyrolean playwright who can be seen as part of that same tradition and whose work is also featured occasionally at the *Tiroler Volksschauspiele* is Franz Kranewitter.

The Zauberspiel Tradition

While it is correct to say that Mitterer often follows the naturalist/ realistic tradition, it must however be pointed out that he also often transcends it. According to Hugo Aust, Peter Haida and Jürgen Hein, the *Volksstück* genre follows two separate streams. The *phantastische Volksstückstrang* (the fantastic type) was best exemplified in the Viennese Popular Comedies, the *Zauberspiele* (magical plays) and Zaubermärchen (magical fairy tales) of the eighteenth and nineteenth centuries,[33] while the type that is more concerned with social issues and which uses realistic/ naturalistic devices[34] has become the dominant one since the middle of the nineteenth century.[35]

While this distinction between the two main streams of *Volksstücke* may be useful, it is in my opinion doubtful that the fantastic type has more or less perished since the end of the last century.[36] Mitterer, in any case, makes use of both traditions. Like the great writers of magical operas and magical plays, Emanuel Schikaneder and Ferdinand Raimund, and like their satirical successor Johann Nestroy, Felix Mitterer has been playing on stage or in film some of the roles he created. For example, he cooperated in the writing of the script of *Egon Schiele*, the television film of 1979 in which he also played the title role,[37] and two years earlier he had played the idiot Wastl in the first performances of his first play *No Place for Idiots*.[38] But this is not the only link tying him to the tradition of the Viennese Popular Comedy. In some of his plays he has successfully used the mix of realism and the fantastic that characterizes the Viennese plays of the eighteenth and nineteenth centuries.

In those plays the world was divided into a supernatural and a human sphere. The two spheres usually come into contact either because a higher being (for example a fairy) and a human fall in love or because an inhabitant of the higher sphere needs the help of a human in order to be free of a curse, a ban or some such thing. Often enough both reasons apply. By helping the higher being the human gets a chance for self-improvement.[39] In Raimund's *The Farmer as Millionaire* (Der Bauer als Millionär), to give but one example, the fairy Lakrimosa tries to use the peasant Fortunatus Wurzel as a means to regain the lost favor of the queen of the fairies. Seen from Wurzel's perspective something miraculous, something supernatural breaks into his life and creates an entirely new situation with which to cope.

This is the scheme which underlies Mitterer's short play *The Wild*

Woman (Die Wilde Frau, 1986):[40] Five woodcutters offer shelter from the wintery cold to a strange woman who never speaks. Her silence makes her appear mysterious to the men. Although she is a human being she has a demonic effect on them. Her apparent passivity—the men use her as a sexual object—encourages the men to project all their suppressed anxieties, frustrations and desires on to her. This leads to violent clashes between the men over their possessive rights in which all except the adolescent Wendel lose their lives. At the end of the play the woman wanders off into the snow-covered forest where she has come from.

The immediate source of this play is not a Viennese magical play but Alpine legends. The so-called wild women or *Saligen* are figures from these legends, supernatural female beings who sometimes cohabit with a human male. They normally bring good fortune to the humans as long as they are not asked questions as to where they come from or what their name is. If these questions are asked, in other words, if the human partner tries to possess her, she either simply leaves or, worse, curses him and brings misfortune.[41] Nevertheless, the dualistic scheme is the same as the one employed in the Viennese magical plays whose creators have, in turn, made use of any sources available to them.

It is tempting, and it makes good sense, to interpret this play psychologically. What appears to the men as demonic is, in reality, their own desires and anxieties which they have projected on to the women from where it hits back at them as if it were something strange, demonic, or supernatural. The famous exorcism scene in *Stigma*,[42] where the demons Schnalljuza (representing lust), Hatzes (rebellion), and Saggera Taggera (blasphemy) escape from the farm-hand Moid into the Monsignor who carries out the exorcism, alludes to the same dualistic world view. Taken literally, they are demons and belong to the other (supernatural) sphere. Yet it is easy to see them as personifications of suppressed desires of Moid as well as of the Monsignor. This view is, in fact, taken at the end of the play by the priest who says to Moid: "And as far as the demons are concerned ... Each of us, each person, has demons within! One only has to awaken them! And sometimes I think that such a demon is nothing devilish, nothing evil, but simply our desire for freedom!"[43]

One can, of course, interpret Raimund's plays in a similar fashion. Allegorical figures such as *Neid* (Envy), *Haß* (Hatred) or *Zufriedenheit* (Contentment) whom Fortunatus Wurzel encounters in *The Farmer as Millionaire* can easily be seen as personifications of his states of mind. However, while Raimund makes them appear on stage as truly supernatural beings, there is nothing supernatural about the wild woman. Her passivity, the fact that she never speaks (we do not know whether she cannot or refuses to speak), encourages the men to project their own demons on to her. It is this which gives her seemingly supernatural power. Furthermore, the title of the play which alludes to the old legends of the *Saligen* facilitates the readiness of the audience to share the woodcutters belief in the demonism of the woman.

Mitterer deliberately uses the dualistic scheme of the old magical plays but in a secularized fashion which encourages a psychological reading. The traditional dualistic scheme which once reflected man's belief in another world thus acquires a new meaning in a world whose hallmark is its total secularization, the loss of any other dimension but the experiential one. What appears to be supernatural and demonic is really natural, as it comes from within ourselves. Yet, as we no longer recognize that which comes from ourselves, as we are, in other words, alienated from ourselves, our own desires become as uncontrollable and dangerous as the old demons had been. The disastrous potential of the (male) tendency to idolize and to demonize women which still exists even in our secularized world is effectively exposed in the play. The play pretends to be about supernatural forces while really dealing with human behavior. Equally, the play pretends to be about a woman, a wild woman as it were. Yet, as the woman could not be more passive than she is, the play turns out to be rather about *wilde Männer* (wild men). The irony of the title underlines Mitterer's technique of turning old structures, schemes and meanings on their head, thus giving new meaning to familiar traditions.

Notes

1. See for example Viktor Šklovskij, Theorie der Prosa, ed. and transl. by Gisela Drohla (Frankfurt a.M.: S. Fischer, 1966). See especially the essay "Kunst als Kunstgriff," ibid., pp. 7-27.

2. I use henceforth the German term Volksstück, as English translations such as popular play, folk play, or play for the people are misleading in so far as they only cover certain aspects of the term. A Volksstück is all of these together and a bit more.

3. Bertolt Brecht, "Anmerkungen zum Volksstück," B.B., Gerammelk Werke in 20 Bänden, Vol. 17 (Frankfurt a.M., 1967), p. 1162.

4. The German term for this genre is erneuertes Volksstück.

5. The German term is kritisches Volksstück.

6. See Dorothy Prohaska, Raimund and Vienna. A critical Study of Raimund's Plays in their Viennese Setting (Cambridge: University Press, 1970), Anglica Germanica Series, 2, p. 53.

7. Herbert Herzmann (Moderator), "Podiumsdiskussion," Ursula Hassel/ Herbert Herzmann (Ed.), Das zeitgenössische deutschsprachige Volksstück: Akten des internationalen Symposions. University College Dublin, 28. Februar - 2. März 1991 (Tübingen: Stauffenburg Verlag, 1992), Stauffenburg Colloquium, Vol. 23, p. 305.

8. Günther Nenning, "Werkstattgespräch mit Peter Turrini," Peter Turrini, Lesebuch. Stücke, Pamphlete, Filme, Reaktionen etc., Ed. by Ulf Birbaumer (Wien, München, Zürich: Europa, 1978), p. 346: "ich kenne keinen, der nicht aus dem Volk stammt" (I know nobody who does not come from the people).

9. Compare Erika Fischer-Lichte/Harald Xander (Ed.), *Welttheater. National-theater. Lokaltheater? Europäisches Theater am Ende des 20. Jahrhunderts (Tübingen and Basel: Francke, 1993), Mainzer Forschungen zu Drama und Theater,* Vol. 9, p. XI.

10. The years given in the text are, in the case of television series, those of the first broadcast, and, in the case of plays, those of the first performance.

11. Felix Mitterer, *Verkaufte Heimat: Eine Südtiroler Familiensaga von 1938 bis 1945. Drehbuch* (Innsbruck: Haymon, 1989).

12. See Felix Mitterer, *Verkaufte Heimat* (note 11), p. 5.

13. Erika Fischer-Lichte, "Die Verklärung des Körpers: Theater im Medienzeital-ter," E. Fischer-Lichte (Ed.), *Welttheater* (note 9), especially pp. 100-102.

14. Quoted in the foreword of Fischer-Lichte/Xander (Ed.), *Welttheater* (note 9), p. X-XI. The same idea has also been expressed by Peter Turrini who said: "Lit-eratur, auch die größte Weltliteratur, ist in ihrem Ursprung immer provinziell und gegenwärtig." (Literature, even the greatest world literature, is in its origin always provincial and based on the present situation). Quoted by Brita Steinwendtner, "Interview mit Peter Turrini: Geduld und Genauigkeit," *Salz,* Jg. 14/III, 55 (March 1989), p. 3.

15. See for example Jürgen Hein, "Das Volksstück. Entwicklung und Tenden-zen," J. Hein (Ed.), *Theater und Gesellschaft: Das Volksstück im 19. und .20. Jahrhundert.* (Düsseldorf: Bertelsmann Universitätsverlag, 1973), *Literatur in der Gesellschaft,* Vol. 12, p. 9.

16. See H. Herzmann, "Podiumsdiskussion" (note 7), p. 311-321; Gustav Ernst is here quoted (p. 312) as saying: "Also Volkstheater ist ... eigentlich komischerweise gegen jenes Volk gerichtet, für das es eigentlich ist." (Volkstheater is, strangely enough, directed against the people whom it really is trying to help).

17. Herbert Herzmann, "Interview mit Gustav Ernst," Hassel/Herzmann (Ed.), *Das zeitgenössische deutschsprachige Volksstück* (note 7), p. 273: "Mit konventionellen Theaterformen käme ich nie zurecht, das funktioniert nicht, ständig falle ich hinein in ein gemachtes Bett, wo ich alle Zustände krieg', da werd' ich narrisch." (I could not cope with conventional theatrical forms, that does not work, it would be like falling into a made-up bed, I would get into a state, it would drive me crazy); p. 279: "Und dazu kommt, daß ich das Gefühl habe, daß diese alten Formen zu sehr den Inhalt prägen ... Man kann noch so kritisch sein, über bestimmte Formen kommt man nicht hinweg, die erscheinen letztlich immer als unkritisch, egal wie kritisch man ist." (I should add that I feel that these old forms influence the content too much ... No matter how critical one is, one cannot escape the power of certain forms which appear uncritical even if one wishes to be critical).

18. See Jürgen Schröder, "Auf der Suche nach dem Volk," Hassel/Herzmann (Ed.), *Das zeitgenössische deutschsprachige Volksstück* (note 7), pp. 75-84.

19. Ursula Hassel and Deirde McMahon, "Interview mit Felix Mitterer," Has-sel/Herzmann, *Das zeitgenössische deutschsprachige Volksstück* (note 7), p. 289. This interview has also appeared as "Felix Mitterer im Gespräch mit Ursula Hassel und Deirdre McMahon" in *Modern Austrian Literature,* Vol. 25 (1992), Nr. 1, pp. 19-39.

20. For biographical details see Herbert Herzmann, "Felix Mitterer," James Hardin (Ed.), *Twentieth Century German Dramatists, 1919-1992* (Detroit, London: Bruccoli Clark Layman, 1992). *Dictionary of Literary Biography,* Vol. 124, pp. 325-332.

21. In a curious way, however, Thomas Bernhard who has all his life worked very hard to write himself out of Austrian society, has by this very attempt ulti-

mately managed to become viewed as a quintessentially Austrian writer. But this is the subject for another article.

22. Mitterer told me that in the making of the series the Italian actors enjoyed learning about the Alto Adige about which they had previously known nothing. The cooperation of Austrian and Italian actors and actresses in making this film about their past (the history of their countries/regions) brought about a new understanding of their own situation and of each other. In contrast to the actors, however, the Italian authorities did not appear to have learned anything, neither were they interested that a wider Italian public would learn about South Tyrol/Alto Adige.

23. See for example Felix Mitterer, "Zur Entstehungsgeschichte des Stückes" [the play referred to is *Kein Platz für Idioten - H.H.*], F. Mitterer, *Kein Platz für Idioten: Volksstück in drei Akten* (München: Friedl Brehm, 1979), p. 73-74. He again expressed this opinion in a discussion with students at University College, Dublin on 15 November 1988.

24. Felix Mitterer, *Munde: Das Stück auf dem Gipfel* (Innsbruck: Haymon, 1990), p. 78: "Der Aufstieg gehört genauso zur Vorstellung wie das Stück selbst." (The ascent is just as much a part of the performance as the play itself).

25. See Michael Skasa, "Skandal im Tiroler Theater? - Mitterer's 'Stigma' in Telfs (doch) gespielt," *Theater Heute*, 10 (1982), p. 60. See also Felix Mitterer: "Die Tiroler Volksschauspiele und der Wirbel um STIGMA," F. Mitterer, *Stigma: Eine Passion* (Feldafing/Obb.: Friedl Brehm Verlag, 1983), p. 101-103.

26. Hassel/McMahon, "Interview mit Felix Mitterer" (note 19), p. 287-288.

27. Quoted by Kurt Palm (Ed.), *Vier österreichische Stücke. Elfriede Jelinek: Burgtheater. Heinz R. Unger: Zwölfeläuten. Käthe Kratz: Blut. Felix Mitterer: Besuchszeit* (Berlin: Henschel, 1986), p. 252.

28. Ibid., p. 253.

29. See Felix Mitterer, *Kein schöner Land. Ein Theaterstück und sein historischer Hintergrund* (Innsbruck: Haymon, 1987), p. 82.

30. 'Perchten' are frightful figures with horns and chains etc. who roam the streets around February in order to drive winter away. They are part of the folklore in many Alpine regions.

31. Georg Hensel, *Spielplan: Der Schauspielführer von der Antike bis zur Gegenwart*, Vol. 2 (München: Paul List, 1992), pp. 850ff., discusses Mitterer's plays under the heading "Dramatiker, die man Naturalisten nennt" (dramatists which one may call naturalists) (p. 737). Hensel does not confine the term naturalists to writers who belonged to the naturalist school at the end of the nineteenth century but extends it to contemporary manifestations: certain productions of the theater, large parts of television and film, in particular American film (pp. 737-738).

32. Gerhart Hauptmann's *Rose Bernd* is a case in point. Arthur Schnitzler initially planned his play *Liebelei* to be a *Volksstück*. See Hartmut Scheible, *Schnitzler: In Selbstzeugnissen und Dokumenten* (Reinbek bei Hamburg: Rowohlt, 1976), *rowohlts monographien*, Vol. 235, p. 57.

33. Hugo Aust, Peter Haida, Jürgen Hein, *Volksstück. Vom Hanswurstspiel zum sozialen Drama der Gegenwart* (München: C. H. Beck, 1989), p. 290.

34. Ibid., pp. 340-341.

35. Ibid., p. 290.

36. See Herbert Herzmann, "Ghosts, Fairies and Magicians: Elements of the Old Viennese Popular Comedy in Contemporary *Volksstücke*," Ricarda Schmidt and

Moray McGowan (Ed.), *From High Priests to Desecrators: Contemporary Austrian Literature* (Sheffield: Sheffield Academic Press, 1993), pp. 189-199.

37. The TV film was a co-production of ORF (Austrian Broadcasting Association) and ZDF (Second German Television). Director was John Goldschmidt.

38. See Felix Mitterer, "Zu meiner Rolle," F. Mitterer, *Kein Platz für Idioten* (note 23), p. 74.

39. See H. Herzmann, "Ghosts, Fairies and Magicians" (note 36).

40. Book edition: Felix Mitterer, *Die Wilde Frau: Ein Stück* (München: Friedl Brehm, 1986).

41. Program of the first performance of *Die Wilde Frau*, 16 September 1986, pp. 6-13.

42. Felix Mitterer, *Stigma* (note 25), pp. 65-82.

43. "Und was die Dämonen anbelangt ... Jeder von uns, jeder Mensch hat Dämonen in sich! Man braucht sie nur zu wecken! Und manchmal, denk i ma, is so a Dämon gar nix Teuflisches, gar nix Schlechtes, sondern nur unsere Sehnsucht nach Freiheit!" Ibid., p. 90.

'Sie ist keine Jungfrau mehr!' Sexuality and Religiosity in Felix Mitterer's *Stigma*

Todd C. Hanlin

Felix Mitterer's drama *Stigma*[1] focuses on a dichotomy inherent in traditional *Volksstück* motifs. Two major elements of provincial life are depicted: the omnipresence in such a rural setting of pairing and reproduction—the "profane" aspect of human sexuality which peasants confront daily in their surroundings—and the competing spiritual commandments, the "sacred" ideals embodied in institutionalized religion. The former provides temporary and earthly relief from the cares of the day; the latter offers eternal and extra-worldly release from the peasants' woeful existence. Though there are areas where the two "officially" intersect, for example, in the Church's sanction of sexual union between man and wife, they may also clash, as in the taboo against pre- and extra-marital intercourse.

Sexuality and religious faith have always been important natural elements of provincial life. In several of Mitterer's *Volksstücke* we see the enormous impact of the erotic on rural daily life, frequently in conflict with religious tenets and social mores, as mentioned above. For example, in the mythic play *The Wild Woman* (*Die Wilde Frau*), four woodsmen share a mysterious woman, in conscious violation of their own moral codes, eventually chaining her in their isolated cabin to insure that their sexual desires will be satisfied. Eroticism and sexuality are equally pervasive in Mitterer's historical drama *The Children of the Devil* (*Die Kinder des Teufels*). Enduring a fate similar to that of many of the itinerant boys, Magdalena Pichlerin must burn for her alleged complicity in unholy (primarily sexual) acts, as well as for her insolent and salacious remarks to the judge.

Like *The Children of the Devil*, *Stigma* is an authentic *Volksstück*, set in a rural Austrian province in the historical, and therefore implicitly verifiable past—ostensibly around 1830. Formally, it is a "Catholic" play,[2] portraying the stations of a martyr's cross. *Stigma* is also remarkable in that it depicts the inherent complexity of rural life: within the parameters of sexuality and religiosity, Felix Mitterer illuminates specifically the competition and the conflict between members of the same class, as well as among various social classes.

Stigma's heroine is Moid, her name an etymological allusion to both "Mary" and "maid." Though the male characters may perceive her as either a *femme fragile* or a *femme fatale*, Moid's individual, complex nature only gradually surfaces: her calm innocence masks her own natural desires. However, beginning with her simple, naive "gift" to Christ of her menstrual bandage (representing the woman's "sacrifice" or "suffering"), she experiences the stigmata and sufferings of Christ. Because of this unique transformation, she is envied or feared by some, coveted by others, and incomprehensible to all. As woman, maid, and stigmatized virgin, Moid's character is somewhat opaque at the outset and is defined—both before and after her stigmatization—by the different interpersonal relationships with each of the seven main male characters who treat her respectively as sex object, prospective mate, friend, icon, laborer, medical specimen, and scapegoat.

Ruepp, the Landowner's son, is interested in Moid solely as an object of his sexual desire, and he has no qualms about her virginal or sacred status. He has no intention of marrying her, as he knows that public union with a saint is impossible, and a union with a maid is socially unacceptable and would thus be forbidden by his father. Since Ruepp cannot persuade Moid to have sex with him—either by flattery, by innuendo through his songs, or by pleading—he resorts to deception and force, donning a devil's mask and raping Moid.

Bast, the senior field-hand, sees Moid as a potential wife and mother, as keeper of his hearth, a symbol of his eventual though modest independence with his own small farm. A pragmatist, Bast is not averse to committing a sacrilege to attain his goals (such as the communion wafer inserted in his palm, to allow him a steady hand so that he can hit his hunting targets), nor to committing a crime (with the illegal and thus life-threatening poaching which should eventually provide financial independence). Following Moid's stigmatization, he is discouraged by her representative status as permanent "virgin" and thus both envies and hates Christ as his insuperable rival. Ever the realist, Bast is able to forsake Moid, though with great reluctance; if he cannot attain her, he vows to seek a replacement. Nevertheless, he sees Moid's rape as the simultaneous despoliation of his dreams; in a jealous rage, he murders Ruepp for revenge.

The farm-hand Seppele is simple, innocent, generous and good in an altruistic sense, willing to share his ill-gotten food with Moid, willing to protect her at the risk of his own life without asking anything from Moid in return. He supports her when she is too weak to work, allies himself with her when she begins her quest for social justice. Mitterer emphasizes their affinity in stage directions that emphasize a Joseph-Mary Relationship (*'Josef und Maria'-Konstellation*). Significantly, Seppele drinks the blood of sacrificial animals—a mirror of Moid's own bleeding, menstrual and mystical, and consequently her melding with the blood of Jesus. Seppele thus reinforces their mutual tendency toward goodness, though without the implication of marriage or offspring who could continue their ideals. It is ironic that their collaboration proves "fruitless" and that both are sacrificed as martyrs to a cause neither fully understands.

The remaining male characters—both good and evil—are designated by their professional roles in society and not by their "Christian" names. The only individual who demonstrates concern and understanding for Moid as a human being is the village Priest (*Pfarrer*). The Priest is a pawn of the Church, shuttled from one provincial pastorate to another. He can identify with Moid and with his rural flock as a result of his own impoverished background (though he does betray bitterness regarding his involuntary vows of celibacy). In a brief monologue, he reflects on a life which can also be seen as representative for the peasants' serfdom as well:

> Oh, Lord Jesus! Now she's married to You, on top of everything else. A husband ... At least she has that consolation. I'm in the same boat as the hired hands. I've got to stay single, too. No wife, no children. That wasn't my choice. You've known that from the beginning. I was the second son of poor farmers, we had two choices: I could work for a farmer or for the Lord. I preferred working for the Lord. I starved all through school. Year in, year out, I ate nettle soup and potatoes. Slept in a corner of the cellar, and on the side I worked as a mason's apprentice at the age of fifteen. Was the weakest student in seminary, never really did learn Latin. Afterwards served as assistant priest, was transferred from one filthy little village to the next ... Everyday early Mass, no matter how cold it was, my fingers were numb and the wine was frozen solid in the cup. And for a bed I had a sleeping bag with hot plum pits to warm me up a little bit ... They sit around in the confessional and blabber about carrying on with the opposite sex, and as for me, I do this (makes the sign of the cross for absolution) and they're free from sin once again, and can go back to living like pigs until their next confession! And what about me, eh? What've I got? (lifts his flask). This is it![3]

The Priest believes in Moid as a representative of good in the Church and thus encourages her sainthood; later, he is willing to smuggle communion wafers to her following her excommunication.

Other male characters (or groupings) represent different, higher social classes, all interested in the exploitation or suppression of Moid's new status. For example, the city folk (*Stadtleute*) who pilgrimage to the farm to view Moid do so out of curiosity, as if on a visit to the zoo or on safari to the exotic hinterlands (with possible side benefits, such as a cure for constipation, etc.). They do not actually believe in Moid's transformation, especially after she rebukes them for their various sins.

The Landowner (*Bauer*) sees Moid as cheap labor and nothing else— she will be dismissed if she cannot work due to her pregnancy. She will be retained, not out of charity, but only if she can attract crowds of people who will buy the Landowner's beer and wine. Moreover, the Landowner resents her individuality, the audacity that she can have her own prayer apart from that of the head of the table—that is, the Landowner himself. He reprimands Moid (and indirectly the other assembled hands) with an explicit threat: "You know, saying grace is still up to the Landowner! Or the foreman says it. But never the maid! Don't you know that? Next time you're gonna get it!"[4] When Moid later questions his authority and de-mands social justice, the Landowner recognizes her actual threat; even the thought that she bears his only grandchild is scarcely enough for him to retain her.

The Monsignor (*Monsignore*) doubts Moid's "miracle," as he has little faith himself. He is a climber within the Church hierarchy, a lecher, an "unholy" man. It is he who believes in the devils, conjures them up, and is properly claimed by them at the conclusion of the exorcism. The Professor of Medicine (*Professor der Medizin*) is a coldly disinterested party, an acade-mician who cannot wait to finish his examination of this phenomenon and hurry back to a faculty meeting in the capital. An objective scientist, he wants Moid's body donated to science following her imminent death, so he can study her as a freak of nature.

Though all are now intrigued by Moid's new role as saint incarnate, her other, simultaneous transformation has gone largely unnoticed: the development of her individuality and social conscience. This latent trait is first noted in the scene mentioned above, when she says her own grace at mealtime; she is admonished as being out of place. This independence grows in importance with her stigmatization, which legitimizes her social criticism as divine injunction against injustice. In her admonition to the wealthy farmers and city folk alike, Moid pronounces in Biblical incanta-tion a three-fold curse of social damnation: "Woe unto you, you wealthy of the earth, you'll have no consolation! Woe unto you, you gluttons, you'll starve! Woe unto you, you who are now laughing. You'll regret it, regret it for all eternity!"[5]

Following this outburst, she is examined by the Professor and by the Monsignor, in hopes of finding a rational explanation or at least a "cure" for her unusual behavior. It is here, at the mid-point of the play, that the Professor offers his critical diagnosis: Unsuspecting and disinterested in the repercussions of his examination—influenced neither by Moid's sexuality nor by her religiosity—the Professor unleashes chaos with his impartial judgment. On the one hand, the Professor's diagnosis allows an unbiased, scientific explanation for the events:

> The periodic occurrence of convulsive spasms and of fever, as well as the accompanying symptoms, lead me to conclude that we are dealing with an hysterical epileptic. Along with her actual illness—epilepsy—her hysterical condition is compounded by an abnormal craving for attention, by religious fanaticism, and an over-active imagination.[6]

His scientific appraisal explains Moid's mysterious behavior in a logical, concise manner, while drawing attention to the titular implications of "stigmata" vs. "stigma": the stigmata, while "scientifically" questionable, are simply a manifestation of her status as a religious figure. Paradoxically, this status becomes a stigma, requiring her exemption from everyday (sexual, romantic) concerns: as a sacred virgin, she was not available as a prospective bride.

Following a subsequent examination, the Professor makes a fatal discovery: "She is no longer a virgin!"[7] Her reception of the stigmata and the resultant "miracle" of her virginity are challenged by his sobering words. While Moid insists on her innocence, each of the main characters must now deal with this revelation in his own way, depending on his original relationship to Moid. With the loss of her virginal status, Moid loses "value" as both divine figure and as ideal lifemate. The men are stripped of their illusions and are confronted with crass, indeed trivial reality: Moid is simply another hysterical woman, albeit an epileptic one. Yet upon the Professor's departure, the demons appear, complicating the picture. (In fact, the theater audience has seen more than the Professor—Moid's earlier union with the Christ on the cross, for example, as well as the later appearance of the demons, etc.—to seriously qualify the Professor's diagnosis.) Nevertheless, without the protection of her holy status, Moid is now suddenly vulnerable. She has attracted the authorities' attention, and now they must deal with her, make her harmless. Here the exorcism scene provides an apt image of the new Moid: Tied to a chair, she must be bound by the men in order to control her (political) outbursts as much as to control her demons! She is threatening as a worker with her outspoken courage and her knowledge of the Landowner's exploitation. In this sense, her normal human attributes are life threatening, since they make her a target for the privileged upper classes. The establishment, initially represented by the Monsignor, the Professor, and the city folk, are later reinforced by a Policeman (*Polizist*) and two Gendarmes (*Gendarmen*), who are called in to restore public order—and thus the status quo.

Though having lost her special stature as a local saint among most of the male figures mentioned above, Moid has gradually established yet another, independent relationship—with the *Volk* (and thus with a theater audience comprised primarily of rural *Volk*). If the play's action (that is, the men's behavior) has now changed and turned against Moid, there is an equal but opposite reaction on the part of the peasants. They gather round Moid as their idol, their spokesperson, their defender in their struggle for social justice with the prevailing powers. The Farm-hands (*Dienstboten*) have become true believers and, much like a Greek chorus, represent, influence, and share the author's intentions with the actual theater audience.

Moid's transformation was a blessing to the provincials who enjoyed a worldly incarnation of the Passion that encourages and confirms their blind faith and helps them endure the travails of their brutal daily existence. Significantly, despite the "loss" of her virginity and thus the loss of her sanctioned status as saint, the common people continue to support her and to believe in her, to protect her from those who would destroy her as a representative and as a person. Here her virginity is of little consequence, for she has become a political figure, questioning authority (as represented by the Landowner, and, by extension, the Professor and the Monsignor). Although Moid's loss of virginity is of personal importance to the few individuals mentioned above, it is of no consequence to her greater role as agitator, as a symbol of justice. In this role she is most threatening to the establishment figures; in this role she has the greatest significance for the *Volk*—and for the theater audience. While her personal travails and psychological makeup are fascinating for the audience (who sees and knows much more than any of the individual players), she is a fulcrum that, because of her unique status, tilts the old world on edge. Still, her personal fate, her martyrdom, will have no lasting historical impact—after all, there is no world-famous Saint Moid![8] She has performed no verifiable miracles (at least none that the Church will wish to recognize), and she dies an inconsequential death. It is only as a legend that she will live on, not as a symbol of religious purity in her virginal incarnation, but as a political radical, a populist who incites the hired hands to criticism of the establishment, to disrespect and, ultimately, to insubordination. The Church excommunicates her in a feeble attempt to undermine her (religious) status as a saint—not realizing that she is more important to the peasants as a social reformer. The final monologue of the Old Woman (*Alte Dirn*) conjures up an apocalyptic vision of insurrection, revenge and murder:

> And there will appear in the heavens a great sign—a woman, cloaked with the sun, the moon beneath her feet, and on her head a wreath of twelve stars. And the woman will commence to speak in a loud voice, saying:
>
> Gather unto me, you poor, gather unto me, you who have no voice, gather unto me, join in the great feast, to eat the flesh of kings, and the flesh of warriors, and the flesh of those who feast on our flesh and blood. Thus the woman will say, and we shall come, with hoes and sickles and scythes, and will harvest what is rightfully ours.[9]

Thus the play's final words curiously signal the beginning of yet another drama, that of social and political developments throughout the remainder of the nineteenth century, culminating in the revolutions of the 1830s and

1848—which were also put down forcefully by the establishment through-out Europe.

The traditional designation *Volksstück* has become problematic as a result of twentieth-century developments,[10] yet we should not hesitate to employ this term to categorize *Stigma*. Mitterer has taken great pains to develop, cast, and stage this play with a certain *Volk* in mind: the peasants and hired farm-hands of Telfs, so reminiscent of the characters in *Stigma*.[11] Those characters who portray the *Volk*—Moid, Bast, Sepple, the Priest, and the large group of peasants—represent the earnest tribulations of this class; in contrast, Ruepp, the Landowner, the Monsignor, and the Professor are stock characters who have inhabited *Volksstücke* for centuries, demonstrating their timeless "antagonism, exploitation and an almost feudal disregard for human decency."[12]

Thus, the play's primary impact is not to examine Moid's fate or her relationship with any other single character, but rather her significance for the *Volk* who accurately mirror Mitterer's contemporary, rural, theater-going audience. For today's audience, the discovery that Moid is no longer a virgin comes as no surprise; her resistance to the three men's entreaties, her struggle against her own carnal desires, and her subsequent rape at the hands of the masked Ruepp all attest to her virginal character. She has demonstrated her self-sacrifice, her denial and suffering, and later her intent to work despite the painful stigmata. Moreover, the theater audience has witnessed her union with the Christ on the cross and can judge its authenticity. Perhaps the only implausible element is the discovery that she is possessed by the three demons: they are presented theatrically as reality, and not merely as a delusion of the wicked Monsignor. It is not Mitterer's intent to question or disparage the peasants' reliance on sexuality or on religion: he does not deny the primary if primitive function of sexuality,[13] nor does he mock the simple beliefs or even the superstitions of the *Volk*. He knows their importance in the peasants' everyday existence—after all, Mitterer is one of their own.[14] He thus presents the demons realistically, with differentiated characters and voices that divulge secrets about the other characters that no human could know, secrets that are corroborated by all present at the exorcism. If, indeed, the demons have the power to inhabit the Monsignor, then they were conceivably present in Moid—but with what outcome? From the beginning her behavior has not been "devilish" or improper, she has not done anything that could be attributed to Satan. Is the audience to conclude that she has been strong enough to suffer the three demons inside her without giving in to normal human (sexual) temptation—and is therefore indeed a saint? Whether the demons have had any deleterious effect on Moid's morals is an interesting point for conjecture. Suffice it to say that, whether sanctioned piety or heretical superstition, both elements are inseparable aspects of belief and faith in the province. Mitterer's Moid is the more fascinating for these aberrations, discrepancies, and unresolved mysteries.

In the end, however, our two prime considerations—sexuality and religiosity—no longer define Moid's role in her community. She has become "stigmatized" both in terms of her sexual being (she has a child but no husband and no prospect of ever attracting one, thus she is in worse straits than a widow, who could conceivably remarry), and of her religious status (no longer a saint, she is excommunicated by her Church and thus no longer exists in the eyes of her chosen religion). Her attraction as a possible (sexual) mate or as that of a potential saint are nullified, while her representative value as a political firebrand increases. Her eventual threatening nature first emanates from piety, when she prays audibly before the evening meal. Her later accusations concerning the sins of the wealthy and the farmers' profits at the expense of the farm-hands are merely a heightening of this trend toward individualization, independence, and thus criticism of the "other." And it is this aspect of Moid's personality and development that survives her experiences, survives her premature death; the final monologue of the play, the prophecy spoken by the Old Woman, has by now become a rabid appeal to revolt, to attain justice, if not revenge.

While Moid, the woman, originally appealed to the personal desires of individual men in a limited, intrapersonal sense, her transformation through the stigmatization gradually projected an idealized persona of religious dimensions. Nonetheless, her ultimate distinction lies somewhere between. Her worldly role as political agitator is symbolic yet human. Moid is, finally, a worldly authority, opposed to social and political injustice, belonging not to any single man as his property or wife, nor to any supra-natural community as its religious idol.

With the play's ambiguous title, *Stigma*, Felix Mitterer focuses our attention in Brechtian fashion on Moid, the Shen Te of the nineteenth-century Austrian provinces. Her purported blessing—the stigmata—is, as we have seen, a curse—a stigma—from which she cannot escape and to which she must succumb. The Professor's discovery—"Sie ist keine Jungfrau mehr" (She's no longer a virgin)—simultaneously reveals Moid's loss of innocence in a political sense. She has begun to express the plight of the poor, to calculate their financial exploitation at the hands of the powerful, and to fulfill the Biblical imperative that the meek shall indeed inherit the earth, though not without struggle. The theater audience—Mitterer's rural peers—is thus left with the conclusion that the time-worn provincial elements of sexuality and institutionalized religion are both, to expand Marx's dictum, opiates of the masses, mere diversions intended to distract the peasants from the reality of political power, that element which has the most direct impact on their everyday lives in the provinces. The audience ultimately should be unconcerned about Moid's double-edged "virginal" status, since her primary function for them is that of social revolutionary who embodies their grievances—with or without a maidenhead.

Notes

1. Due to editorial changes in subsequent editions, I cite here the original play script in Tyrolean dialect: Felix Mitterer, *Stigma: Eine Passion* (Wien: Österreichischer Bühnenverlag Kaiser & Co, no date). All following page references to this edition will be indicated in the notes below; the English translations are my own.

2. For a thoughtful overview of Mitterer's debt to the popular play, see Herbert Herzmann, "The Relevance of the Tradition: The *Volksstücke* of Felix Mitterer," in *Modern Austrian Literature*, XXIV (1991), pp. 173-182.

3. Ach, Herr Jesus! Mit dir soll si oana auskennen. Bräutigam ... Die hat jetzt wenigstens ihren Trost. Mir gehts ja genauso wie den Dienstboten. I muaß a allein bleiben. Koa Weib, koane Kinder. Aus freiem Willen war des nia, du woaßt es eh. Bin a weichender Erbe von an notigen Bauern, zwoa Weg samma offen gstanden: Bauernknecht oder Gottesknecht. Gottesknecht war mir lieber. Hab mi durchs Gymnasium ghungert. Kochte Brennessel hab i gfressen und Erdäpfel jahraus, jahrein. Und gschlafen in an Kellerloch und nebenbei mit 15 Jahren als Maurerbub garbeitet. Am Priesterseminar der letzte Depp, des Lateinische nia richtig derlernt. Nacha als Aushilfsgeistlicher von oan Dreckloch ins andere Dreckloch versetzt ... Jeden Tag Früahmeß bei aller Kälten, die Finger klamm und der Wein im Kelch gfrorn. Und im Bett an Sack mit hoaße Zwetschgenkern, damit i's a bissl warm hab ... Da hockens broat in mein Beichtstuahl und derzählen, wia sies treibein mit dem andern Geschlecht und i, i mach so (Kreuzzeichen wie zur Absolution) und sie sein wieder frei von aller Schuld und können sich wieder aufführn wie die Säu, bis zur nächsten Beicht! Und was is mit mir? Ha? Was bleibt mir? (hebt die Flasche hoch) Des da! (pp. 26-27).

4. "Das Tischgebet is eigentlich no immer dem Bauer sei Sach! Oder der Großknecht machts. Aber nia die Dirn! Woaßt du des nit? 'S nächste Mal kriagst oane übers Maul!" (p. 5).

5. "Wehe Euch, Ihr Reichen, Ihr habts Euren Trost empfangen! Wehe Euch, Ihr Vollgefressnen, Ihr werdets hungern! Wehe Euch, die Ihr jetzt lachts. Ihr werdets rearn, rearn, bis in alle Ewigkeit!" (p. 41).

6. [D]as periodische Auftreten von konvulsivischen Krämpfen und von Fieberanfällen sowie die ganzen übrigen Umstände lassen mich zu dem Schluß kommen, daß es sich bei dieser Person um eine hysterische Epileptikerin handelt. Zu ihrer eigentlichen Krankheit, der Epilepsie, gesellten sich durch übermäßige Geltungssucht, durch religiöse Schwärmerei und erhitzte Einbildungskraft ihre hysterischen Zustände (p. 63).

7. "*Virgo intacta non iam est* ... Sie ist keine Jungfrau mehr!" (p. 61).

8. Involuntarily one thinks of one of the more publicized stigmatizations in our time, that being the case of Therese Neumann, also known as Therese von Konnersreuth (1898-1962), whose story was the subject of numerous articles and books in the international press since her initial stigmatization in 1926.

9. Es wird erscheinen am Himmel a großes Zeichen: A Weib, umkleidet mit der Sonn, der Mond unter ihre Füaß, und auf ihrem Kopf a Kranz von zwölf Stern. Und des Weib wird anfangen zu reden, mit lauter Stimm, und wird sagen:

Kommts her, Ihr Armen, kommts her, die Ihr nix geltet, kommts her, versammelts enk zum großen Mahl, um Fleisch von Königen zu fressen und Fleisch von Heerführern und Fleisch von denen, die sich mästen an enkerm Fleisch und

Bluat. So wird die Frau reden, und mir wern kemmen, mit Hacken und Sicheln und Sensen, und wern ernten, was uns zusteht (p. 105).

10. For a thorough discussion of the genre's development, see Hugo Aust, Peter Haida, Jürgen Hein, *Volksstück: Vom Hanswurstspiel zum sozialen Drama der Gegenwart* (München: C.H. Beck, 1989).

11. On several occasions Mitterer has taken his plays first to rural communities for performance there, casting local actors and actresses in leading parts. *Stigma* was first performed in the rural Tyrolean hamlet of Telfs (Inn Valley, population 1,000) in 1982—a village where the players and the audience could readily identify with the conditions and the characters of the play.

12. Alan Best, "Ödön von Horváth: The *Volksstück* Revived," in: *Modern Austrian Writing: Literature and Society after 1945*, ed. by Alan Best and Hans Wolfschütz (London: Oswald Wolff, 1980), p. 110.

13. See also *Die Wilde Frau*, where the mythological, beneficial aspects of the woman as sexual blessing are explored.

14. Critics have correctly identified Mitterer's social criticism concerning working and living conditions which Mitterer personally experienced. Here his plays appear to diverge from recent trends in Austrian theater, namely that preoccupation Jutta Landa accurately describes in her book *Bürgerliches Schocktheater: Entwicklungen im österreichischen Drama der sechziger und siebziger Jahre* (Frankfurt: Athenäum, 1988). Though a cause for scandal even before its premiere, *Stigma* is less intended to shock the middle class audience than it is to identify and empathize with the hardships of the peasants.

Confronting the Past: Felix Mitterer's
Kein schöner Land and *Verkaufte Heimat*

Jennifer E. Michaels

As the motto for his play *There's No Finer Country* (*Kein schöner Land*, 1987), Felix Mitterer chose a quotation out of George Santayana's *Life of Reason*: "Those who cannot remember the past are condemned to repeat it." With this quotation, which also appears in the museum at Auschwitz, Mitterer succinctly expresses his main goals not only in this play but also in the television film script *Homeland, Sold Out* (*Verkaufte Heimat*, 1989). In these works, Mitterer grapples with the painful issue of Austria's complicity during the Nazi years, a topic that many Austrians have tried to "remember to forget."[1] As the quotation from Santayana suggests, Mitterer is convinced that without confronting and understanding the past, the same mistakes will inevitably be made again. In *There's No Finer Country* Mitterer examines the Nazism and anti-Semitism in a small village in Tyrol, a setting that he uses as a model not only for Tyrol but for Austria as a whole. *Homeland, Sold Out* thematizes the issue of the Option of 1939 in South Tyrol, which even nowadays still causes bitterness there. Although Mitterer briefly mentions the Nazi period in other works, for example in the plays *Visiting Hours* (*Besuchszeit*, 1985) and *Siberia* (*Sibirien*, 1989),[2] *There's No Finer Country* and *Homeland, Sold Out* are (as yet) his only two works in which the Hitler years are central.

To understand why Mitterer would choose in 1987 and 1989 to deal with the Nazi period in Austria and the Option in South Tyrol so many years after the end of the Second World War, it is useful to look briefly at the Austrian response to the Nazi years. Unlike Germany, Austria for many years largely avoided confronting its Nazi past. Although the Moscow Declaration of 1943 mentioned Austrian complicity, it also declared that Austria was a victim of German aggression. This helped Austrians "to convince themselves and the world that the Nazi bacillus had been a foreign germ."[3] They refused to remember that Nazism originated in Austria, and they minimized the role that Austrians played in the Nazi regime. They chose to forget, for example, that Austrian Nazis often treated Austrian Jews more brutally than German Nazis treated the Jews of Germany, and that Austrian Nazis "manned some of the most notorious concentration camps."[4] As several historians have pointed out, Austrians comprised 13 to 14 percent of the SS even though the Austrian population was only about 8 percent of the Greater German Reich.[5] This "selective loss of memory"[6] was also apparent in Austrian literature. Unlike such German authors as Heinrich Böll and Günter Grass, most Austrian writers did not deal extensively with their country's Nazi past in the years after the war ended.[7] Only at the beginning of the sixties did some start to confront the Nazi period critically in their literary works.[8]

This neglect of the past changed radically, however, after the presidential campaign and election of 1986. The questions raised during the campaign about Waldheim's involvement in the Nazi period aroused some Austrian writers, like Felix Mitterer, and historians, like Erika Weinzierl and Anton Pelinka, to reexamine their country's recent history and to protest against its suppression.[9] Pelinka and Weinzierl express the concerns of many young Austrians when they observe that Austria is seen as a country that has learned little or nothing from its past despite the fact that it was the breeding ground of National Socialism.[10] They are, however, less troubled by Austria's image in the world than by their fellow citizens' refusal to come to grips with their moral responsibility as collaborators. In their historical and literary texts, these writers and historians examine the continuity between Austro-Fascism and National Socialism.[11]

For Austrians like Mitterer, the presidential election was shocking since it became painfully clear that many Austrians refused to accept any guilt or responsibility for the past. The campaign was also distressing to them because it revived anti-Semitic prejudices. Some Austrians, for example, blamed the Jews for raising questions about Waldheim's past: "Instead of confronting the difficult questions of complicity and concealment—of not just Waldheim's but their country's real role in the war—Austrians began increasingly to dismiss the matter as an irrelevant controversy that would have died out long ago had it not been for the efforts of a few media-wise, Holocaust-obsessed American Jews."[12] Austrians continued to suffer during the campaign from what has been called "Waldheimer's Disease,"[13] that is, the refusal to admit that many in Austria had collaborated with the Nazis.

Yet although the Waldheim campaign reawakened anti-Semitism in Austria, it also encouraged awareness of Austria's Nazi past, especially among young Austrians.[14] In an interview with Elfriede Schmidt, the writer Wolfgang Georg Fischer, who was forced into exile from Austria as a child because he was half Jewish, stresses this positive aspect of the election. He likens Waldheim's features to those carved on the cork of a schnapps bottle. This bottle, however, contains not schnapps but poison: "The cork is out and the bottle is tipped up. For the first time, perhaps, we can really fight this poison."[15] It is within this context of taking a critical look at Austria's past for the sake of Austria's future that Mitterer wrote these works.

It is not surprising that Mitterer would turn his attention to this period. In the introduction to the play *Lost Homeland* (*Verlorene Heimat*, 1987), which deals with the expulsion of the Protestants from the Zillertal in Tyrol in 1837, Mitterer writes that he considers it important to discover as much as possible about the past and the mistakes committed in order, perhaps, to learn a little from them. Although Mitterer hopes that literature can effect social change, at least in some small way, the "perhaps" suggests that he is less optimistic than writers such as Bertolt Brecht and Heinrich Böll that people can or will in fact learn from literature. In the same introduction Mitterer remarks that, although the play was generally well received, some conservative priests and their flock thought that it was wrong to rake up old stories and create conflict again,[16] a remark that applies equally well to some reactions to the topics of *There's No Finer Country* and *Homeland, Sold Out*. Mitterer believes that learning from literature is important. In his introduction to the play *No Place for Idiots* (*Kein Platz für Idioten*, 1977), which deals with the theme of the outsider, here a mentally handicapped boy and his harsh treatment by society, he cautions, however, that one should not overestimate the effect of drama or literature in general since the impact can only be a small part of the attempts of all people of good will who want to contribute to a positive change in our society.[17]

Mitterer's conviction that literature should make people aware determined the form and language he chose for *There's No Finer Country*. By writing a *Volksstück* in dialect, Mitterer could reach a wide audience. As he relates in the introduction to *No Place for Idiots*, which was first performed at the Tiroler *Volksbühne Blaas* in Innsbruck on September 15, 1977, he saw that this stage could reach an audience that would be more difficult to reach at another theater, or that could not be reached at all. The people who attended the *Volksbühne*, Mitterer observes, were quite normal people with quite normal prejudices. Some of them began to reflect after seeing his play, which was at least a beginning (p. 11). He was pleased that his play aroused discussion since it encouraged handicapped people to talk about themselves and their treatment by society and thus contributed to making people more sensitive to their plight. *There's No Finer Country*, which premiered at the Tiroler *Landestheater* on April 12, 1987, reached a similarly wide audience. By choosing this genre, Mitterer managed to avoid the problems that some Austrian authors experienced when they wrote socially critical works; in Austria there was often no broad audience for such works. They mostly reached only a small audience which found their portrayals rather shocking, but did not draw any other lessons from them.[18] Mitterer combines elements of the peasant farce, popular in Tyrol, with the *Volksstück*, and uses and transforms the stock characters traditional to these genres, such as the village idiot, the mayor, and the gendarmes. In addition, he draws on the socially critical *Volksstück* that emerged at the end of the sixties. This tradition, which is indebted to Brecht, Fleißer and Horváth, seeks not only to entertain but also to offer critical analyses of model situations.[19] Through his use of the popular *Volksstück*, Mitterer can attract an audience which might otherwise be reluctant "to see a play about Austria's Nazi past."[20]

In his introduction to the edition of *There's No Finer Country* in his collected plays in 1992, Mitterer tells why he wrote the piece. In 1980 he came across an article by Hans Thöni that described the fate of Rudolf Gomperz, a man of Jewish ancestry, born in Vienna, who loved the mountains and who worked tirelessly to develop tourism and skiing in St. Anton. Gomperz married an Aryan woman and had two sons, Hans and Rudolf, who, like many young people growing up in Austria in the thirties, became enthusiastic Nazis. Although Gomperz was one of the most respected citizens of St. Anton, he was forced from the various offices he held after the *Anschluss*. Mitterer relates how nearly all the inhabitants of St. Anton, who had much to thank Gomperz for, turned from him. In order to save her sons, Mrs. Gomperz declared that their father was an Aryan with whom she had had an adulterous affair. Both Hans and Rudolf joined the SS: Hans fell in the war and Rudolf shot himself after the war. Gomperz was deported to a concentration camp in the East—in Minsk, according to Thöni—where he disappeared.[21] Mitterer writes that the fate of this man moved him so deeply that when he was asked in 1986 to write a play for a co-production of the *Südtiroler Ensembletheater* with the Tiroler *Landestheater*, he suggested this topic because he believed that in Tyrol there had never been any attempt to confront the Nazi period.[22]

Mitterer stresses in his introduction that he does not intend to write a documentary but rather to use the story of Gomperz as a model and a stimulus for the play. In his view, the theater is poorly suited for a documentary. The documentary is particularly problematic, he observes, when an event is not far in the past and when people who were involved are still living. Mitterer therefore makes several changes in the historical facts. For example, he changes Gomperz's name to Adler, an ironic name within the context of the play because of its association with the German eagle. He sets the play in an unnamed village in Tyrol instead of in St. Anton. The village thus becomes representative of any village in Tyrol or in fact in Austria, and Adler's fate becomes a typical one: it represents the treatment suffered by many Austrian Jews. In the play, Adler has a son and a daughter, instead of two sons. Mitterer changes Gomperz's religion from Protestant to Catholic to make Adler more like the other villagers.[23] Adler is a cattle dealer which, like the change in religion, makes him an integral part of the village. Several of these changes reinforce Adler's role as a model and not an individual case and they stress how deep his roots are in this community and in Austria.

Yet Mitterer is concerned with basing the play on historical fact. He spoke with witnesses of the time and studied court records from the war and the post-war period, a methodology that he often employs.[24] In the introduction to the book version of the play in 1987, Mitterer remarks that since his play is not a documentary, he is pleased that the book includes Thöni's article because Gomperz's fate thus becomes known to a wider public.[25] In addition to Thöni's article, the book version contains an article by Gretl Köfler on the Jews in Tyrol as well as other historical materials that document not only the treatment of the Jews, but also of the Catholic Church and the mentally handicapped in Tyrol during the Nazi period, topics that Mitterer added to the original Gomperz story.

For Mitterer, this is a story about opportunism, cowardice, going along, self-interest and political blindness. It is also a story about society's brutal treatment of those who are different. The victims are, Mitterer notes, the "others," a theme that preoccupies him in most of his works. Mitterer observes that a large part of humankind is constantly afraid of the "others" and feels aggression toward them. This aggression can begin for such reasons as differences in hairstyle, clothing, ways of behavior or views. It can be caused by differences in language, color, religion or customs. As a result of this, a loved and respected fellow citizen is suddenly stamped a villain and murdered, just because he is a Jew (p. 91).

Mitterer's remark in his introduction that the Nazi past has never been confronted in Tyrol is pertinent. As several historians have pointed out, there has long been a tradition of anti-Semitism in Austria.[26] It was a major force in Austrian politics in the thirties, a fact that the Austrian Nazi Party managed to exploit successfully. Anti-Semitism was widespread in Tyrol, even though the Jewish population there was very small. It was, as several have observed, an anti-Semitism without Jews. Austrian anti-Semitism was and still is often strongest in the provinces "where almost no Jews live today and very few have lived in the past."[27] Although there were never many Jews in Tyrol—Köfler estimates that at the time of the *Anschluss* there were only about one thousand Jews in the entire Tyrol (p. 130)—the Tyrolean anti-Semitic League was founded in 1919 and its definitions of a Jew were in fact stricter than those contained later in Hitler's Nuremberg Laws. The League proposed that Jews should be excluded from many professions and not be allowed to buy property in Tyrol.[28] In 1935 a play written by Gottfried Schöpf, a local priest, was performed at Rinn-Judenstein in Tyrol. The play was based on a legend that claimed that the child Andreas from Rinn was the victim of a ritual murder, a fiction that had led to the Anderl cult. Although after protests by the Jewish community in Innsbruck some of the most offensive parts of the play were toned down, it nevertheless was allowed to be performed. It was enormously successful, and there were special performances for Innsbruck school children.[29] Despite the small numbers of Jews, the *Gauleiter* of Tyrol, Franz Hofer, was strongly anti-Semitic and was proud to report to the *Führer* that his district was the first in the Reich to be "Jew free."[30]

In *There's No Finer Country* Mitterer uses an abundance of documentary facts from his research to depict the increasingly murderous persecution of the Jews in Austria. He begins the play in the fall of 1933 and shows Adler to be fully integrated into Tyrolean village society. After the *Anschluss*, however, Mitterer documents the various stages of Adler's exclusion from society and his persecution. Once it is discovered that Adler is Jewish, his cattle business is "Aryanized," he is beaten unconscious in the night after the *Kristallnacht*, the North German Nazi District Administrator who visits the village forbids him to wear the Tyrolean national costume (a particular irony since this North German is also wearing the Tyrolean national costume to which he has much less right than Adler), he is forced to wear a Jewish star, he is not allowed to have rations for such food as milk, cheese and meat, his electricity is cut off, he is deported to Vienna in January 1942 to make Tyrol "Jew free," and finally he is sent to a concentration camp in Eastern Europe.[31]

Mitterer shows at the beginning of the play the enthusiasm of the young people for Nazism. Both Adler's son, Hans, and the mayor's son, Erich, support the Nazis and smuggle weapons across the border in defiance of the Austrian government, which had made the Nazi party illegal. The play opens with a swastika, formed out of torches, burning on the mountainside, with the enthusiastic response of most of the villagers to this swastika, and with the words "Sieg Heil" that the Nazi teacher, Hopfgartner, bellows. Through this opening, Mitterer stresses that Nazism was not imported from Germany, as many would have preferred to believe, but existed in Austria *before* the *Anschluss*. Right from the outset, he makes his audience confront Austrian complicity and guilt. The swastikas that quickly appear on the villagers' houses after the *Anschluss* are another indication of this enthusiasm. Later in the play, Mitterer depicts Austrian complicity in carrying out the laws against the Jews. When, for example, Adler protests about the "Aryanization" of his property and accuses the village Nazis of being robbers, the mayor states that this is quite legal. The mayor is content to go along with the new laws and tries to turn them to his own profit.

Mitterer shows that the Nazi version of the *Kristallnacht* as "a spontaneous popular outburst of indignation" caused by the assassination of a German diplomat in Paris by a Polish-German Jewish refugee was a fiction. Instead, he accurately documents how the pogrom was carefully planned.[32] Not wanting to be less zealous than his fellow Nazis in Innsbruck in their attacks on Jews and Jewish property on the previous day in which three Jews had been killed, many injured, and the synagogue destroyed, Hopfgartner, following orders, organizes his own pogrom a day later. The three participants, two of whom are the former *Heimwehr* men from the opening scene, are in civilian clothes to disguise their official capacity. Through this example, Mitterer underscores the enthusiasm with which the persecutions were carried out in Austria and the anti-Semitic fury of the Austrian Nazis that several historians have noted.[33] Adler's attackers are more zealous than they are supposed to be, partly in the case of the former *Heimwehr* men to show their loyalty to the new regime. Besides beating Adler unconscious, they also destroy some of his property, to the chagrin of the mayor who hopes to profit from Adler's business. Although Erich, who is now in the SA, and Hans, who has joined the SS, do not participate in the brutality to Adler, they do nothing to prevent it. Only two people try to stop it, Adler's daughter, Anna, and Hopfgartner's mentally handicapped son, Toni. The other villagers let it happen, and Olga, the mayor's wife, watches with curiosity (p. 54).

Mitterer holds the Catholic Church partly responsible for promulgating anti-Semitism. When the play opens, a large crucifix dominates part of the stage, giving an impression of deeply rooted religious faith in the village. Most of the villagers do not, however, follow the commandment to "Love thy neighbor." One of the worst offenders at the beginning is the priest, who has contributed to the growth of anti-Semitism by preaching that it was the Jews who crucified Christ. He tells his congregation that Jews have spread like a plague over the whole world and determine everything with their lack of morality and their greed (p. 13), an example of the religious anti-Semitism that had been prevalent in Austria for a long time. After the First World War, the Catholic Church in Austria "bitterly resented and resisted the trend toward liberalism, democracy, Marxism, capitalism and especially secularism, all of which it associated with the Jews."[34] The priest's role in supporting and encouraging anti-Semitism is particularly disturbing, since because of his religious office he should represent the moral and religious conscience of the village.

There is a sharp contrast in the play between the idyllic, picture postcard setting amidst the beauty of the surrounding mountains, and the callousness of Adler's former friends and neighbors. By September 1939, all the windows in his house have been broken. Maria, Adler's former wife, asks who broke the windows and learns that it was anyone who was passing by. She finds this treatment all the more shocking because Adler always treated the villagers decently. He paid good prices for their cattle, was always punctual with payment, and in times of hardship he lent them money. Now they break his windows, she comments bitterly (p. 63). Nobody in the village protests when the Gestapo men take Adler away.

Although most of the villagers do not do Adler any physical harm, they allow the persecution to happen which, as Anna tells her husband Erich when he defends himself by saying that he did not take part in the village's *Kristallnacht*, is the same as doing it (p. 56).

Three main characters, Erich, Hans, and the teacher, Hopfgartner, are committed Nazis. Although Mitterer is critical of Erich and Hans, he does not condemn them as strongly as he does Hopfgartner. Erich and Hans have some redeeming qualities since they refuse, for example, to participate in the brutality toward Adler. They also pay for their complicity and political blindness: Erich is killed in the fighting, and Hans is inwardly destroyed by the brutality of what he has participated in and witnessed in the East. That he is not entirely cold and heartless but misguided is shown when he returns to the village in 1941. Tormented by his experiences, he goes to Adler for comfort and breaks down sobbing. Mitterer makes no such excuses for Hopfgartner, the local Nazi party leader. From the beginning Mitterer depicts him as a brutal man who has driven his first wife into the grave by treating her callously and who treats his son, Toni, cruelly. He is rabidly anti-Semitic and anti-clerical. The Nazi regime gives him the opportunity to exercise the intrinsic brutality in his nature by organizing, for example, the attack on Adler. He is also intent on profiting materially from his position, as when he expropriates Adler's car.

Most of Mitterer's criticism in the play is directed at the opportunists and the conformists. In the play, these are represented by the two *Heimwehr* men who quickly join the Nazi party once it is in power, and by the policemen who join the Gestapo. Of all the opportunists in the play, the mayor is the worst. Throughout the play, the mayor swims with the tide, as Adler tells him (p. 48), a character trait that the changing pictures on the walls of his inn underscore. When the play opens, the mayor has a picture of Dollfuss prominently displayed. He betrays his son's friend, Hans, to the police for being a Nazi in the hopes that if Hans is arrested Erich will give up his Nazi activities. He does this not because he opposes the Nazis, but because he fears that his son's illegal Nazi activities will make him lose his position as mayor. His plan backfires, however, since Hans escapes and the police arrest his own son instead. The mayor also assures Hopfgartner that he supports the Nazi party in secret (p. 14). As he tells his son, one has to be cunning to survive in hard times (p. 20).

This cunning, demonstrated by the picture of Hitler now displayed in the inn, enables him to remain mayor under the Nazis. He is not openly brutal to Adler, which is not out of any humane reasons but out of fear and opportunistic motives. When he discovers that Adler is Jewish, he expresses his attitude toward Jews succinctly. In the whole country there are perhaps only 80 Jews, he moans, and one of them has to live in our village (p. 41). His fear is caused because Adler overheard him betray his son to the police and threatens to make this devious behavior public if the mayor does not leave him alone. The opportunistic motive is because he hopes to gain from Adler's business. He later employs Adler in the business, not because he wishes to help Adler but because he does not know how to run the business without him. Throughout the play he tries to ingratiate himself with those in power. After the attackers have beaten Adler during the village's *Kristallnacht*, the mayor offers them a beer. At the end of the play, he reveals Toni's address to the Gestapo men who have come to take Toni away to be killed. As the priest and Adler are taken away at the end he does not try to save them, but murmurs with relief, "finally it is quiet" (p. 81).

Most disturbing, however, is the last scene. When the curtain drops and the audience thinks that the play is over and begins to applaud, the mayor appears on the stage wearing a national costume with a red/white/red armband. He gives a speech in which he proclaims that he is mayor again because "our American friends" trust him. His speech is an example of what others have called Waldheimer's disease, the determination of some Austrians to rewrite history and suppress the past. The mayor justifies his behavior during the Nazi years by telling his audience that he has helped many in those hard times. In his speech, he makes the following points: We have terrible times behind us. Many of our sons and fathers have fallen for an idea in which they believed with all their hearts. Even though some things may have happened which have been exaggerated, that often happens in war. Let us honor those who fulfilled their duty as soldiers. Nobody should be reproached since nobody knew that we were led by a madman. Now we need to be concerned with reconstruction. Let us obliterate this time, let us erase it from our hearts and memory (pp. 85-86). The name of his inn, "The White Lamb, " is an ironic comment on his behavior since he adeptly plays the role of the innocent victim. He whitewashes the past and absolves the villagers and especially himself of complicity and guilt. Herzstein's characterization of Waldheim is relevant here: like Waldheim, the mayor has gotten along by going along.[35] The mayor mentions no word about those like Adler, the priest, and Toni who lost their lives in concentration camps or through resistance to the Nazis, and he minimizes any atrocities. In the mayor's version of the Nazi period in Austria, the Nazis, opportunists and cowards become the victims, and the actual victims are forgotten. Remarkable also in the mayor's speech is the absence of even the slightest feeling of remorse.

Set against the Nazis and the opportunists is Adler. When he first comes onto the stage, Adler seems just like any other Austrian. He joins the Nazi party in 1933, and the mayor considers him to be a "super Nazi" (p. 17). Even in 1938, he has a picture of Himmler on his wall. Like many Austrian Jews, Adler is, or thinks he is, thoroughly assimilated. In 1938, he appears wearing the Tyrolean national costume. After the introduction of the Nuremberg Laws into Austria on May 20, 1938, his situation deteriorates rapidly. He cannot produce proof that he is Aryan and has to confess to his wife and family that he is Jewish. At this revelation, his Nazi son, Hans, knocks him unconscious and then wants to commit suicide, and Anna's marriage to Erich is threatened. To protect her children, Adler's wife, Maria, declares that they are illegitimate: Hans is the son of Hopfgartner, and Anna is the daughter of a railroad signalman. She later divorces Adler and marries Hopfgartner, partly to try to protect Adler but also, as she later confesses, to try to save herself because she was afraid. Mitterer makes Adler more isolated than Gomperz. Without consulting her husband, Maria decides to say that Hans and Anna are illegitimate, a lie that intensifies Adler's pain until he later realizes that it is a subterfuge. In the Gomperz family, this lie was a *family* decision, as Thöni notes (p. 110). Revealing that he is Jewish robs Adler of his family since Hans goes to live with his supposed father, Hopfgartner, and Maria divorces him. Although Anna and Maria both try to help, Adler is nevertheless left alone in his house, forced to face his persecution without the immediate support of family members, a sharp contrast to the Gomperz family who did everything they could to help him.

Throughout the play, as Adler is increasingly stripped of his possessions, his relationships, and his national identity, he grows as a human being. He does not accept his fate passively but fights back, as when he calls Hopfgartner a "Scheissnazi" and hits him. Adler originally joined the Nazi party because he was afraid. When Hopfgartner expels him, however, Adler says that he could spit on himself for joining in the first place. Adler angrily tells Hopfgartner that he was born in Tyrol, grew up there, worked there, paid his taxes there, and went to war for Austria. He declares proudly: "I am a Tyrolean" (p. 44). Because of this strong feeling of being at home in Tyrol, Adler refuses both his wife's and the priest's pleas for him to flee. What is there for him in Switzerland, America or Palestine? He tells the priest: "This is my home. This is a beautiful country. I don't know of a country that is more beautiful"(p. 72). In this conversation the priest expresses fears about what the Nazis plan to do with the Jews in the resettlement areas in occupied Eastern Europe (p. 72), an indication that at least some people not only knew about the existence of the camps but also suspected what took place there.

Until his Jewish heritage makes him an outcast, Adler's religion and his ethnic background play no significant part in his life. He is Catholic, and has not even told his wife that he is Jewish. In his eyes, he is an Austrian and, specifically, a Tyrolean. As he is increasingly excluded and mistreated he unpacks a dusty box containing the clothes and ritual objects of an orthodox Jew: the black hat, black pants and caftan, prayer shawl, prayer book, and phylacteries. While he is sewing the Jewish star onto the caftan, he recites psalm 59, a prayer to God to deliver him from his enemies. Instead of the forbidden Tyrolean national costume he puts on the caftan and hat and transforms himself into the stereotypical Eastern European Jew, a sharp contrast to his Austrian image at the beginning. Like Andri in Max Frisch's *Andorra*, Adler is forced into a role: he is forced to assume an identity that at first means nothing to him but which at the end grows in meaning for him, as his prayers suggest. Another indication of his growing spirituality is his decision not to denounce the mayor for his betrayal of his own son.

Why would Mitterer choose to depict such a totally assimilated Jew as the protagonist of his play? In part, this is because of his historical source: like the majority of Austrian Jews, Gomperz was fully assimilated. But his reasons go further than this. By making Adler such an integral part of a community, Mitterer intensifies the horror of persecution. In a small village, people cannot claim that they did not know what was happening. Unlike the persecution in big cities where the attackers frequently did not know their victims personally, here the villagers persecute a fellow human being who has lived for many years peacefully and in harmony with them, someone who has been a friend and neighbor.

Mitterer not only looks at the anti-Semitism of the Nazis, but broadens his picture by including the persecution of the Catholic Church and the mentally handicapped. Mitterer depicts clearly the conflict between the Church and the Nazis. In May 1938, two members of the Hitler Youth destroy the crucifix and then make this sacrilege worse by playing soccer with Christ's head. The Nazis allow the traditional Corpus Christi procession that has been held for hundreds of years to go only through the fields. They expropriate the Catholic youth center for the Hitler Youth, and Hopfgartner forbids the priest to give religious instruction. Hopfgartner states that National Socialism does not need religion because it is a religion (p. 35). Later, the priest is arrested for preaching against the Nazis in his sermons. During the course of the play, the priest changes from a religious anti-Semite to a person who accepts his responsibility for contributing to anti-Semitism and belatedly tries to make amends. He offers to hide Adler, and he refuses to stop preaching against the Nazi regime in his sermons. As he tells Adler in 1941, he had been anti-Semitic but had not known any Jews. Once he knew Adler, his prejudice ceased (p. 71). At the end he is led away, handcuffed to Adler.

Mitterer also addresses the brutality toward the mentally handicapped in the Nazi period. Toni, Hopfgartner's son, unconsciously mocks the Nazis by wearing the SA uniform and by parroting his father's Nazi slogans. Although the village idiot is traditionally the object of fun in the *Volksstück*, in this play his fate is tragic since he becomes a victim of the Nazi euthanasia policy. Toni is forced to be sterilized, and at the end he is killed by injection after the mayor's wife brings his existence to the attention of the visiting North German Nazi, an example of the complicity of the villagers in the Nazi crimes. Yet Toni is the only one of all the villagers, be-

sides Anna, who tries to help Adler when he is beaten during the village's
Kristallnacht. Although he at first thinks it is fun, his innate decency rebels
at the brutality and he attacks the perpetrators. He is thus much more
humane than the other villagers.

As Bernhard Natter points out, the closing scenes exemplify how
difficult it is to portray the horrors of Nazism on the stage, a problem that
such dramatists as Rolf Hochhuth and Peter Weiss also struggled with.
Scene 10 shows Toni's death by injection, and scene 11 the priest's death by
torture in a concentration camp. Scene 12, which takes place in an unspeci-
fied concentration camp in the East, is more problematic. Adler, who is
carrying a heavy rock, is emaciated and at the end of his strength. He is
horrified to see Hans, who (at first) does not recognize his father because
he has changed so much. When he does, he embraces him, shoots him,
kisses him, and then shoots himself. In death they are locked in an embrace. The unlikely coincidence that Hans as an SS guard would meet his
own father in a camp makes the ending melodramatic. Natter criticizes this
scene because, in his view, this personal death hides the anonymous death
machinery of the camps and misrepresents the Nazis' racial extermination
policies.[36] Although Adler's death is melodramatic and a weak part of an
otherwise powerful play, it is important that Mitterer includes these three
scenes to counter those like the mayor who claim that the atrocities have
been exaggerated. These scenes stress the murderous brutality of the Nazis
and thus also the guilt of those who went along and are now intent on
down-playing Nazi crimes.

Homeland, Sold Out (1989) deals with the Option of 1939, another sensitive topic that, until recently, has been taboo.[37] As his introduction indicates, Mitterer explores here why 86 percent of South Tyroleans, a people
closely tied to their home, opted to leave South Tyrol. The introduction also
sheds light on the genesis of the work. At the end of 1985, ORF, the Austrian broadcasting company, suggested that Mitterer write a film about the
Option that would be broadcast in 1989 on its fiftieth anniversary. Mitterer's methodology for the film script was similar to the one he used for
There's No Finer Country. He studied literature and documents, he inter-
viewed witnesses of the time, and even visited Czechoslovakia to talk to
people who had been expelled from their farms during the war to make
room for the South Tyroleans. Mitterer does not want, as he puts it, to tear
up new graves. Instead, he treats those who left and those who decided to
remain fairly. He wonders how people today would have chosen at that
time: would we also have fallen into the propaganda trap of the Nazis and
the Fascists? As Mitterer points out, there is still a gulf between those who
left and those who remained. The wound still hurts, and people do not like
to talk about it. Mitterer is emphatic that one must discuss it, even if it is
painful: only what is expressed, he observes, can be overcome.[38]

As in *There's No Finer Country,* Mitterer wants to reach a wide audience for his discussion of this topic, and thus the television film was for him an attractive medium. Like his play, the film is not a documentary despite the fact that it is based on substantial research. Instead, Mitterer shapes the vast amount of material he collected into a story that powerfully depicts the human dimensions of the Option. Mitterer sets his film in an unnamed and therefore representative village in South Tyrol. His film contains a large number of characters who represent the various groups involved: those who opted to stay and those who opted to go, the Italians and the South Tyroleans, the poor and the more well off, the Nazis and the Fascists. Among this array of characters, he focuses on three families in particular: the Tschurtschenthalers and the Rabensteiners, who opted to go, and the Oberhollenzers, who chose to stay. Through this technique, Mitterer makes his audience aware of how the Option tore families and communities apart. He wants, as he remarks in his introduction, to depict the suffering of that time so that the television viewer could sympathize and understand.

The first part of the film begins in March 1938 and concludes on December 31, 1939, the last day for deciding whether to stay or leave. Gradually Mitterer relates the suffering that the South Tyroleans were forced to endure since Italy acquired South Tyrol at the end of the First World War. The earliest scenes document the destruction of South Tyrolean culture by the Italian Fascists. In the school, the teacher, an Italian, who is also the mayor, wears the Fascist party uniform and dictates in Italian an episode from Mussolini's life to the children. The schools thus serve as a place of indoctrination. Worse, however, is the suppression of South Tyrolean culture and language. The teacher hits Siegfried Tschurtschenthaler for writing an "s" in German script on the board. He accuses Siegfried of being a barbarian who will never learn Italian, and makes fun of his name, Tschurtschenthaler. No civilized person can pronounce it, he declares, showing his disdain for their culture. Mitterer depicts the reluctance of most South Tyrolean German-speaking children to learn Italian. Only a few, such as Hanni Rabensteiner, sing the Italian national anthem enthusiastically. The others sing half-heartedly at best. Although some children like Alfons Rabensteiner wear the uniform of the Balilla, the Italian young Fascists, most are strongly opposed. Mitterer points out, however, that Alfons has joined because of the free uniform and school books since his parents are poor. He and his sister Hanni, who also wears a Fascist youth organization uniform, are subjected to taunts from the other children, who throw Alfons into a cesspool.

Through this opening, Mitterer documents the suppression and discrimination that South Tyroleans suffered in the years since Italy acquired the region in the treaty of St. Germain. As soon as the Italian Fascists gained power they began to Italianize South Tyrol and destroy its culture, a policy shaped by the fanatical nationalist senator, Ettore Tolomei, whom Mitterer mentions in the film. The Fascists decreed that Italian was to be the language of instruction in South Tyrolean schools: by suppressing the German language they sought to destroy the cultural identity of South Tyroleans. The German elementary school was gradually abolished starting with the school year of 1923/24 and ending in 1927/28. German teachers were fired and replaced with Italian teachers. Encouraged by their parents, South Tyrolean children resisted learning Italian.[39] The film shows how the children learn German in the "catacomb schools," the illegal secret schools. Despite their caution, the Italians discover the school, arrest the teacher, and exile her to southern Italy, a typical punishment.[40] Mitterer gives other examples of discrimination. The old school custodian, for example, is fired because she only spoke German. After Kathl Rabensteiner forces her husband, Sepp, to Italianize their name to Pietracorvo, she becomes the new custodian. As Kathl observes, they have to get by since they have three children to support and Sepp is unemployed. The other South Tyroleans in the village consider them traitors. As the film shows, such suppression caused a great deal of bitterness. Anna Tschurtschenthaler tells the Italian gendarme, Ettore, whom she later marries: "We are South Tyroleans. We speak German. Why do you want to take our language away?"(p. 26).

Mitterer points out how the persecution by the Italian Fascists led the South Tyroleans to view Hitler as their salvation, the main reason why their response to the *Anschluss* was so enthusiastic. Kofler, the local leader for the *Völkischer Kampfring Südtirols* (VKS), expresses the hope of many when he declares that in a few days Hitler will be in South Tyrol. Peter Hofer, however, the district leader of the VKS, has a more sober assessment of the situation. He notes that Hitler cannot bring his politics into danger because of South Tyrol since he needs Italy as an ally (p. 34). As the film shows, he was right. Although in 1920 Hitler had favored the unification of the North and South Tyrol, he began to change his mind as early as the fall of 1922 with Mussolini's rise to power. Mussolini gave Hitler money for his Putsch in exchange for Hitler's abandoning claims to South Tyrol. For Hitler, the Italian alliance was more important than South Tyrol, a view that made him break with other nationalists in Germany and Austria.[41] In May 1938, Mussolini promised to support Hitler's claims to Czechoslovakia on the condition that Hitler renounce claims to South Tyrol. Hitler was willing to sell South Tyrol for Czechoslovakia, which was more important militarily.[42]

In the film, the South Tyroleans realize that their hopes that Hitler would rescue South Tyrol from the Italian Fascists are illusory when the priest reads from the speech Hitler gave during his visit to Mussolini on May 7, 1938. In it, Hitler reiterated that the Alps should remain the border between the two countries. As the priest notes bitterly, Hitler traveled home in a curtained train without stopping to see their betrayed and sold homeland (p. 43). Both Hitler and Mussolini wanted to solve the festering problem of South Tyrol by resettlement. Mitterer documents in the film, however, how the two countries understood this resettlement differently. The Italians did not want all South Tyroleans to leave but only those they suspected of irredentism, the poor, and the workers in the cities whose jobs could easily be filled with Italian workers. They did not, however, want the farmers to leave. This explains the confusion in Italian policy toward the Option. At first the Italians did not allow propaganda against opting for Germany since they were eager for some to leave. Once it became clear that not only the poor and people from the towns but also the farmers were opting to go, the Italians banned propaganda for opting for Germany. They feared that with such an exodus the economy of South Tyrol would fall apart (p. 70). Hitler's purpose was different: he wanted the largest possible number of people to opt for Germany to provide him with a propaganda coup.

Mitterer describes with historical accuracy the reactions of the VKS. At first, Kofler considers the agreement between Hitler and Mussolini criminal and says that before they leave their home they would prefer to be shot (p. 53). As a leader of their delegation to Berlin, Peter Hofer bitterly tells Himmler that they did not believe that Hitler would abandon them and that Hitler's determination to separate blood and soil is incompatible with Nazi ideology. Himmler, however, persuades the VKS that it is their duty to obey Hitler in his goal of solving the problem of South Tyrol forever. Himmler promises that the South Tyroleans will be resettled together. He orders that at least 90 percent must opt for Germany. After this meeting, the members of the VKS support Hitler's policy. They are actively involved in shaping the propaganda for leaving, encouraged, in part, by Himmler's promise that members of the VKS will continue as leaders in the resettlement areas. Some, like the VKS, were thus not merely passive victims of the Option but were active participants.

Although the word option implies choice, the choice was rather between Scylla and Charybdis.[43] As Mitterer shows, the South Tyroleans were confronted with the choice of either abandoning the farms where their families had lived for many generations for an uncertain future in the German Reich, or staying on their farms and continuing to experience the persecution of the Italian Fascists. Mitterer points out that the large number who opted for the Reich does not necessarily mean that they voted *for* National Socialism but rather *against* Fascism. Most just wanted to flee from Fascist Italy. Although the Italian gendarme, Ettore, says that they should stay since the Italian Fascists will not be in power forever, his voice of reason does not prevail in the heated and emotional debate.

Mitterer documents the vicious propaganda for the Option. Hofer tells the South Tyroleans that they are strangers in their own land, hated and oppressed by the Italians. In a generation none of them will speak German any more. In Germany, in contrast, they will be free and will belong to the most powerful and courageous people on earth (p. 65). The Nazis offer them better land than the steep, rocky soil of South Tyrol and promise even second and third sons a farm. This was attractive since at that time in South Tyrol only the first son inherited the land, as can be seen in the case of Hermann Tschurtschenthaler. People wanted to believe the promises, and blinded themselves to the fact that the German army would first have to capture this land before they could have it. In the film, Mitterer shows how the Italian Fascists contribute to the propaganda for leaving. The Italian mayor, for example, declares that those who opt for Italy will be Italian citizens and will not be allowed to speak a word of German (p. 58). Mitterer stresses how influential the Sicilian rumor, a master stroke of the Germans,[44] was in persuading people to leave. According to this rumor, which originated with the Germans and which the Italians only denied later when it was apparent that too many were opting to leave, those who opted to remain in Italy would not be allowed to live in South Tyrol but would be sent to Sicily. The threat of this forced resettlement in the South of Italy and the promise of land for everybody in an area where they would be resettled together were the main weapons of the propaganda in favor of opting for Germany. In addition, this propaganda tried to intimidate people into leaving by denouncing those who decided to remain as traitors and collaborators.

As others have documented, those who opted for Germany treated those who decided to stay badly. Their haystacks were burned down, people threw stones at their children, and their windows were broken.[45] In the film, the Oberhollenzer's dog is shot to death and in the church those who opted to go refuse to sit next to those who decided to remain. Kofler calls those who stay cowardly swine. Mitterer depicts how the Option exacerbated tensions within the community and especially within the family, where it caused conflict and heartbreak and tore families apart. In the Tschurtschenthaler family, for example, Michael and Anna stay but Paula and Hermann's father leave with the other family members, even though they would prefer to stay. In the Rabensteiner family, Kathl wants to stay but Sepp insists on leaving.

The second part of the film deals with the consequences of the Option. It begins in March 1940 and ends in October 1945 at the end of the war. Mitterer shows the gradual exodus of the South Tyroleans to the German Reich. At the beginning, some poor people who are hoping for a better life are seen leaving, and the Italian mayor is happy to see them go. Those who are not tied to the land are sent to work in munitions factories in Germany or are conscripted into the army. He shows the arrival in Innsbruck where already some begin to question their decision since the people in Innsbruck are unfriendly and resent the influx of the South Tyroleans, who may take away their housing and jobs. Single men are immediately drafted.

Mitterer uses the experiences of the Tschurtschenthalers as a model for those farmers who opted to leave. The family is assigned a farm in Moravia where they are surrounded by hostile Czechs. They soon learn that they are benefiting from Nazi plunder since the farm is stolen from Milos and his family and Milos is forced to work there. Paula is horrified when she learns this and wants to leave, but Hermann sees the farm as a paradise and is not overly concerned about the moral issues involved. Paula tells Hermann later when he returns on leave that he has deceived himself from the beginning. He wanted to have property and be free. Where are you now? she asks. You shoot people and take their homes away. We are in a strange land on a stolen farm, she points out (pp. 141-142). Later they lose everything when they have to flee at the approach of the Soviet army.

Although Mitterer shows that many were innocent victims of the two dictators who decided the fate of this small ethnic minority, he does not make them all into innocent victims and does not gloss over their wrongdoing. Toni and Hermann are fanatical Germans, and Toni quickly joins the SS. As Mitterer shows, there were convinced and fanatical Nazis who made the people's misery worse. Those who stay treat the newly arrived Italians with hostility. When Enzo and Francesca arrive on the Tschurtschenthaler farm, Peter Oberhollenzer throws a stone covered with burning straw though their window. Those who opted for Germany are prepared, like Hermann, to profit from the plunder of the Nazi regime. Although Mitterer sympathizes with people's desperate desire to flee from Fascist Italy, he does not deny that those opting for Germany did not express any opposition to Nazism. Mitterer alludes to the brutality of the German occupation of South Tyrol beginning in September 1943 and lasting until the arrival of the Allies. During this time the number of victims in South Tyrol—Jews, those who refused to serve in the army, and opponents of the Nazi regime—who were killed after sentences by special courts or in concentration camps was appallingly high.[46] As Toni warns his brother Michael, some of the leaders of those who opted to stay are already on the way to Dachau (p. 132). Leaders of the VKS were involved in the brutality since they played a leadership role during the German occupation. Toni, for instance, takes advantage of his new power to arrest Ettore, beat him, and try to force him to divorce Anna. At the end, when Kofler is arrested by the Americans, he shows his racism when he calls the victors Jews, niggers, Italians and traitors (p. 150).

Mitterer vividly depicts the hostility between the Italians and the South Tyrolean Germans, between those who decide to leave and those who stay, and between family members, which separates people into warring groups. So much bitterness exists that it seems impossible for these various groups to ever get along with each other. Mitterer does offer some hope, however. Kathl Rabensteiner, for example, has contact with the Italians, not only out of material considerations but because she is open and tolerant. Many of the Italians who are not Fascists are friendly and humane. Ettore, for instance, tries to understand the South Tyroleans and learn their language.

In defiance of orders, he speaks to them in German. He is friendly with Kathl and cooks a Sicilian specialty for her and her husband Sepp, which Sepp refuses to eat. Mitterer depicts Ettore as a humane and concerned person who attempts to build bridges between the two cultures. As Ettore tells Sepp in an effort to persuade him to stay: I am a human being, you are too. Mussolini will not be in power forever. Then you will get your schools, culture and language. Then we will be brothers (p. 81). Mitterer also shows another positive example of the ability of people of different cultures to get along with each other. Although at first the Italians who move onto the Tschurtschenthaler farm are ostracized, Hans and Rosa Oberhollenzer later make friends with them.

The most hopeful sign is, however, the relationship between Anna and Ettore which Mitterer proposes as a model. At first Anna and Ettore hide the relationship, but Anna courageously refuses to hide any longer. Like the other South Tyroleans, Anna's family reacts with great hostility to this relationship: her mother curses her and Anna's brothers, Toni and Hermann, the most fanatical Germans of the family, attack Ettore and beat him unconscious. Although Paula is sympathetic to Anna, Anna's brother Michael is the only one who is supportive and the only family member to attend the wedding. When Anna and Ettore return to their room after the wedding, some South Tyroleans have destroyed their belongings. When they look outside, they see themselves being burned in effigy on their stolen bed. The Italians are much more tolerant of the relationship than the South Tyroleans. Despite the many cultural difficulties that they encounter in the marriage, Ettore tells Anna: "We must show them that it is possible, that a living together is possible"(p. 59), and they succeed. Through their example, they show that people of different cultures and backgrounds can understand each other and work out their differences.

At the end, the priest argues that peaceful coexistence can only be based on freedom, equality and mutual respect. If we don't reject hatred, violence and nationalistic arrogance on both sides, he declares, South Tyrol will never live in peace (pp. 151-152), words that summarize Mitterer's plea in both these works for tolerance and understanding. As both works show, Mitterer is convinced that confronting the past is crucial. If we repress the past, as Santayana observes in the opening motto, and refuse to discuss it, we are condemned to repeat its mistakes. Repressing the past prevents us from understanding the present and poisons both the present and the future. Mitterer thus agrees with Wolfgang Georg Fischer's remark: "The poison in the bottle would be a much worse inheritance for a future generation."[47]

Notes

1. George E. Berkley, *Vienna and Its Jews: The Tragedy of Success 1880s-1980s* (Cambridge: Abt Books, 1988), p. 345. "Remembering to Forget" is the title of Chapter 28 of his study.

2. *Sibirien* is an expanded version of "Abstellgleis," one of the parts of *Besuchszeit*.

3. Robert Edwin Herzstein, *Waldheim: The Missing Years* (New York: Arbor House/William Morrow, 1988), p. 240.

4. Bruce F. Pauley, *Hitler and the Forgotten Nazis: A History of Austrian National Socialism* (Chapel Hill: University of North Carolina Press, 1981), xiii.

5. Bruce F. Pauley, *From Prejudice to Persecution: A History of Austrian Anti-Semitism* (Chapel Hill and London: University of North Carolina Press, 1992), p. 297.

6. Berkley, p. 345.

7. Berkley, p. 346.

8. Joseph McVeigh, *Kontinuität und Vergangenheitsbewältigung in der österreichischen Literatur nach 1945* (Wien: Braumüller, 1988), p. 135. See also Elke Atzler, "Beharren, Adaptieren, Neuorientieren? Aspekte zur literarischen Entwicklung der 70er Jahre in Österreich," in Walter Buchebner Literaturprojekt, *Illusionen-Desillusionen? Zur neueren realistischen Prosa und Dramatik in Österreich* (Wien, Köln: Böhlau, 1989), pp. 56-65.

9. An example of Austrian historians' recent concern with the past is Anton Pelinka and Erika Weinzierl, Eds., *Das grosse Tabu: Österreichs Umgang mit seiner Vergangenheit* (np: Verlag der Österreichischen Staatsdruckerei, 1987). A few Austrian historians such as Gerhard Botz had addressed this issue earlier.

10. Pelinka and Weinzierl, p. 7.

11. Klaus Zeyringer, *Innerlichkeit und Öffentlichkeit: Österreichische Literatur der achtziger Jahre* (Tübingen: Francke, 1992), p. 153.

12. Herzstein, p. 251.

13. Berkley, p. 345.

14. Herzstein, p. 264, and Bruce F. Pauley, *From Prejudice to Persecution*, p. 312.

15. Elfriede Schmidt, *1938 ... and the Consequences*, trans. Peter J. Lyth (Riverside: Ariadne Press, 1992), p. 60.

16. Felix Mitterer, Introduction to *Verlorene Heimat* (1987), in *Stücke* 2 (Innsbruck: Haymon, 1992), p. 9.

17. Felix Mitterer, Introduction to *Kein Platz für Idioten* (1977), in *Stücke* 1 (Innsbruck: Haymon, 1992), p. 11.

18. Peter Gerlich, "Illusionen der Politik—Politik der Illusionen," *Illusionen—Desillusionen*, p. 16.

19. For a discussion of recent developments in the *Volksstück* see Jürgen Hein, Ed., *Volksstück: vom Hanswurstspiel zum sozialen Drama der Gegenwart* (München: Beck, 1989).

20. Herbert Herzmann, "The Relevance of the Tradition: The *Volksstücke* of Felix Mitterer," *Modern Austrian Literature* 24, nos. 3/4 (1991), pp. 176-177.

21. For a more extensive discussion of Gomperz see Hans Thöni, "Das Schicksal des Rudolf Gomperz," contained in Mitterer, *Kein schöner Land: Ein Theaterstück und sein historischer Hintergrund* (Innsbruck: Haymon, 1987), pp. 95-117.

22. Mitterer, *Stücke* I, p. 305.

23. Thöni mentions that the Gomperz family was Protestant which he sees as an argument for the family coming originally from Germany (p. 96).

24. See, for example, Mitterer's plays, *Die Kinder des Teufels: Ein Theaterstück und sein historischer Hintergrund* (Innsbruck: Haymon, 1989) and *Das wunderbare Schicksal: Aus dem Leben des Hoftyrolers Peter Prosch: Ein Theaterstück und sein historischer Hintergrund* (Innsbruck: Haymon 1992). As both subtitles indicate, the book versions of these plays, like the book version of *Kein schöner Land*, contain extensive historical documentation.

25. Felix Mitterer, *Kein schöner Land: Ein Theaterstück und sein historischer Hintergrund* (Innsbruck: Haymon, 1987), p. 91. Further references to this work will be given in the text. The translations are my own.

26. See, for example, Bruce F. Pauley, *From Prejudice to Persecution*; Ivar Oxaal, Michael Pollak, and Gerhard Botz, *Jews, Antisemitism and Culture in Vienna* (London and New York: Routledge and Kegan Paul, 1987); George E. Berkley, *Vienna and its Jews*; Elfriede Schmidt, *1938 … and the Consequences*; and Pelinka and Weinzierl, *Das grosse Tabu*, to mention but a few recent studies.

27. Bruce F. Pauley, *From Prejudice to Persecution*, p. 305.

28. F. L. Carsten, *Fascist Movements in Austria: From Schönerer to Hitler* (London, Beverly Hills: Sage, 1977), p. 99.

29. See, for example, Carsten, p. 284; Schmidt, p. 176; Gretl Köfler, "Die Juden in Tirol," in Mitterer, *Kein schöner Land*, pp. 127-128.

30. Schmidt, p. 175.

31. For a detailed account of the historical accuracy with which Mitterer depicts Nazi policy to the Jews in the play see Bernhard Natter, "'Endlich! Jetzt is a Ruah!' Das Bild nationalsozialistischer Ausgrenzungs-und Vernichtungs politik in Felix Mitterers Theaterstück *Kein schöner Land*," *Mitteilung aus dem Brenner-Archiv* 7 (1988), pp. 49-57.

32. Pauley, *From Prejudice to Persecution*, p. 287.

33. Berkley, p. 306.

34. See, for example, Pauley, *From Prejudice to Persecution*, p. 10.

35. Herzstein, p. 63.

36. Natter, p. 57.

37. Recently two works have dealt with this issue: Klaus Eisterer and Rolf Steininger, Eds., *Die Option: Südtirol zwischen Faschismus und Nationalsozialismus* (Innsbruck: Haymon, 1989) and Benedikt Erhard, Ed., *Option, Heimat, Opzioni: Eine Geschichte Südtirols: vom Gehen und vom Bleiben* (Wien: Österreichischer Bundesverlag, 1989).

38. Felix Mitterer, *Verkaufte Heimat: Eine Südtiroler Familiensaga von 1938 bis 1945, Drehbuch* (Innsbruck: Haymon Verlag, 1989), pp. 5-6. Such a view reflects those expressed by writers in *Die Option*. Future references are given in the text. The translations are my own.

39. Rolf Steininger, "Die Option—Anmerkungen zu einem schwierigen Thema," *Die Option*, p. 12.

40. See Maria Villgrater, "Die 'Katakombenschule': Symbol des Südtiroler Widerstandes," *Die Option*, pp. 85-106.

41. Bruce F. Pauley, *Hitler and the Forgotten Nazis*, p. 44.

42. Max von der Grün, *Wie war das eigentlich? Kindheit und Jugend im Dritten Reich* (Darmstadt und Neuwied: Luchterhand, 1979, Sammlung Luchterhand 1981), pp. 127-128.

43. Alfons Gruber, "Faschismus und Option in Südtirol," *Die Option*, p. 234.

44. See Klaus Eisterer, "'Hinaus oder hinunter!' Die sizilianische Legende: eine taktische Meisterleistung der Deutschen," *Die Option*, pp. 179-207.

45. Steininger, *Die Option*, p. 26.

46. Benedikt Erhard, Hugo Seyr, "Option Heimat—Geschichten und Fiktionen," *Option, Heimat, Opzioni*, p. 4.

47. Schmidt, p. 60.

Ethnic, National, and Regional Identities in Felix Mitterer's *Verkaufte Heimat*

Bernd Fischer

Felix Mitterer continues to reap praise for the ingenuity with which he adapts the traditional folk play for contemporary audiences. He has written remarkable folk plays for the stage, and possibly even more admirable has been his ability to develop the genre for television. The techniques Mitterer employs are so conventional and straightforward they seem to defy many of the claims made by the modernist discourse of our century. He employs a carefully structured poetic realism peppered with interspersions of fantastic or modernist elements. His characters are constructed around a conventional, easily decipherable psychology and function within well-established symbolic configurations. The dramaturgy offers few surprises, and the plot is usually predictable.[1] At times it is as if this author belongs to the nineteenth century, and yet there is little doubt that these 'premodern' aesthetics of poetic and social realism are effective in our times. Mitterer's dramas fulfill many of the clichés which German feuilletons have derided as trivial. And yet Mitterer's stage and television plays have achieved more in terms of spurring critical and self-critical discussions among large numbers of viewers than have most of the intellectualized stages of post-war German theater. Mitterer's success is, at least for this reader, an important indication that, in spite of all the eulogies, the aesthetics of a critical enlightenment are still both possible and adequate today.

What makes these aesthetics suitable in Mitterer's case are, by and large, the particular topics addressed in his plays. They are always of current concern for a very specific region, history, or social group. Mitterer stresses that growing up in Tyrol as the adopted son of a farm-hand was in many ways comparable to living in the nineteenth century. Accordingly he sees himself less influenced by a particular literary tradition than by the continuation of lifestyles and mind-sets that bridge the two centuries. In this sense he understands his plays as expressions of a specific regional mentality and culture; as such, they have been composed to reach an audience that shares many characteristics with the characters portrayed on stage. "These are plays that are written for many people, not for intellectuals."[2] At the same time the topics of Mitterer's major dramas depart from those of the traditional peasant farce, which remains a favorite among amateur theaters in Tyrol.[3] More than other authors, Mitterer has managed to establish topics of extensive political or historical significance for both the professional and amateur *Volksbühne*. Many of his plays deal with difficult contemporary problems or uncomfortable historical questions in a straightforward fashion without unduly shocking or alienating the audience of the typical peasant farce. Of particular importance is that his plays show a sense of responsibility that includes both a closeness to the audience he intends to reach and a high degree of familiarity with the topics that his plays portray. "One has to be incredibly exact in these matters and not simply rely on the testimony of witnesses, since they forget and repress a lot—for this reason, one needs to do extensive archival research, as well."[4] The plays deal with such diverse topics as life in a nursing home (*Siberia*), the fate of a small-town family during Austrian Nazism (*There's No Finer Country*), the biggest known witch burning of seventeenth-century Salzburg (*The Children of the Devil*), or the 1837 expulsion of Protestants from the Zillertal by the Archbishop of Salzburg (*Lost Homeland*). *Homeland, Sold Out* treats the complex events in South Tyrol, when it was squeezed between Nazism from the north and Fascism from the south. It was co-produced by Austrian and German television as a TV play in two parts and was directed by Karin Brandauer.

The play offers a case in point. In spite of its sensitive and politically charged topic, it found a considerable audience in both Austria and northern Italy. Mitterer manages to stay true to the question of historical interpretation and contemporary meaning at hand and neither evades nor circumvents the political potential of his play by engaging in autonomous aesthetic experimentation. While there are certain artistic costs incurred by using these aesthetics of attempted historical justice (predictability, moral discourse, and a harmoniously constructed ending), the play's ability to set into motion a discussion in the midst of the everyday reception patterns of an average TV audience might well be worth the price. For this drama not only understands what it is doing, but also recognizes its limits. In this sense it is truly a worthwhile continuation of critical folk literature. Indeed the play's biggest drawback, which the audience recognizes after the first few scenes, is perhaps also the play's chief merit; namely, its thoroughly planned structure lies openly revealed or, to put it differently, the viewer is always fully aware of the author's hand. The *Volksstück* has no need to hide the means by which it entertains.

Mitterer formulates the central question addressed by his play as follows: How was it possible that in 1939 over 80 percent of the German-speaking population of South Tyrol voted for German citizenship and opted to leave their homeland? The decision seemed to contradict the Tyrolean myth of their strong attachment to this mountainous region.[5] To solve this puzzle Mitterer spent two years studying the available historical accounts and documents, collecting additional materials, traveling to the localities, and conducting interviews with survivors. Only then did he design a story with characters and a plot sufficient to voice all the different opinions and memories that he had encountered. "This story of South Tyrol [*Verkaufte Heimat*] is especially complicated politically. There are so many different points of view and so much that the public should know about the political situation."[6]

In addition to the opposing groups of the Leavers and Stayers, Mitterer presents binary structures of rich and poor, local Fascists and Nazis, ideologues and opportunists in both camps, and demographic politics carried out by the church and politicians in both Berlin and Rome. The play proposes a complex net of interwoven dualisms and oppositions, and yet it hints that these binary structures might actually fail to offer an adequate understanding of individual decisions and collective mistakes. Therefore, each group and ideological camp is confronted with inner contradictions and dissenting voices that break up the simplicity of a dualism common to dramatic conflict. This is, of course, more easily achieved in a TV play, which allows for a greater number of scenes, figures, and localities, than in a stage production which, because of its technical limitations, has no choice but to concentrate on supposedly essential conflicts and is less equipped to provide a panoramic view of a multitude of conflicts and motivations on numerous personal and social levels.

As representatives of those who opted to leave their farm in hopes of acquiring a bigger farm within the German Reich or recently conquered areas, Mitterer offers the family Tschurtschenthaler. The family from the neighboring farm, the Oberhollenzers, on the other hand, represents the Stayers. Aside from these two, there are two other farm families 'in the play: the Czechoslovakians, who are the rightful owners of the farm that Hermann Tschurtschenthaler received from the German Reich, and Enzo and Francesca, the Sicilian family who bought the abandoned Tschurtschenthaler farm. The rugged landscape and the unbending prejudice of the Tyroleans, however, prove too much of an obstacle for their hopes of a better life outside Sicily. In the end they gladly resell the farm to Toni, the younger brother of Hermann Tschurtschenthaler, who had inherited the farm. The prospect of returning to Tyrol from Germany with sufficient political power to acquire by force the farm that had fallen to his older brother has indeed motivated the laborer Toni all along. As the second son and, therefore, a secondary citizen in the society of Tyrol, Toni eagerly embraces a radical Nazism that spreads terror among the Stayers and he joins the *Waffen SS*. Later he returns to South Tyrol as part of the German occupation force in the uniform of the German military police. For a moment the second-born and unemployed laborer is on the top of his world: he can arrest the Italian mayor, the Italian carabiniere, who married his sister, and the Sicilian farmer who bought the family lands. While his triumph is short lived, the SS man Toni remains the owner of the farm even after his arrest by the American troops. Hermann, the returning older brother, will have to find a way to reconcile himself with his younger sibling.

Michael, a third brother who remained firmly on the side of the Stayers and in political opposition to both the Fascist Italian administration and the propaganda and terror of the local Nazis, offers this consolation to Hermann Tschurtschenthaler: "You two will soon reconcile!"[7] Michael had been preparing to enter the priesthood, but now decides to become a politician. The consolation to his brother suggests that his politics will not be interested in revenge and punishment, but rather in reconciliation and appeasement. While there may be a slight change in the power structure of the Tschurtschenthaler family, Toni and Hermann will soon be back on their father's farm and will enjoy their traditional rights in spite of their misdeeds. Just like the Stayer Hans Oberhollenzer, who becomes the town's first mayor after the war, Michael and the local priest belong to the victorious side of history. They have made the right moral and political decisions all along and inspire hope for the political future of Mitterer's fictitious Tyrol. However, it is difficult to imagine how they will reconcile themselves with the 80 percent of German-speaking Tyroleans who opted for Germany and put the Stayers under considerable psychological and physical pressure. Ultimately the play, like Michael, has no answer to the question of what to do with the perpetrators of Nazism and Fascism and those seduced by it, other than to propose their unconditional reintegration. Given the sheer numbers involved, there might indeed have been no other answer; and yet this solution is at best problematic. Can a broader audience accept the fact that Toni, the SS man, and Hermann, who not only listened to the local Nazi propagandists Hofer and Kofler, but also clearly sought to enrich themselves with the help of the German army, are able to return to their farm and possibly dominate once again? Mitterer obviously aims at an integrative message in view of the contemporary political situation in Tyrol and in the process avoids any condemnation aside from the state and party offices in Italy and Germany. When the U.S. army arrives, the Fascist Italian mayor and teacher, the Nazi innkeeper Kofler, Toni, and his SS comrade Willi are arrested for a time. But it is clear they will be back, and more importantly, so will the xenophobia and prejudice they have politically exploited. In the play it is this prejudice against the Italian way of thinking, living, and working that is the defining characteristic of what can be called the German culture of South Tyrol. The dislike of anything

Italian is in part the result of Mussolini's politics of forced romanization, which had forbidden the use of German in schools, had excluded Germans from political offices, and was basically directed towards freeing the area of its German character. It was also, however, a result of their understanding themselves as the "others" of Italy, which has indeed been the crux of the German identity in South Tyrol all along. Having been persecuted themselves, the German-speaking Tyroleans assume the role of the victim, in spite of their own crimes. Kofler vividly expresses one possible post-war mind-set while he is being arrested: "And those are the victors now (*looks back*): Jews, niggers, foreigners and traitors!"[8]

The most convincing attempt of the play to portray the character and function of this particular xenophobia lies in the figure of Hermann Tschurtschenthaler's mother. Without hesitation she washes her hands of her daughter Anna, who has fallen in love with the Italian carabiniere Ettore, and later even refuses to acknowledge their child. She pushes her son Hermann to opt for emigration against the wishes of her husband and her daughter-in-law. Mother Tschurtschenthaler represents the evil soul of German South Tyrol and later becomes the evil soul of the German occupation in Czechoslovakia. For it is here that the family Tschurtschenthaler receives a farm from the German Reich that, as promised, is much bigger and richer than their old one in Tyrol. The decisive ethical question regarding the family's role in Czechoslovakia arises when Milos, the Czech farmhand who is forced to work for Hermann, explains why he does not work as hard as the Tschurtschenthalers expect. He declares that he is the rightful owner of the farm, and that the Tschurtschenthalers have stolen it from him with the help of the German army. Hermann's wife Paula sits down and says: "We didn't know, Milos, honest we didn't!" Hermann's father says: "Well I wouldn't be working for someone who stole my farm!" Hermann yells: "I didn't know it! They told me it was a gift of the Reich!" Hermann's mother, however, remarks: "Well, that cannot be changed anymore. Fate! I said you should look for another job."[9] Realizing the family's ethical bankruptcy, Hermann's father wanders out into the cold night and dies. Hermann, on the other hand, using his mother's pragmatic ethnic hatred, eases his conscience by denouncing Milos as a lazy inferior: "You're a lazy dog! While I've plowed ten acres, you've only done two. You're all probably the same lazy pack of foreigners as back home." From there it is only a small step to his embracing official Nazi propaganda: "I don't give a damn who used to own the farm, you get it?! I've been working my ass off for two years now. And whoever works should reap the rewards of his labors. The Führer is proud of us. We are fighting peasants, like a thousand years ago. And now I'm off to defend my property."[10] It is not until his experience on the Russian Front and his realization that the Reich is coming to an end that Hermann recognizes his mistake. Paula finally brings his motivations to a point: "But no, you wanted to own property, a big farm. You wanted to be free. And are you now free? We're here in a strange country on a stolen farm." Hermann sighs and answers: "I know now it was all wrong. I know we're going to lose the war and we'll have to leave again. But what should I do? What should I do?"[11] The motivation of both Hermann and his mother lies within their identity as proud, independent, and prosperous German farmers. Under the Fascist domination of Tyrol, it is precisely this existence that seems out of their reach. They have sunk to the position of a politically powerless minority which ekes out an existence on a miserably poor and work-intensive farm. Faced with this kind of oppression, both are willing to go anyplace where they are offered the chance to realize their pride and greed as dominant German farmers. No price is too high to achieve this position—not accepting a stolen farm or even having to fight other countries to maintain their new riches. In Hermann's opinion, "Everyone has to make sacrifices—everyone! We once again have a fatherland! And this fatherland gave us this farm—we've never had it so good, never! We are wealthy—I'm a wealthy farmer!"[12] This ambition defines the principal difference between Hermann and Hans Oberhollenzer, who chose to stay in Tyrol and accept his fate. Hans works in an Italian quarry, since his farm cannot sustain his family. He even finds a way to develop a neighborly relationship with Enzo and Francesca. While the play leaves no question that all citizens of Tyrol are mere statistics in a demographic numbers game between Mussolini and Himmler—the latter is mainly interested in gaining workers for the war industry and soldiers for the eastern front—there is also no question that individual ethical decisions did in the end make a decisive difference. Both Toni and his mother threaten the Stayers as well as the Czechs with the concentration camp, and Mother Tschurtschenthaler actually denounces a Czech worker to the military authorities.

On the other hand, the play provides almost too many model German-speaking Tyroleans in its search for an optimistic future: besides Hans, his wife Rosa and their four children, there are Michael and Anna Tschurtschenthaler, their father, and the priest. While these citizens offer hope for a brighter future in South Tyrol, it is an Italian character that more radically defines an integral and *inter*-cultural future for the region. The Sicilian carabiniere Ettore Magalone falls in love with Anna, learns German, and marries her against the prejudices of both the German and the Italian camps. There is a decisive moment in the play, just before the German occupation of South Tyrol, when Ettore suggests that it might be best if Anna and he leave for the south. Anna refuses. After the Germans have arrived, and Ettore has been jailed and beaten by her brother Toni, Anna admits that Ettore had been right—they should have left. Ettore answers: "No! No! We're staying!" ("Nein! Nein! Wir bleiben!" ibid., p. 131). He joins the resistance and fights, hoping to bring the war to a quick end. Although he was not born in Tyrol, Ettore makes a conscious decision to live in and work for an *inter*-cultural South Tyrol. He does not inherit but builds a home—this is what defines his concept of *Heimat* (Homeland). At the end of the play an alternative concept of *Heimat* is proposed in the political program of the *Südtiroler Volkspartei* (South Tyrolean Folk Party), as well as the new Italian parties.[13] It promises a peaceful co-existence of the two nationalities on the basis of freedom, equality and mutual respect (ibid., p. 152). Because of their political nature, the parties are oriented towards a *bi*-cultural Tyrol, in which the differences of the two groups of people ("Volksgruppen," ibid.) are preserved—although peacefully this time. Ettore and Anna, however, stand for a model of mutual acculturation and assimilation. While Hermann's and Paula's youngest son bears the name Andreas, Ettore's and Anna's son bears the name of their compromise in assimilation: Andrea.

With the exception of the characters of Anna and Ettore, Mitterer's play presupposes ethnic identities that deserve further investigation. The play offers numerous examples of political and ideological exploitation based upon presumed ethnic differences. Mitterer not only shows how thin the basis for these prejudices actually is, but also explores the psychological reasoning behind prejudice and bias. Nevertheless, one is left with the impression that the play itself proceeds upon the assumption that there are defining national differences between the groups in question that cannot be analyzed further. This becomes particularly obvious with the characters of Sepp Rabensteiner and his wife Kathl. Throughout much of the play there is the implicit accusation that Kathl has assimilated somewhat too readily and enthusiastically. In fact her overeagerness to become Italian may be considered opportunistic. She hopes to rescue her family from poverty and discrimination by going along with the dictates of the Italian authorities, and she and her husband are rewarded with jobs as school custodians and an apartment in the school building. The play accuses her of pretending to be something that she is not and, more importantly, of forcing her husband to become something that he cannot become. The family name illustrates this point. In order to be employed by the Fascist mayor and principal, Sepp Rabensteiner has to change his name to Guiseppe Pietracorvo (a literal translation of his German name). With the loss of his name, Sepp also loses his sense of self-worth. His anger wells up until he threatens to blow up the school. During an evening with Anna and Ettore, who have their own difficulties trying to find a name both can agree on for their son, Kathl and Sepp argue about the quality of Sicilian wine and their decision to take on an Italian name for economic reasons. Kathl suggests that the name does not make the man. Sepp gets up angrily and replies:

> Well what else? If I'm Chinese, I have a Chinese name. If I'm German, I have a German name!

KATHL: Oh, stop it, Sepp! Bertolini! Pizzinini! Ferrari! Crazzolara! Those are all South Tyroleans from our village!

SEPP: But they all have German first names.[14]

What defines national or ethnic identities? Since most characters in the play speak German and Italian, and, as suggested by their last names, many have intermarried with Italian families, what remains is the first name that one receives at birth. There is also the question of acquired cultural taste. However, no matter what Sepp claims, he does drink the Sicilian wine. While emotions run high when it comes to national identity, there is actually no defining difference other than these emotions themselves. They are in fact the cause and not the result of the differences. Indeed it seems that the emotional drive behind ethnic/national identity is so strong because it is without any defensible basis. In Sepp's case, he finally succumbs to a German recruiter and leaves with Kathl and their three children for Essen to work in an arms factory.

SEPP: (*screams*) "Fare thee well, my South Tyrol! My name is Sepp Rabensteiner. And all of you can kiss my ass!"

He ends up at the front, of course. After the liberation of South Tyrol, Sepp and Hermann are able to return, claiming that they were forced laborers in Germany. Kathl, who had made it back some months earlier, provided Sepp with the necessary papers.

SEPP: (*In a weak voice.*) "My Kathl was an angel of God! An angel of God! And she was always right! (*Begins to cry.*) Always! God, I should have listened to her!"[15]

Mitterer's play is bilingual and the stage directions suggest that the language individual characters use in specific situations is not without significance. There are those with a highly developed willingness and interest in using both languages like Anna, Kathl, Ettore, and others. And there are those who avoid using the other tongue whenever possible. But even the readily bilingual characters use their first language whenever they talk about sensitive issues, especially those that concern their own sense of self. Not only the ideological politics of the play's Fascists and Nazis, but also the psychological dispositions for particular identity constructs fall alongside the lines of the characters' first and second languages. In the end, this is the deciding factor. The play leaves us with the impression that the future of South Tyrol might well hinge on the possibility of introducing true bilingualism—in itself a difficult and open question.

Possibly the most inconspicuous and at the same time one of the most interesting characters of the play is Dario Nardelli, a Trentinian street cleaner. He speaks the Tyrolean dialect as well as German and Italian, and with his 'gothic' beard, he looks, according to the Fascist mayor, like "Andreas Hofer, a damned Tyrolean!"[16] He is always around with his dog and his cleaning wagon. He knows everyone—Sicilian, German, Leavers,

Stayers. He talks to everyone and seems to understand everyone on a certain level. He hates the Fascists (p. 31) and German nationalists (p. 87) and dislikes the Leavers as well as the southern Italians who were lured into offices in Tyrol. Dario has found a way out of the dualism of *Deutsch* or *Walsch*.[17] When Sepp attempts to project his own identity crisis on Dario—"You're a foreigner. And if you stay here for a hundred years, you'll still be a foreigner!"—Dario replies: "What am I? A foreigner? I'm a Trentiner, a Trentiner, I tell you! Porco dio!"[18] In the final scenes that portray a kind of tableau of the good Tyrol, Dario greets the Sicilian Ettore, who has returned from his partisan hide-out, in a mixture of German and Italian, and he greets Michael in an equally inclusive manner. If Hermann's mother, the old mistress Tschurtschenthaler, is the evil ghost of German nationalism and divisive greed, then the street cleaner Dario is the good fairy of Italian regionalism. In the first decade after the war Dario's vision indeed seemed to prevail, as the province Bozen was combined with the province of Trient into a common autonomy. However, this placed the German-speaking population in a minority status once again, and the *Südtiroler Volkspartei* did not rest until Bozen was separated from Trient and granted its own autonomous status, in which the German-speaking population now holds a 75 percent majority.

If not explicitly, the play implicitly qualifies ethnic and national identity constructs by connecting them to a psychology of an inferior sense of self that is compensated by opportunism and aggression. This holds true for the preposterous Italian mayor and teacher, who obviously has been put in offices that are clearly beyond his abilities, for Hermann Tschurtschenthaler's loss of pride, for Toni's inferiority complex as the younger brother, and for Sepp, who fears loss of identity more than unemployment. All these identities are constructed around the psychology of overcoming fears of economic inferiority by erecting ethnic fences and positing national differences. Although the play offers explanations for this kind of xenophobia, it allows for another set of differences in its own right. However, while there are differences between the mentalities of the southern Italians who have just moved north and the Tyrolean farmers as well as between Hermann and Milos, questions of ethnic origins are exposed as ideological. Many Tyroleans have, as mentioned above, Italian last names and German first names; many are bilingual. The differences that are supported by the play—in contrast to those propagated by the local Fascists and Nazis—are regional but not national or ethnic. In that sense, possibly more than in many others, Mitterer's play is truly in the tradition of the Tyrolean folk play. His play still suggests that what makes someone Tyrolean is a specific way of life, a mentality or mind-set that results from living and working in this particular mountainous region with its particular pleasures and hardships. This is the meaning of identity constructs around the concept of *Heimat*. Hermann was mistaken when he believed he could be a Tyrolean in Czechoslovakia. Ettore, on the other hand, has opted to be Tyrolean simply by deciding to stay and to work for a Tyrol worth living in.

In Mitterer's poetic framework, the Tyrolean folk play is possible as long as the specific Tyrolean way of life finds some kind of continuation—as it clearly did in spite of the time period treated in the play. While Mitterer maintains that rural structures of the nineteenth century still prevailed in Tyrol of the 1950s and 1960s, he also knows that an entirely new era might have begun with the decline of agriculture and the emergence of tourism, an era in which the concept of *Heimat* as well as the folk play might be no more than folklore.[19]

Notes

1. Herbert Herzmann points out the traditional elements and stock characters and sees many of Mitterer's dramas in the tradition of "Tyrolese/Bavarian Passion Plays." Cf. Herbert Herzmann, "The Relevance of the Tradition: The *Volksstücke* of Felix Mitterer." *Modern Austrian Literature* 24, 3/4 (1991), p. 174. Hans Weigel stresses parallels to Fritz Hochwälder and Karl Schönherr. Cf. his review in *neue tiroler zeitung* (5 Aug. 1989).

2. "Das sind Stücke, die für viele Menschen geschrieben sind, und nicht nur für Intellektuelle." Ursula Hassel, Deirdre McMahon, "Felix Mitterer im Gespräch." *Modern Austrian Literature* 25, 1 (1992), p. 21.

3. Cf. Herzmann, p. 174.

4. "Da muß man wahnsinnig genau sein und sich aber auch nicht nur auf die Zeugen verlassen, weil die ja viel vergessen und verdrängen, sondern in die Archive gehen und lesen." In "Felix Mitterer im Gespräch," p. 35.

5. Cf. Felix Mitterer, *Verkaufte Heimat: Eine Südtiroler Familiensaga von 1938 bis 1945*. Drehbuch mit Fotos von Petro Domenigg (Innsbruck: Haymon-Verlag, 1989), p. 5.

6. "Vor allem diese Südtiroler Geschichte [*Verkaufte Heimat*] ist politisch wahnsinnig kompliziert. Es gibt so viele Standpunkte und so viel, was das Publikum über die politische Situation wissen müßte." In "Felix Mitterer im Gespräch," pp. 38–39.

7. "Ihr werds euch schon einigen!" *Verkaufte Heimat*, p. 151.

8. "Und des sein jetzt die Sieger (*schaut zurück*) Juden, Neger, Walsche, Verräter!" Ibid., p. 150.

9. "Des hamma nit gwußt, Milos! Wirklich nit! ... Also i tat nit bei jemand als Knecht arbeiten, der mir den Hof gstohlen hat! ... I habs doch nit gwußt! Die haben gsagt, der Hof is ein Geschenk des Reiches! ... Ja, des kann ma jetzt alles nimmer ändern! Schicksal! I tat sagen, du suachst dir an anderen Posten!" Ibid., pp. 115-116.

10. "A fauler Hund bist! Wenn i zehn Ackerfurchen mach, machst du zwoa! Ihr seids wahrscheinlich genau des gleiche faule Gsindel wia bei uns dahoam die Walschen! ... Und mir is des wurscht, wem der Hof zerst gehört hat, verstehst du?! I hab nämlich gearbeitet! Wie ein Viech hab i jetzt gschuftet da, zwoa Jahr lang! Und wer arbeitet, der soll besitzen! Der Führer is stolz auf uns! Mir sein Wehrbauern! Wie vor tausend Jahr! Und jetzt geh i, mein Besitz verteidigen!" Ibid. p. 123.

11. "Aber na, an Besitz wolltest du haben, an großen Besitz! Frei wolltest sein! Ja, bist du jetzt frei? ... Mir sein in an fremden Land, auf an gstohlenen Hof! ... I woaß eh, daß alles falsch war! I woaß eh, daß ma den Krieg verlieren! Und daß ma wieder gehn müaßen! Aber was soll i tuan? Was soll i tuan?" Ibid., p. 141-142.

12. "Jeder muaß Opfer bringen! Jeder! Mir ham jetzt wieder a Vaterland! Des Vaterland hat uns den Hof da geben! So guat is es uns no nia gangen! No nia! Mir sein wohlhabend! I bin a reicher Bauer!" Ibid., p. 123.

13. About 90 percent of German-speaking Italians have consistently voted for the *Südtiroler Volkspartei*, which was led by Sylvius Magnago, an "Optant" (Leaver), who also has been the Landeshauptmann of the province Bozen.

14. Ja, was denn sonst? Bin i a Chines, hab i a chinesischen Namen! Bin i a Deutscher, hab i an deutschen Namen! KATHL: Geh, hör auf, Sepp! Bertolini! Pizzinini! Ferrari! Crazzolara! Alles Südtiroler aus unserm Ort! SEPP: Aber deutsche Vornamen hams! Ibid, p. 91.

15. "SEPP: (*schreit*) Leb wohl, du mein Südtirol! Sepp Rabensteiner hoaß i! Leckt's mi alle am Arsch! (p. 96) ... SEPP: (*mit schwacher Stimme*) Mei Kathl war ein Engel Gottes! Ein Engel Gottes! Immer hat sie recht ghabt! (*Beginnt zu weinen.*) Immer! Mei, hätt i ihr doch gfolgt!" Ibid., p. 150.

16. "Andreas Hofer, wie ein verdammter Tiroler" Ibid., pp. 48–49.

17. *Deutsch*, derived from *theodiscus*, signifies all those who did not speak a Romance language. In turn, *Welsch* or *Walsh* signified all those who did not speak a Germanic language. Cf. Rudolf Walther, "Erfindung der Vergangenheit durch die Gegenwart." *Die Zeit* 3 (14 Jan. 1994), p. 48.

18. "A Walscher bist! Und wenn du hundert Jahr bei uns bist, du wirst immer a Walscher bleiben"—Dario replies: "Was bin ich? ein Walscher? Trentiner bin ich! Trentiner! Porco dio!" *Verkaufte Heimat*, p. 74.

19. Mitterer deals with the end of *Heimat* in a number of recent plays, as well as in the acclaimed *Piefke* series written for Austrian television.

Heimat Sold Out: Felix Mitterer's Television Plays

Jutta Landa

Felix Mitterer's contributions to Austrian television can be divided into three major groups. He wrote original scripts for the television plays *Homeland, Sold Out (Verkaufte Heimat*, 1990), *The Fifth Season (Die fünfte Jahreszeit*, 1983 and 1990), *The Piefke Saga* (1991 and 1993) and *The Fool from Vienna (Der Narr von Wien*, 1983). He adapted works by the Austrian writers Peter Rosegger (*Earth's Blessing* [*Erdsegen*, 1986]), and Alfons Petzold (*The Rough Life* [*Das rauhe Leben*, 1987]). Lastly, there have been televised broadcastings of his stage plays *Siberia* (1992), *Stigma* (1982), and *Munde* (1990). Mitterer has also acted for TV (in John Goldschmidt's *Schiele* (1979) and written scripts for the cinema: his murder mystery *Wilderness (Wildnis*, 1992), directed by Werner Masten, followed Robert Dornhelm's docudrama *Requiem for Dominic* (1990), in which Mitterer also played a leading part. Given the demands of a mass audience, the highly collaborative nature of a TV production and the aesthetics of a small screen, it is interesting to see how these altered circumstances affect a playwright's choice of subject matter and representation.

For the purpose of this article, I will concern myself with the television plays or series based on Mitterer's scripts. Commensurate with its cultural mission, Austrian Television has a strong commitment to the *Fernsehspiel* or television play, devoting an entire department to this genre. The objective of the television play is to combine "artistic quality with appeal for the mass viewing public."[1] Therefore it seems only natural that a stage author of Mitterer's repute should be commissioned to write for TV.[2] Conversely, the author himself welcomes the reception possibilities inherent in television—a broad audience and exposure beyond national boundaries (especially in co-productions with the ZDF or ARD)—and the fact that television represents "nothing culturally respected."[3]

Nonetheless, it is surprising that Mitterer took to the medium so readily. Usually performed by lay acting troupes such as the *Volksbühne Blaas*, his productions, taking place in community halls or inns, involve the nearly physical participation of an audience composed of locals. Identifying themselves with the actors on the stage, the spectators respond to the mirror effect with strong affective emotions. For example, in order to experience the performance of *Munde*, directed by the Southern Tyrolean Rudolf Ladurner in 1990, the theater-goers had to brave the elements by literally climbing a mountain (*Die Hohe Munde*) and camping out overnight. In this way, the reception of the play became a "total or complete experience,"[4] an experience tied to physical exertion and the confrontation with untamed nature. Such a gut reaction of the audience, which stands in stark contrast to the passive "couch-potato" viewing habits of the average TV consumer, is quite in line with Mitterer's premise that theater "has to hurt."[5] Considering the visceral nature of his theater, one cannot but find the small screen inadequate for Mitterer's style. Moreover, the sexual and verbal explicitness of Mitterer's plays does not lend itself well to television family entertainment. Scenes already shocking to a restricted theater audience, such as when Moid sacrifices her menstrual blood in *Stigma*, are even more controversial on prime time television. (Of course, the situation is different in the case of a televised stage production which retains or rather quotes the theatrical reception conditions.)

Another possible ratings problem could have been the decidedly regional character of most of Mitterer's writings. In keeping with his premise that he only writes about the world he knows (Hassel, p. 300), Mitterer's preferred location is the Austrian province Tyrol, where the author himself was born and raised as the adopted child of farm laborers.[6] At first sight such a geographically confined segment of reality would seem to offer only limited interest, especially to viewers in Germany or even in the eastern regions of Austria. But as the success of the series *Homeland, Sold Out, The Fifth Season*, and *The Piefke Saga* indicates, Mitterer's focus on *Heimat* or the homeland, with all its political, social, environmental, and emotional connotations, has struck a nerve in his audience. The main reason for the popularity of Mitterer's brand of regionalism can be traced to the long tradition of the *Volksstück* (folk play) as represented by authors such as Ludwig Anzengruber (1839-1889) or Ludwig Ganghofer (1855-1920), and, especially significant for Mitterer, the Tyrolean playwrights Karl Schönherr (1867-1943) and Franz Kranewitter (1860-1936). During the postwar years German film appropriated the *Volksstück* in its all-time favorite genre: the *Heimatfilm*, "cliché-ridden, Agfa-colored images of German forests, landscapes, and customs, of happiness and security."[7] These two strands then merged, as TV became the "secret" *Volkstheater*, unifying various populist genres.[8] Another, less overt reason for the unbroken popularity of the

Heimat theme can be found in the fact that the very vagueness of the term allows the coexistence of reactionary and progressive discourses. After the corruption of the concept *Heimat* by the Nazis and its consequent rejection, the vacuum was soon filled with the re-awakened national pride of the post-war era and a veritable boom of *Heimat* films. With low production costs, these films offered escapist fare which not only revived a sense of patriotism, but also addressed the problem of war refugees and restored traditional family values and patriarchal structures. In the late sixties, the notion of *Heimat* underwent a complete revision, as a strong movement of regional writers deconstructed the homeland myth, portraying the average village as a haunt of Fascism, bigotry, reactionary behavior, nationalism, ossified prejudice and xenophobia (an Austrian example can be found in Peter Turrini's *Hog Slaughter* [*Sauschlachten*] of 1972). In the eighties, in the wake of such political movements as the Greens, the progressive thrust of environmentalism was combined with an attempt to reincorporate such retrospective values as love for the land and pre-industrial methods of farming. Since then, the neo-Nazi movement in unified Germany or the rightist orientation of politicians such as Jörg Haider in Austria have given a new, if not frighteningly familiar ring to *Heimat*, yet again redefining it as an enclave that needs to be purged from foreign elements.

It is through this ideological minefield that Felix Mitterer tiptoes in most of his TV plays. He succeeds in doing so by sustaining a careful balance of all connotations of *Heimat*, both positive and negative. In the process, he salvages folklore motifs and legends which have been ideologically exploited in an attempt to restore them to literary quality.[9] To this effect, his scripts conform to genre expectations on the one hand and transcend them on the other. The author utilizes stock motifs from provincial literature: the generation gap acted out in the father-daughter or father-son conflict, the feuding brothers, the corrupt and flighty citizen vs. the stable, solid peasant, the clash of progress and tradition. He also follows the typical family-centered dramaturgy. All of Mitterer's teleplays discussed here are centered around the family—more specifically, the extended family of traditional peasantry, which, by its very anachronism, offers an example of old-fashioned values. The dramatic opportunities of the proliferation of characters lie in suspense-enhancing subplots which criss-cross the main plot. As the family's unity and coherence is threatened by external as well as internal forces, the dramatic conflict is intensified. Internal forces manifest themselves in the revolt of the sons, often more right wing than the fathers. External forces are usually the unholy alliance of the Catholic Church, the land-owning aristocracy, national politics and economic progress. Trite as this formula may appear, it is unsurpassed in its effectiveness for identification. As a rule, Mitterer employs it in the version of ideologically opposed families pitted against each other, their respective members displaying different degrees of conformism or protest.

The medium of television affords the author a genre of its own which captures and, above all, sustains audience interest: the mini-series. By sending his viewers through family sagas (a format established with Peter Turrini's and Dieter Berner's six-part *Saga of the Alps* (*Alpensaga*, 1976-1980), Mitterer creates a bonding process with his characters. In fact, if the topics addressed by Mitterer were not so loaded with cultural references, his television dramas could remind one of soap operas whose viewers vicariously live and suffer with their sprawling TV families. But the playwright brings to these well-worn patterns a degree of seriousness and political information which lifts his plays and series above the prosaic norm. He succeeds in expanding the *Heimat* theme and compressing it. Expansion takes place through a carefully researched and documented historical framework, both distant and more recent. Thus Mitterer presents histories of persecution and treason as they appear in the sellout of South Tyrol by the Nazis in *Homeland, Sold Out*. In *The Fifth Season* he combines a hundred years of political history in a Tyrolean village with the more mundane, but economically significant evolution of Alpine skiing into a commercialized industry. Compression is achieved through the author's representation of marginalized groups within an already peripheral Tyrolean peasantry. In *Homeland, Sold Out* he depicts the South Tyrolean mountain peasants who are politically and economically reduced to minority status as they literally scrape a living from the soil. The author does not stop there, as he also protests the pauperization of the farm laborer, painfully embodied in the itinerant old couple of *Earth's Blessing*, who upon being denied social security or a home after a lifetime of hard manual labor, have to beg for food and shelter. In his concern for the endangered homeland, he adds the new, more current twist of the destruction of traditional social structures and the ravaging of nature by mass tourism. This is nowhere else more true than in the *Piefke Saga*, where Mitterer drives his dystopia of Tyrol as a Disneyland for German tourists to its logical extreme.

In relation to the theme of *Heimat*, Mitterer's treatment of Peter Rosegger's epistolary novel *Earth's Blessing* (1900) allows insights into the author's agenda, precisely because it is an adaptation of an original. It is above all the homage paid to Peter Rosegger (1843-1918) that illustrates Mitterer's deeply felt affinity for the popular Styrian author. In an ORF press release, Mitterer points out the similarities in their respective biographies under the title "Two Poor Farmboys" (Zwei Waldbauernbuben), concluding his article with the humble words: "I was now allowed to make a script out of the novel, meaning that the two poor farmboys have met. I hope the 'Lenzen-Peterl' is satisfied with the 'Maurer-Felix'."[10]

Although he considers Rosegger to be a little too *beschaulich* or inoffensive, Mitterer has always been intrigued by Rosegger's sympathy with the Styrian mountain peasants, whose marginal existence strongly resembled that of their Tyrolean counterparts. In addition, Mitterer recognized a certain topicality in the drop-out theme. In the play, the business editor of the *Wiener Zeitung*, Hans Trautendorffer, "The dandy, the pencil pusher, the frequenter of coffeehouses,"[11] has wagered a bet that he will work as a farm hand for a whole year. Initially rejected by the Styrean mountain peasants, he prevails, eventually cultivating his own field of wheat which is then sadly destroyed in a hailstorm. Interwoven with Trautendorffer's adventure is the story of the farmer Adamshauser's daughter Barbel, who gets pregnant by the village school teacher Guido Winter. Bringing disgrace to her family, she contributes to her father's death which in turn causes her to miscarry. At the end of the play, Hans Trautendorffer returns to Vienna with his new wife Barbel.

Mitterer approaches this formulaic story of city corruption versus country solidity with an acute sense of a precarious balance to be established. The play essentially describes the rapprochement of the forces of traditionalism and progress, as represented by the Adamshauser peasant family on the one hand, and Trautendorffer on the other. This approximation of antagonistic values is only possible because both camps have the courage to act independently. Thus, the old Adamshauser breaks with the prejudices of his fellow farmers and even his close family to hire the city slicker. While the extreme hostility of the peasants toward the stranger is presented with an accusatory gesture, the city people do not fare much better. Whereas the peasants use their fists or the goriness of animal slaughter to oust Trautendorffer from their midst, the city people use more sophisticated weapons, such as breaking contractual obligations, to the same effect. Within the closely knit family drama, the outsider represents an invading, but also a rectifying force. When her own daughter becomes the target of bigotry and cruelty, the religious fanaticism of Adamshauser's wife is broken: "It's not always the worst who have bad luck." She is ultimately turned to rebellion against God's seemingly willful acts of destruction: "with human beings, everything is wrong right away; only the one above can do whatever he wants."[12] On the other hand, the agnostic Trautendorffer sinks to his knees to join the family in prayer in the same scene. Trautendorffer is also pitted against Rocherl, the younger son of Adamshauser, who is on a moral crusade for the honor of his sister. In the end Trautendorffer wins over the aggressive Rocherl and marries his sister. Forced to suffer the punishment of a brutal code of sexual repression, Barbel succeeds in directing the frivolous Trautendorffer to the path of true love. On one side of the spectrum, the narrow-mindedness of the peasants goes too far, when soap, toothbrush and above all newspapers are seen as manifestations of sinful pride. On the other side, Trautendorffer comes to the conclusion: "Why furnish man with 1000 fine organs and indulging hearts? The perfect human being owns nothing and enjoys everything."[13] In order to lend Trautendorffer the critical voice granted by the epistolary format, Mitterer provides him with an "educated" dialogue partner in the figure of the teacher, a victim of an outdated code of honor (duelling) and thus a displaced person himself. Ultimately, however, the conversations between the two rivals (both are vying for Barbel) seem somewhat strained, with the teacher only adding the obvious to the discussion: "Western culture has, after all, evolved in the sin-infested cities."[14] The play's ending is unsatisfying in that its underlying conflicts are not resolved. While the mother is happy that the daughter has married "a peasant and not a teacher," Trautendorffer is quick to point out that he certainly is not a peasant. Barbel's uprooting is presented as surprisingly unproblematic. In the final analysis, the abrupt ending more or less reduces Trautendorfer's one-year stay to a vacation, which permits the regeneration of physical and mental forces and perhaps a slight reorientation of values, thus de-valorizing the entire experience. As Willi Winkler indicates, "[Trautendorffer's] offertory procession was a recovery trip with a return ticket."[15]

Nevertheless, *Earth's Blessing* makes a valuable contribution to filmed rural literature. Under the direction of Karin Brandauer the television play was awarded the Erich Neuberg-Preis and the Silbernen Enzian at the International Bergfilm Festival in Trier in 1987. The drama constitutes an attempt to represent the dilemma of the mountain peasants, increasingly marginalized in the twentieth century. Despite modest landholdings and back-breaking work, in terms of real income, they fall far below the poverty line. Victims of austere weather conditions and of geographically imposed ignorance and illiteracy, they are reluctant to embrace progress and thus stand to lose their autonomy. Even the socialist forces which break into the hermetic world of these poor farmers are described with skepticism. The rebel Schlosser, whose command *"zuoschlogn"*(strike out) only results in attacks against him instead of the real exploiters, serves as an example of ill-advised violence. In *Earth's Blessing*, Mitterer, together with Karin Brandauer, unmistakably voices a timely plea for the rescue of a nearly extinct peasant tradition. (The status of its Alpine peasants was a subject of contention in the negotiations for Austria's entry into the European Union.) Tying their backwardness to economic causes, Mitterer hopes to awaken understanding for these marginalized peasants. To achieve this effect, Karin Brandauer, in turn, opted for an unsentimental, documentary film style, utilizing authentic Styrian dialect in her screen transformation of his script. In her attempt to capture the extreme frugality and hardship of the peasants' life she tactfully abstained from "anything colorful and folkloric."[16]

Closely following Rosegger's original, Felix Mitterer's *Earth's Blessing* comes across as a very conciliatory text. In contrast, Mitterer injects more controversy into the nine-part series *The Fifth Season* (1983 and 1990), for which he wrote segments 4-9.[17] The German production, which covers the time span of 1880–1980, intercuts the evolution of the Tyrolean village Waldberg (a thinly disguised Kirchberg) from the Monarchy to post World War II with the history of Alpine skiing. As these histories unfold, the local peasantry is described in less than flattering terms, greed and opportunism governing their actions. In typical *Heimat* dramaturgy, Mitterer pits two representative families, who are in fact blood related, against each other.

Episodes 4-6, "The Thousand Mark Tax" (Die Tausend Mark Sperre), "Judas," and "Return Home to the Reich" (Heim ins Reich), describe the fate of the Perwanger clan before the war. The owners of the *Gasthof Roter Adler*, the Kilian Perwanger branch with wife Rosa, and sons Sepp and Klaus, are loyal supporters of Hitler. The Franz Perwanger branch, whose brothers Toni and Georg work for the *Hahnenschwanzler* (a nickname for the *Heimwehr*), resists the Nazis until the family is forced into submission. Reduced to the status of farm hands since their own farm has been auctioned off to Mayor Schlatter, *Obmann der Vaterländischen Front* (Commander of the National Front), these former Hitler opponents can only benefit from the 1938 annexation of Austria. In the ensuing shift of power, the head of the third Perwanger branch, Heinrich, owner of the *Pinzgermühle*, is coerced into becoming a party member, Toni is thrown into jail by a vengeful Klaus, and Schlatter is forced by Kilian to restore the property to Franz. These measures are followed by well-calculated acts, such as a moratorium on forced auctions, the protection of the farm under Nazi property laws, and the distribution of food and clothes, all of which eventually swing the vote of even the staunchest opponents to Naziism. The story is riddled with a variety of subplots, which contribute to the main theme of seduction by political power and money. Thus Franz's brother Toni goes through a series of trying experiences. He is forced to work as a male prostitute to earn money to salvage the farm, and later becomes embroiled in the melodrama surrounding Georg's betrayal of Klaus, who had defected from Germany because of homesickness. An additional subplot is found in the fate of the Jewish Tyrolean brother and sister Felix and Katharina Silbermann, who are confronted with vicious antisemitism, bringing about Katharina's suicide and Felix's flight to America.

The last three episodes, shot in 1990, represent a shift from the political arena to the economic realm of mass tourism. They are centered around two generations of descendants of the Perwanger clan, whose family strife is now dominated by their conflicting attitudes toward tourism. The Perwangers of the Pinzgermühle have embraced the tourist business to the fullest, devoting their entire existence to running their hotel and the ski schools. The peasant faction of the Perwangers has remained on their farm, living frugally, but happily, if it were not for the two rebellious sons Eddi and Erwin, who have betrayed their family heritage. Once again winners and losers emerge, although the script underlines that economic gain is equated with a loss of identity and self-worth. Consequently, Erwin's transformation from a xenophobic mountain peasant boy to the husband of an American-Chinese film star (an episode modeled after the factual story of the marriage of a ski instructor to Nancy Kwan) leaves him empty and, in the end, destitute. The locals, in particular the ski instructors, eager to cash in on their rustic virility, prostitute themselves in the name of tourism. Corruption prevails, as they expect a commission for bringing their students for après ski drinks at the local inns.

The Fifth Season makes generous use of the stock elements of *Heimatfilm*. One is the poacher motif which is transformed in the seventh episode to the economically driven smuggler motif. Thus the rebellious rejection of official power inherent in this motif is eventually perverted to a consumer attitude, in which the well-stocked shop on the Swiss side appears as a "paradise." Another standard motif, that of the feuding brothers, is also carried on throughout this teleplay. In earlier times it is the struggle between the eldest son Franz as the inheritor of the land and the less fortunate younger brother Toni; in later times it is not the farm, but money and women that spark jealousy between the brothers Erwin and Eddie. Mitterer, however, clearly makes use of these stereotypical situations for didactic purposes. For example, in the first three episodes the educational goal is to delineate the rise of Austrofascism. Well-researched glimpses of history, such as the Thousand Mark Tax for German tourists, one of Hitler's measures to economically isolate Tyrol and thus prepare the path for surrender, serve as the structural backbone of the family drama. Mitterer also has his characters mention some embarrassing historical facts, such as the Austrian referendum's 99.75 percent vote in favor of the annexation, with 106 of 266 Tyrolean communities voting unanimously for Hitler. In the last three episodes, a new concern with *Heimat* takes over, one that was voiced by many Austrian writers in the eighties. Here the focus on *Heimat* shifts from the people to nature. The perspective "from below" with its concomitant description of discrimination and exploitation of peasantry is replaced by a strong concern for nature and the environment.[18] Thus the closing episodes of *The Fifth Season* focus on the damages wreaked by the tourist industry, in particular the erosion of valuable Alpine landscapes through ski runs and lifts. Tour buses, snow plows and caterpillars are seen carving paths of destruction and noise through the no longer pristine scenery. Mitterer links the destruction of nature with moral decay, as in the scene where the mundane baron and his friends pay top money for the privilege to ski virgin powder snow. As they prepare for the descent, they drink champagne and don white capes just as the smugglers or refugees in previous episodes have done in order to remain invisible against the white glare from their pursuers. With these decadents however, the clothes have been perverted to carnivalesque sheik costumes, adding excitement to their adventure. The locals' corruption and loss of identity is demonstrated in their language, which in Mitterer's teleplays is always the local dialect. At first Toni and then later Eddi and Erwin speak an aborted English, in an attempt to sell themselves off to rich women. That the expansion of tourism, the accumulation of wealth and the break with tradition go too fast for human comprehension is poignantly captured in Eddie's ever-recurring insipid comment, "that's awesome!" ("des is a Wahnsinn!").

Mitterer's probing analysis of *Heimat* in *The Fifth Season* caused a typical pre-broadcast controversy in Austria, where the series was televised two years after its premiere in Germany. As to be expected, the Austrian tourist industry disliked the negative portrayal of its most profitable source of income. By paralleling the evolution of Austrofascism and the ski industry, Mitterer insinuates that both are equally destructive forces, endangering the cultural and political identity of his homeland. At one point the collaboration between Fascism and skiing is merged seamlessly, as when Klaus boasts that the Innsbruck Ski Association insisted on an all-Arian membership as early as 1927. Nevertheless, in spite of its provocative potential, the series was hardly noticed by television critics or the audience. Karsten Visarius sees the cause of the lukewarm response in the benign meshing of "the entertaining family series that invites sympathy and compassion with the critical teleplay."[19]

Since this mixture is fully intentional, one is more inclined to blame the serialization process for the lukewarm reception. Not only do the time gaps and new actors make it difficult to keep track of the generations of Perwangers, but there are also inconsistencies in the character treatment. Thus the figure of Heinrich Heysen is at the same time a ski sport fanatic, an impoverished bookstore owner, who is willing to pay the 1000.-- DM in order to spend a vacation in his "second homeland," and the spreader of the Nazi gospel. To our surprise we learn later that Heinrich has died in a concentration camp, after having turned away from the Nazis. In fact, the absence of most of the earlier characters in episodes 7, 8, and 9 is for the most part accounted for verbally, leaving the viewer confused as to the family configurations of the new cast. Characters such as Erwin or Klaus strike the viewer as one dimensional in their quests for power and money. The audience's credulity is further stretched when the endangered Silbermanns still enjoy taking ski vacations in an area where they have been the target of unbridled hostility. The figure of the ski-jumper Leo is potentially controversial, in that he represents a good-natured Nazi, who evens out all hostility with a glass of the local liquor ("*Schnapsl*").

Another possible reason for the muted response lay in a visual translation of the script to the screen that seemed to shun controversy. Visually, *The Fifth Season* is to a large extent a continuation of the *Heimat* films, the director being familiar with the genre. Reminiscent of Alfons Stummer's 1954 film *The Forester in the Silver Forest* (*Der Förster im Silberwald*), the series—especially in its establishing sequences—features the beautiful landscape of the Tyrolean Alps, with eternal snow, glaciers, wildlife, and a picturesque village nestled in the valley. Again and again we observe the main characters skiing these mountains, be it as refugees, as smugglers or as tourists. The Tyrolean music is strictly mood enhancing, with an occasional ominous note at the sight of a swastika chalked onto a rock. Editing is smooth and unobtrusive, with meaningful graphic matches, as when Franz's desperate strike at the unsold calf is visually matched (and thus replaced) by his daughter jumping down from a bench. The film establishes a rhythm between outdoor and indoor scenes, contrasting the grandiosity of nature with the frugal and cramped living conditions of the peasants, who cannot afford shoes for their children to go outside and play in the snow. When the series shifts interest to the skiing industry, the mise-en-scène changes. Camera pans reveal that the majestic mountain panoramas are now invaded by herds of tourists who ski into the frame or clutter it as they swarm onto the decks of the mountain cafeterias. With its continuous capturing of a sublime landscape (even when crowded with tourists) the series visually undercuts its own goal, presenting itself as a virtual commercial for Tyrol. Shot on location, the snow-covered scenery provides an authenticity which is somehow lacking in the representation of the Nazi take-over. The use of standard Nazi iconography of swastikas, be they formed by candles in the mountains, carved on the door of the prison cell, or even painted on a squealing pig is too simplistic to evoke a sense of believability. Kilian Perwanger's get-up as a look-alike Hitler is in the same way jarring in its obviousness. Likewise, the director has trouble capturing the sentiments evoked by old peasant traditions without falling into sentimentality. He comes dangerously close to exploiting yet another cozy *Heimat* cliché in the scene that contrasts the peaceful Christmas celebration in the old farm house (complete with hand-carved crèche and angelic children's voices) with a cold and rushed gift exchange in the hotel. A visual leitmotiv is the corner with a crucifix (*Herrgottswinkel*) at the Perwanger Hof, which the camera pans at poignant moments of the narration. These are moments of loss, dramatizing the eviction of the Franz Perwanger family or, later, Eddie's denouncement of the faith of his parents, when he blasphemously compares the tortured position of Christ on the cross to a "perfect Arlberger Hüftknick" (hip turn).[20] All in all, Mitterer's educational project is visually undercut by too many concessions to mainstream tastes and expectations. One has to agree with Visarius: "One recognizes behind it all an ambitious project that has filtered and dampened its potential dramaturgical, acting and thematic pointedness by its predominant interest in entertainment."[21]

Compared to *The Fifth Season*, the series *Homeland, Sold Out* (1990) is much more overtly political. The two episodes, entitled "Burning Love" (Brennende Lieb) and "Goodbye, My South Tyrol" (Leb' wohl, du mein Südtirol), again directed by Karin Brandauer for the German network ARD, describe the sellout of South Tyrol by Hitler and eventually by the South Tyroleans themselves, who were conned into leaving their homeland. Again Mitterer uses the device of the opposing families, this time the Tschurtschenthalers and the Oberhollenzers, who are divided according to their political allegiance, and again the split goes through the families. Even more than in the *The Fifth Season*, the positing of ideological factions against each other is described as the result of political oppression, first engendered by the Italian regime and then by the Nazi regime. Accordingly, *Homeland, Sold Out* succeeds in demonstrating how individual fate is affected by political arbitrariness. Initially, the inhabitants of the South Tryolean village suffer discrimination at the hand of the Italians. They are not allowed to speak German, their children are forced to attend Italian schools where they are indoctrinated by Italian teachers, and in order to get a job they have to Italianize their names (as when Frau Rabensteiner can only become the school janitor as Signora Pietracorvo). In addition, the peasants are under constant surveillance by the much-hated Carabinieri who themselves react with violence to the unfamiliar environment.[22] In their effort to retain their national identity, the villagers bank on Hitler as their savior. However, it soon becomes apparent that for Hitler, South Tyrol is only a pawn in his political game. Hitler's shifting allegiance to Mussolini culminates in the Resettlement Treaty (*Umsiedlungsvertrag*) of July 1939, in which the South Tyroleans were urged to emigrate to Germany. Pressured into accepting the treaty, the South Tyroleans were split into two fiercely antagonistic groups, the "Remainers" (*Dableiber*) and the "Optants" (*Optanten*). Tricked by political rhetoric into leaving their homes, the optants are not sent to Germany, as they had hoped, but instead to Galitzia, where their new land is claimed from the hostile, disenfranchised Bohemian peasants. To complete this senseless uprooting, the mountainous farmland of the South Tyrol is settled with Sicilian farmers, who in turn are hated by the remaining German-speaking population. The insanity is resolved at the end of the war, when the remainers are finally vindicated. The series ends with the return of the homecomers from Galitzia and yet another overturn of the local power structures. From the viewpoint of the *Ortsgruppenleiter* Kofler, this is the ultimate end of his homeland: "Jews, Negroes, Italians, traitors—those are now our winners."[23]

Homeland, Sold Out follows the tried serial principle of individual sample families in order to show how the political rift in fact went through the families and destroyed their closely knit structure. Ironically, in an ingenious political ploy the remainers were branded as traitors (*"Walsche Judasse"*) and the deserters praised as the true defenders of the homeland. It is in the capturing of this dialectic that the strength, and, as Mitterer hopes, the healing quality of the series lies. Intolerance only drives alienation further: when Anna Tschurtschenthaler defects to the enemy camp by marrying Ettore she is henceforth ostracized by her kin. It is at this juncture that the director Karin Brandauer makes the connection to the asylum and immigrant problems of the nineties: "The film is a plea for widespread tolerance."[24] In her attempt to downplay the didactic intent in favor of an emotional engagement for the victims, Karin Brandauer's visual style sometimes underscores the homeland sentimentality too much. A case in point are the titles, "Burning Love" and "Goodbye My South Tyrol," which smack too much of homesickness (*Heimweh*) to suggest the cosmopolitan attitude the director attempts to instill in the viewer. The same phenomenon occurs in the imagery of *Homeland, Sold Out*, where glorious landscapes, rustic peasants, and sentimental scenes of leavetaking are underscored by authentic South Tyrolean dialect and plaintive folk songs. The series also has to cope with excessive historical baggage, which leads to an imagery composed of ominous icons: "Cross and swastika are moved into the frame like Cain and Abel marks, in order to denote the parties"[25] Nonetheless *Homeland, Sold Out* succeeds in confronting the repressed traumas of South Tyrolean history.

Mitterer's most popular television series dealing with *Heimat* was the *Piefke Saga*, directed by Wilfried Dotzel. The main idea for it came from the producer of *The Fifth Season*, Walfried Menzel, who showed Mitterer an issue of the Viennese magazine *Wochenpresse* with the derogatory title caption "Who Needs the Piefkes?" (Wer braucht die Piefkes?). Menzel also handed Mitterer piles of protest letters of German tourists, which had arrived in the aftermath of Joachim Fuchsberger's television show "Let's Get Going" (Auf los geht's los) of 28 August 1982. In the show Fuchsberger had asked the Austrian participants: "How many of you call the Germans Piefkes?" As it had turned out, the derogatory epithet, branded on the Germans since the days of the Prussian military bandmaster August Piefke, was widely used to denote the "arrogant" nature of affluent German tourists. Mitterer immediately recognized the potential for comedy in the subject matter. After two years of close observation in his native Tyrol, he wrote the story of the German Sattmann family, who become increasingly intertwined with two Tyrolean families, one a mountain peasant family of the Rotterhof, the other the hotel-owning Wechselbergers. Placing the Sattmann family in an Austrian setting, the series investigates the ambivalent relationship between the Austrian tourist industry and their most profitable guests—the Germans—as well as the enormous strains that tourism puts on an endangered landscape. Mitterer insists that he is not out to satirize the Germans, that the mechanisms are always the same and that he could have shown a Viennese family in Caorle with the same results.[26]

Divided into four parts, "The Scandal," "The Animation," "The Business," (Das Geschäft), and "The Fulfillment" (Die Erfüllung), the series again juxtaposes families, whose individual members cross over into the other camp. In the first part, "The Scandal," by way of an exposition, the original controversy is replicated: the infamous Fuchsberger show is viewed by the Wechselberger family, owners of the Hotel Alpenfrieden in Lahnenberg (that is Mayrhofen in Tyrol), by the Austrian Trade Minister in Vienna, and by the Sattmann family in Berlin. Appalled by the Austrian "jurors" in the show who define Piefkes "as Germans who throw about their German Marks because the Shilling is worthless" or "who think they are something better and show off in foreign countries" (*Piefke Saga*, p. 19), the respective viewers (captured simultaneously on split screen) vent their anger through telephone calls. Whereas Franz Wechselberger sees his income threatened and is angered at the stupidity of his own countrymen, Heinrich Sattman calls him to task: "One should keep in a good mood the cow that one is milking"[27] After having finally cooled off, the controversy flares up again as the *Wochenzeitung* publishes its issue with a picture of a fat German tourist on the title page. In this episode, which is satirical in its overall outlook, Mitterer nevertheless addresses some serious issues, such as the exploitation of the labor force in the hotel sector. As is typical for his television style, Mitterer tries to balance his sardonic attacks evenly. Thus the local philanderer Joe with his noisy motorbike is juxtaposed with the Berlin punker Gunnar with his colorful Cherokee hairstyle. The grand-father Sattmann stems from the old guard, hardly concealing his nostalgia for the Nazi era. On the other side of the political spectrum stands Weizen-berger's renegade brother Hans, who agitates against his hotel-owning brother by passing on information to his journalist friend. In the second episode, "The Animation," the lives of the characters from the opposing camps become more closely interwoven, as Gunnar gets Anna pregnant and discovers his love for a peasant lifestyle, and Sabine's jealousy reveals that she really cares for Joe. Gunnar's troubles continue as he and Wechsel-berger's son are booked for the possession of marijuana, which Georg grows on the Alpine meadows. The episode also finds Karl-Heinrich Sattmann in pursuit of the hiking certificate, and in an even more trying quest he tries to climb his first mountain peak in typical tourist fashion— equipped to the teeth with climbing gear, but lacking preparation and good judgment.

The comical tone of the second episode becomes more serious in the third episode, entitled "The Business." Here the symbiosis of tourism and big business is consummated when Sattmann opens a factory in Lahnen-berg that will provide 300 season-independent jobs by producing snow guns. In return for the favor he wants to fulfill his lifetime dream and pur-chase land in Tyrol, which is not feasible according to Tyrolean property laws. In an intrigue of criminal proportions, Niedecker intends to dupe old Andreas, the owner of the Rotterhof, into a deal that will circumvent the law. The patriarch, who has been ailing since his farm was converted into a Pension, and will hopefully soon die, makes for the ideal straw man. In order to complete the deal, Andreas has to be persuaded to sign three documents, first a sales contract which officially declares that he bought the land for three million Schillings, then a will in which he deeds his land to the German citizen, and thirdly the "Land Use Declaration" which pro-vides for quick usage of the land. But Andreas only signs the first docu-ment which, to the conspiring parties' dismay, transfers ownership to him.

Although the ploy has been discovered and threatens to be publicized, the corruption continues as the governor, *Landeshauptmann*, interferes on Sattmann's behalf. But even with his house built and his daughter married off to Joe, Sattmann cannot enjoy his success: the house stands in an avalanche zone and has to be retrofitted. Sattmann's struggle continues, as his son-in-law becomes a poacher in order to add excitement to his affluent, but utterly directionless lifestyle. The last straw is the scandal that Sattmann's snow guns are polluting Lahnenberg's drinking water. In an attempt to dissociate himself from his buddy Sattman in a bid to win re-election as mayor, Wechselberger evokes the old hatred against the Piefkes. In a campaign speech he vilifies Sattmann "as a colonialist among Negroes": "Unfortunately, he *is* a Piefke! He is everything one imagines by this term: boastful, a show-off, greedy, avaricious, and arrogant."[28] This glaring ingratitude induces Sattmann one more time to swear never to set foot in this land again. The episode ends with the seductive charms of Tyrolean folklore insinuating themselves back into the Sattman lifestyle, as the local band, *Trachtenkapelle*, takes a trip to Berlin, serenades Sattmann from below his window, offers an apology, and extends an invitation to return to Lahnenberg. Although the series comes full circle with the third episode, owing to its popularity, a fourth episode (directed by Werner Masten) with a different, much more somber tone was conceived. In sci-fi style, Tryol is now represented as a nightmarish Disneyland with artificial snow, staged hunts with computerized stuffed animals, and organized sex orgies. Human beings are reduced to robots, who retain their sunburned, healthy vacation looks on the operating table.

Claimed to be one of the most successful television productions of the last decade, although more so in Austria than in Germany, the *Piefke Saga* owes its popularity to its blend of entertainment with social critique. As in his previous series, Mitterer takes some of the critical edge off by bringing the colliding political and economic controversies down to the level of a family drama. Many of the plot twists are consolingly familiar: the convention of associating the German tourist with capitalist take-over schemes can already be found in Ralph Benatzky's operetta *Im Weißen Rössel*, thus conforming to traditions of bourgeois entertainment. Mitterer also follows other conventions of slapstick comedy, such as asynchronicity, repetition, and escalation, as well as garbled communication.[29] Asynchronicity is achieved by the hectic pace of Karl-Friedrich Sattmann, which stands in comic contrast to the local tempo, but is even more absurd since he is on vacation. Repetition (and escalation) is assured by the numerous times Karl Friedrich threatens to leave Lahnenberg ("ich reise ab"). The clash of the indigenous dialect with Berlin German results in humorous communication breakdowns, which ascribe emotional value to the dialect. In the scene in which Anna confesses that she is "of good hope," that is, pregnant, she sounds almost lyrical in contrast to Gunnar's hip street slang.

Although overall he bought into standard fare, Mitterer took risks with this series. As he points out, he discarded the principle of uniformity by changing the tone in each episode: the first part is conceived as a satire, the second as a comedy, the third as a tragic comedy and the last a horror vision "zum Totlachen" (Preface, p. 6). Underlying the character configurations is an analysis of the different appropriations of *Heimat*. Thus, in a speech following his acceptance of a biathlon prize, the old Heinrich Sattmann evokes the Nazi nostalgia: "Here in the beautiful land of Tyrol one sticks to the old values! Here there is no terrorism, no house squatting, no violent demonstrations, no drug addiction, no female gunslingers. And why? Because one sticks to the old values. Because the male virtues are still held high." The ideological receptivity of his audience reveals itself in the unanimous calls "Schi Heil, Schi Heil, Schi Heil."[30] His son, on the other hand, represents the sentimental tourist approach, which praises the healing and restoring powers of untouched nature, while at the same time conspiring to destroy them. Hans Wechselberger, the teacher, represents the Greens, who go too far in their "back-to-nature" romanticism. In a scene in which Hans, quoting Pasolini, waxes romantic about poverty, he is confronted by Anna, who reminds him of his carefree upbringing as the son of wealthy hotel owners. Franz Wechselberger appears as the typical entrepreneur, who perceives *Heimat* as a profitable commodity. His greed is only topped by that of Max Niederwieser, President of the Tourist Association, who turns the folklore of his homeland into hard currency in his souvenir store. Among other kitsch items he sells "Tyroleans wearing leather shorts packaged in cans" (*Lederhosentiroler in Dosen*) and does not shrink from crime. He is the creator of the silver hiking pin which turns love of nature into a relentless mileage game only to be survived with the help of anabolics. The true purpose of the pin, however, is to provide remote Alpine cottage owners with the chance to share in the milking of tourists. In Niederwieser's service we find the small-time profiteers of tourism, the likes of animators and ski instructors, whose services often border on prostitution. Since nature is apparently not stimulating enough on its own, the animators organize games in which farming tasks such as milking cows and mowing grass become a matter of competition with plenty of innuendo to boot. Pitted against these corrupted natives, Mitterer posits two "originals," the old peasant woman Elsa Anderka (who plays old Lena) and Peter Kluibenschädl (who plays old Andreas), whose seniority and nature-bound existence make them appear like extinct species, bound eternally on film in a touching wedding ceremony. Throughout the series Mitterer paints the downside of an economy and a lifestyle that is based on the exploitation of mass tourism. The damage goes from the destruction of natural resources to the loss of identity and the exposure to "urban" decadence. A case in point is Anna with her illegitimate child, who was not allowed to serve an apprenticeship at the local co-op because a waitressing job, while exposing her to sexual advances, would bring in more money. With acute perception Mitterer also portrays the destruction of male identity, as Joe is split into a seasonal Casanova who turns peasant during the off season.

In spite of this unabashed critique, the conciliatory tone typical of all of Mitterer's television series also prevails in the first three episodes of the *Piefke Saga*, as unlikely friendships or allegiances are formed, such as the punker Gunnar helping the octogenarian Andreas to escape from the hospital. Overly romantic as this ironing out of conflicts might appear, one has to keep in mind that it is not Mitterer's goal to accuse, but rather to render understandable the pecuniary motivations for the unchecked greed of the peasants, to whom tourism is a necessary source of income. Again the script is transformed to the screen in a visual language which does not stray from the conventional. The unobtrusive cuts, limited dialogue, luscious exterior shots, and the normal TV proximity ranges (medium and close-ups) are all geared to present non-jarring entertainment. That the outward gloss hides a deeper antagonism than the series cares to reveal is perhaps indicated in its signature music: the opening Bavarian *Blasmusik* is soon overtaken by traditional Austrian zither music. This antagonism manifests itself in the mutilation of Karl Friedrich Sattman in the fourth, much more acerbic episode: he is surgically transformed into a Tyrolean.

With his regionalism Mitterer has found himself in the same dilemma as other *Heimat* authors, such as Peter Turrini. Their style of journalistic realism all too often results in misinterpretation; the analysis of deformations is taken as denunciation of the victimized rural population by one in their midst. Where these writers seek to expose ingrained prejudice as caused by centuries of marginalization and exploitation, such honest efforts are often misinterpreted as downright betrayal. Mitterer has been attacked for his lack of critical distance by reviewers who apply Brechtian categories to Mitterer's *Volksstücke*.[31] The initial reception of Mitterer's *Stigma* or *No Place for Idiots* (*Kein Platz für Idioten*) was paramount to a scandal. It took years until the Tyroleans realized, in Mitterer's own words "that he wrote for them, not against them."[32] However, this realization did not come in the wake of a new dramaturgy, but rather through the playwright's personal interference. Typically, appeasement was achieved through close interaction with the lay actor troupes. In *No Place for Idiots* (1977) Mitterer played the title role himself for lack of a more suitable actor, thus doing his share in guiding the reception of the play. In addition, the lay aura of the performances offered the opportunity for ensuing discussions and clarification. It should also be mentioned that the persona of Mitterer himself, his heart-wrenching biography and his unassuming, caring attitude tend to nip any suspicion of self-aggrandizement or exploitation in the bud. By working for television, Mitterer had to forego the close contact with actors and audience alike as a means of steering the reception of his plays, although there have been televised discussions. What is more, in the collaborative effort of a TV production the script writer has less control over his material than the playwright. Mitterer himself points to the difficulties he encountered when he had to condense his scripts to 90 or 105 minutes and to present highly complex political events in a simplified, action-filled format (Hassel, p. 304). It is because of all these "cuts and changes" that Mitterer's TV plays appear less stringent and more commercialized than his stage plays and leave him vulnerable to charges of exaggerated decency: "Mitterer's naive clean conscience seems to snuggle to the cynical hardness of the television medium to particularly touching effect. To his decency one can delegate compassion wonderfully: Mitterer touches the heart, but nothing else: sentimentality without regret."[33]

This brand of criticism, while justly acknowledging the absorption of television drama into the general conditions of mass communication,[34] fails to understand Mitterer's educational intentions: "One has to tell about human beings. Why do they act like that, where have they lost the overview, when were they drawn into something."[35] In depicting this process, Mitterer is neither a purveyor of change, nor a hard-core traditionalist. Instead, all of Mitterer's provincial dramas revolve around the critical point when the private and the public collide, or in other words when coercion and lack of integrity combine into the sell out of values and beliefs, resulting in the loss of the real, inner *Heimat*. In *Homeland, Sold Out* above all, Mitterer is keenly successful in delineating the impact of politics on the personal lives of the peasants and at bringing the "terribly complicated" political history of South Tyrol (Hassel, p. 304) within understanding of an audience that wants primarily entertainment. It must nonetheless be admitted that the visual language used for carrying out Mitterer's agenda is anything but innovative. While it is possible that the author himself wanted the camera work to appear as unobtrusive as possible in order not to distract from his characterization, most of the burden of responsibility should go to the respective director. Karin Brandauer, at least, chose to opt for a more intimate style in *Earth's Blessing* and *Homeland, Sold Out* than the director of the much slicker *Piefke Saga*.

Most importantly, it should be pointed out that Mitterer's mimetic style is firmly grounded in everyday reality. A region that has added a pro-tourism party "The Independent Tyrolean" (*Unabhängige Tiroler*) to its political spectrum, but where the Greens are also increasingly successful, proves that the family split of Mitterer's television plays is symbolic of the contending parties in Tyrol. It is also no wonder that Parts 3 and 4 of *Homeland, Sold Out* were just recently shot under the direction of Gernot Friedel. Threatened by the increase of transit traffic and land purchase options in the wake of Austria's membership in the European Union, Tyrol, and all of Austria, senses its *Heimat* once more under attack.

Notes

1. Michael Kehlmann, "Preface," *Austrian Films 1889/90*, published by the Austrian Film Commission (Wien, Zürich: Europaverlag, 1989), p. 104.

2. According to Mitterer, his collaboration with Austrian Television started in 1976, when the ORF, in an effort to promote new script authors, ran a competition under the motto "Geschichten aus Österreich." Mitterer's script "Schießen" was selected for Tyrol and produced in 1977. Felix Mitterer, personal (written) interview, 28 March 1994.

3. Ursula Hassel and Deirdre McMahon, "Interview with Felix Mitterer," *Das zeitgenössische deutschsprachige Volksstück*, Stauffenburg Colloquim, vl. 23 (Tübingen: Stauffenburg Verlag, 1992), p. 290.

4. Felix Mitterer in *Personenbeschreibung: Felix Mitterer: Ein Platz für Idioten*, broadcast on sat 3, German TV, directed by Georg Stefan Troller.

5. Felix Mitterer in an interview with Kurt Palm in *Burgtheater, Zwölfeläuten, Blut, Besuchszeit: vier österreichische Stücke*, edited by Kurt Palm (Wien: Edition Frischfleisch, 1987), p. 255.

6. With Mitterer's success his world has expanded to include the cities. Three of his TV projects describe Vienna at the turn of the century: *Schiele, Der Narr von Wien*, and *Das rauhe Leben* (see Hassel, p. 300).

7. Anton Kaes, *From Hitler to Heimat: The Return of History as Film* (Cambridge, Massachusetts: Harvard University Press, 1989), p. 15.

8. Cf. Hugo Aust, Peter Haida, and Jürgen Hain, *Volksstück: Vom Hanswurstspiel zum sozialen Drama der Gegenwart* (München: H.C. Beck, 1989), p. 320.

9. He is not alone in this project. Barbara Frischmuth has attempted similar rescue operations in her novel *Sophie Silber* or in her as yet unpublished short story "Wildfrau."

10. "Ich durfte nun ein Drehbuch aus diesem Roman machen, womit die zwei Waldbauernbuben sich getroffen haben. Ich hoffe der 'Lenzen-Peterl' ist zufrieden mit dem 'Maurer-Felix'." Felix Mitterer, "Zwei Waldbauernbuben," ORF (Austrian Television) press release, 21 March 1986. All translations are mine.

11. "Der Stadtfrack, der Federfuchser, der Kaffeehaushocker," *Erdsegen*, directed by Karin Brandauer, ORF/ZDF, 1984.

12. "Die Schlechtesten san's net, die a Pech ham." She is ultimately turned to rebellion against God's seemingly willful acts of destruction: "Beim Mensch is alles glei g'föhlt, nur der oben derf tuan wos a will."

13. "Warum dem Menschen 1000 Feinorgane und Genußherzen anzüchten wollen? Der vollkommmene Mensch besitzt nichts und genießt alles."

14. "Die abendländische Kultur ist nun mal im Sündenpfuhl der Städte entstanden."

15. "[Trautendorffer's] Opfergang war eine Erholungsreise mit Rückfahrkarte." Willi Winkler, "Ein Gang aufs Land," *Die Zeit* 14, 28 March 1986, p. 56.

16. "Alles bunte und folkloristische"; Karin Brandauer quoted in "Rosegger im Originalton," *Südost Tagespost* (Graz) 4 March 1986, p. 16.

17. Parts 1 and 2 were written by the Bavarian author Reinfried Keilich, and the third by the director Franz Josef Gottlieb himself. The last episode "Ski Total" was filmed by Reinhard Schwabenitzky, not by Gottlieb.

18. Cf. the chapter "Literatur/Landschaft—Fremden/Verkehr" in Klaus Zeyringer, *Innerlichkeit und Öffentlichkeit: Österreichische Literatur der achziger Jahre* (Tübingen: A. Francke, 1992), pp. 229-242.

19. The meshing of "die unterhaltsame, Sympathie und Mitgefühl heischende Familienserie mit dem zeit-und sozialkritischen Fernsehspiel." (Karsten Visarius, "Familienepos mit kritischen Obertönen," *Frankfurter Allgemeine*, 29 December 1982.

20. The perfect posture for traversing slopes.

21. "Man erkennt hinter allem ein ambitioniertes Projekt, das seine möglichen dramaturgischen, darstellerischen und thematischen Schärfen durch ein vorrangiges Interesse an Unterhaltung gefiltert und abgedämpft hat."

22. Cf. entry "Verkaufte Heimat-Brennende Lieb' (1)" in *Austrian Film 1988*, edited by Austrian Film Commission (Wien Zürich: Europavelag, 1989), p. 96.

23. "Juden, Neger, Welsche, Verräter—das san jetzt die Sieger."

24. "Der Film ist ein Plädoyer für übergreifende Toleranz." Quoted in Uwe Schmitt, "Deutschsprechen verboten," *Frankfurter Allgemeine* 32, 7 February 1990, p. 30.

25. "Kreuz und Hakenkreuz werden ins Bild gerückt wie Kains—und Abelsmale, um die Parteien zu kennzeichen" (Schmitt).

26. Felix Mitterer, "Vorwort," *Die Piefke-Saga: Komödie einer vergeblichen Zuneigung. Drehbuch* (Innsbruck: Haymon-Verlag, 1991), pp. 5-6.

27. "Eine Kuh, die man melkt, soll man auch bei guter Laune halten!" (*Piefke-Saga*, p. 19).

28. "Er *ist* leider ein Piefke! Er ist alles, was man sich unter dieser Bezeichnung vorstellt: großspurig, protzig, gierig, habsüchtig und arrogant" (*Piefke-Saga* p. 167).

29. For a further exploration of these conventions see Volker Klotz, *Bürgerliches Lachtheater* (München: dtv, 1980).

30. "Hier im schönen Land Tirol hält man noch an den alten Werten fest! Hier gibt es keinen Terrorismus, keine Hausbesetzungen, keine gewalttätigen Demonstrationen, keine Rauschgiftsucht, keine Flintenweiber. Und warum das? Weil man an den alten Werten festhält. Weil die männlichen Tugenden noch hochgehalten werden" (*Piefke-Saga*, p. 76).

31. See Sigrid Löffler, "A netts Büabl," *Profil* 5, 29 January 1990, pp. 73-75.

32. Renate Wagner, "Mitterer hier, Mitterer dort," *Neues Volksblatt* 22, 27 Jan 1990, p. 10.

33. "Mitterer's treuherzige Gewissensfrische scheint sich der zynischen Abgebrühtheit des Mediums Fernsehen zu besonders rührender Wirkung anzuschmiegen. An seine Lauterkeit kann man das Ressort Mitleid wunderbar delegieren: Mitterer greift ans Herz, aber an nichts sonst. Rührung ohne Reue" (Löffler, p. 75).

34. Cf. Gerhard Melzer, "Konsolidierung der Gattungen in den neuen Medien: Hörspiel und Fernsehspiel," *Zeit ohne Manifeste: österreichische Literatur in den siebziger Jahren* (Wien: Österreichischer Bundesverlag, 1987), pp. 259-270 and Geoffrey Howes, "Is there a Postmodern 'Volk'? Some Thoughts on the *Volksstück* in the Television Age," *Modern Austrian Literature* 26 (3/4), pp. 17-32.

35. "Man muß von Menschen erzählen, warum handeln sie so, wo haben sie den Überblick verloren, wann wurden sie in etwas hineingezogen." Quoted in Ruth Rybarski, "Der sanfte Rebell" *Profil* 78, 24 January 1994, p. 80.

Felix Mitterer's *Besuchszeit*

Gudrun Brokoph-Mauch

"I strongly doubt that today's theater is justified," Felix Mitterer wrote in 1980. "But out in the villages theater is still important and useful."[1] In the meantime his plays have conquered not only the provincial stages but also the renowned popular theaters of the big cities as well as television. Therefore he has been able to reach a far greater public than with his first play *No Room For Idiots* (*Kein Platz für Idioten*), which was performed near Innsbruck in Blaas, the small stage in the Wienerwald Restaurant. This play ran for one season, with the author himself in the main role. With the revival of the *Volksstück* beginning in the middle of the 1980s, Mitterer's plays, along with those of Kroetz and Turrini, have become en vogue.

Mitterer's inspiration seems to come from two directions: the Catholic Passion Plays and the provincial comedy (*Bauernschwank*), the roots of which lie in southern Bavaria and Tyrol.[2] He is attracted to religion and especially to religious customs in the provinces, the religious annual cycle,[3] while at the same time maintaining a critical attitude toward the Catholic church. This emotional bond with religion in conjunction with his skepticism toward the church is the modus vivendi for his Catholic plays, the famous-infamous *Stigma* (1982) which is performed annually in Telfs, Tyrol, *Lost Homeland* (*Verlorene Heimat*, 1987) and *The Devil's Children* (*Die Kinder des Teufels*, 1989). These plays depict the persecution of saints, witches, Jews, or Protestants, whose stories Mitterer—drawing upon historical sources—brings to the stage or the village square. Incorporating local historical elements guarantees him the interest of the residents and forms a vehicle for Mitterer's social-political intentions: soliciting empathy and compassion for the outsider—those who think, believe and act differently. Thus the Zillertal community Stumm has adopted the play *Lost Homeland*, whose events actually occurred there, as its very own Passion Play. It plans

121

to perform it every ten years with approximately one hundred and fifty laymen after the role model of Oberammergau.[4] *Everyman* (*Ein Jedermann*, 1990), a new version of Hofmannsthal's play of the rich man's death, belongs to the religious plays but does deviate from the theme of the persecuted outsider.

Also for the plays of the second category, the peasant farce, Mitterer several times draws upon old plays which he modernizes for today's stage. Two of those are *Karrenleut '83* (Wagon People) and *Weizen auf der Auobahn* (1985, Wheat on the Highway), both Ernst Schönherr adaptations. Other plays of this kind are *There's No Finer Country* (*Kein schöner Land*, 1987) and *No Place for Idiots* (1977). This first play of Mitterer (originally conceived as a radio play) already contains most of the elements that characterize his later plays: the main and marginal figures consist of the standing personnel of the peasant comedy with which the public is familiar. The action is simple and linear, the language colored by regional dialects. Mitterer lures the provincial public into the theater with the familiar figures of the popular peasant farce in order to entertain and enlighten it, alienating that which is familiar and breathing new life into the stereotype. Thus he uses the well-known figure of the village idiot in order to reveal the tragic fate of the already mentioned outsider, here in the figure of a mentally disabled child. Already with this first play he succeeds in what soon is to make him famous at home and abroad: the tried and true combination of tradition and renewal as well as entertainment and didacticism, heart and mind.

These ingredients are again working their magic in Mitterer's four-part cycle of one-act plays *Visiting Hours* (*Besuchszeit*, 1985). With this play Mitterer, who in the meantime has conquered Austria's and Germany's metropolitan stages, is being exported to New York, where in 1991 two of the four one-act plays *Female Criminal* (*Verbrecherin*) and *I Don't Understand* (*Man versteht nichts*) were performed at the East Village Theater.[5] This play retains the convention of the *Volksstück* within its structure, language, and personnel while at the same time filling this traditional framework with up-to-date topics.

Each of these one-act plays is a dramatic dialogue between two people, a man and a woman. In every case the visit of relatives is an obligation, characterized by clumsiness, embarrassment and constraint. It is a visit with a person who is hospitalized, imprisoned or otherwise confined. In every case it is a visit with someone who is confined against his will and for the rest of his life. This creates a magnetic field of polar opposites between the two people, of freedom and coercion, of debt and debtor, of sinner and repenter. The roles these polar opposites play in this stress-filled confrontation are, however, not fixed upon one or the other, but oscillate in some scenes back and forth. The place corresponds to this overall theme of inescapability, since it is in every instance a variation of the same prison in which the "criminal" of the second one-act play is actually confined. It is always the last dismal station of life, irrespective of whether it was a good or a difficult life. The life of the simple people seems to run out in a predetermined fashion, directly into the nursing home, the cell, or the intensive care station.

The four one-act plays portray the fate of the common people in their entire misery and inadequacy. The people are "socially underprivileged,"[6] disenfranchised by family and environment, and institutionalized. This is what the one-act plays have in common. In addition they can be divided into two main themes: the generation gap in *Siding* (*Abstellgleis*) and *Wheat on the Autobahn* (*Weizen auf der Autobahn*) and the problem between the sexes in *Female Criminal* and *I Don't Understand*. As is customary on the popular stage, the people are familiar to us: the condescending daughter-in-law, the grumpy old man, the boorish husband, the stubborn peasant, the guilt-ridden daughter, the moribund wife. Also, what happens between the two conversation partners is typical: misunderstandings and suspicion between old and young, the unexpressed and repressed feelings between husband and wife, interrupted only by brief moments of agreement, and helplessness in the face of an overwhelming fate. The title of the fourth one-act play, *I Don't Understand*, is fitting for all the others.

Siding describes life in a nursing home with its monotonous rhythm, its bland food, the stench of old age and the daily little humiliations from the nurses. Among all the sufferings at the inadequate institution, which separates the old people and locks them up like lepers, the loss of identity and dignity is the most bitter. With a fine ear Mitterer exposes shame and disgrace in the way the young dispose of their responsibility toward the old—albeit with a bad conscience but nevertheless—in the dialogue between father-in-law and daughter-in-law.

Daughter-in-law: I know, you are mad at us.

Old Man: No I'm not. Not at all. I understand that alright.

Daughter-in-law: I couldn't have done it any more. And here you are taken care of.

Old Man: Everything is fine. I have everything here. Only the food is terrible, that I have to say. Grandpa, clean off your plate, or else there's no dessert. I don't need a dessert. I am constantly complaining to the administration. But it's useless. Only a grin and behind it he thinks, leave me alone, you old fool.[7]

But the old man's pleas for understanding are in vain with his daughter-in-law, who dismisses his complaints about the food as picky, admonishes him like a child not to make a mess with his snack, looks at her watch every few minutes and interrupts him impatiently when he starts to talk about the "good old times," as old people are wont to do. As is apparent from the quotation above, the disrespect of the young toward the old is concentrated in the word "Grandpa."

Daughter-in-Law: Oh, Grandpa!

Old Man: I'm not your grandpa! I'm your father-in-law! More respect please! (p. 171).

The visit to the nursing home is a bothersome duty that one fulfills as infrequently and as quickly as possible. It is also women's work, for the son has something more important to do. But the alienation is mutual: the old man is more attached to his dog than to his family. His first question is about the old Haika for whom he donates a five hundred shilling bill, while his granddaughter receives only a few coins for her piggy bank. The scene ends with the sad news about the death of the old dog who has left the old man behind, totally alone, staring death in its face.

Later on Mitterer developed this one-act play into a longer monologue drama called *Siberia*. The original dialogue partners, father-in-law and daughter-in-law, were first changed to father and son and later reduced to the father alone. Further changes were structural, dividing the play into two parts, the imaginary dialogue with the son and the imaginary address to the visiting president. In addition Mitterer lengthened the time span in order to divide the various stages of the old man's deterioration into distinct phases. He devises five stages in which he shows, "how an active, sanguine, rebellious old man's legs are being cut off, how they make him small and decrepit and how they prepare him for death."[8]

The central metaphor is the white hospital bed, which dominates the stage and accompanies the individual stages of his physical decay from beginning to end. The old man's constitution is reflected in his relationship with this bed, his freedom or lack of freedom from this bed: initially he can walk around it on crutches and then he needs it to support himself, later on he sits on it, and in the end he is stretched out on this last place of rest. With the relentless waning of his strength, the sense of being delivered up to the administrators' and nurses' indifference, cruelty and greed is growing steadily. His last weapon against total neglect is his bank account, of which they scheme to rob him through spying out his code word. The title of the seventy-five minute monologue refers to the interpersonal frigidity of these institutions and compares the nursing home unfavorably with a labor camp in Siberia. But the play is not just an attack against these kinds of institutions or a sharply critical social study but rather is a dramatic outcry against something very fundamental. "This play deals with the repression of problems of all kinds within a highly developed society."[9] Moreover it offers up "an inventory of human inadequacies when confronted with the phenomenon death."[10]

The old man in *Siberia* is a troublemaker who rebels from beginning to end against the cruel undignified inescapability of death as well as against the inhuman conditions in the nursing home. It is a "dream role for a mature actor who has to fill out an hour and a half by himself and is permitted to pull all emotional registers."[11] Fritz Mulniar demonstrated this in his performance at the *Akademie Theater* in Vienna. However, even with an actor of such caliber, it is undeniable that the second part, the address to the president, is less successful than the first part which already blurs the thin line between accusation and pathos, emotion and sentimentality.

Returning to the other three parts of *Visiting Hours*, the confrontation between old and young is being repeated in the one-act play *Wheat on the Autobahn*. The only difference is that the general conflict between generations in the first piece has become very specific here. It concerns the provinces and the betrayal by the people of the land and the values connected with it. The young people sold the land to the state for the construction of a highway and with the money changed the farmhouse into a bed and breakfast and discotheque, all in the name of progress and wealth. The old farmer who protested angrily and repeatedly—once he plowed the new highway and sowed wheat on it during the inauguration ceremonies—was locked up as "dangerous" in a mental clinic and kept under control with drugs and electric shocks.

There is no doubt that the trauma of losing his land has changed the farmer, who is dreaming of rolling fields of wheat and blossoming meadows, into a paranoic. He talks about a group of conspirators who, headed by his son-in-law, plans to cover the whole world with cement. The mental state of the farmer vacillates between lucidity and confusion until the one-act play ends with the total collapse of communication between him and his daughter. Left alone at the end, the old man—mentally disturbed and without hope for liberation from his captivity—resumes singing the lullaby of the beginning.

All four one-act plays deal with current problems vis-à-vis social grievances. One topic is the escalation of female criminology, especially murder or an attempted murder of the husband. This topic is, if not the most up-to-date, certainly the most sensational and is the center of the play *Female Criminal*. Mitterer succeeds in capturing the frustrations of a modern marriage in very few words. He demonstrates how unexpressed and repressed thoughts and emotions multiply and escalate into a lethal explosion. As a consequence of this explosion the wife has exchanged the prison of her marriage for the prison of the state. The physical and emotional overload of the working wife and mother leads to a murderous attack with a kitchen knife upon the nagging husband. Husband and wife are now sitting opposite each other in the visitation room of the prison, unable even now to communicate, separated by their own ways of experiencing the partnership and imprisoned by conditioning and prejudices. Especially the husband does not understand anything. "How is he supposed to understand what she herself no longer understands?"[12]

He accuses, laments and blames everything on the "feminists." And she regrets and repents but is now more content in the prison than she was at home, since now she is free the entire weekend, free from work and free from the lovelessness and thoughtlessness of her marriage. He "loves" her still, he says, but in reality misses more the daily orderly routine, the comfort of her presence as housewife and mother. Without her he does not get along as well. She on the other hand longs to see her children who, as is evident from his words, seem to understand more than he does. The audience's sympathy is on her side. The end is conciliatory but hopeless and sad for both. He will send the children but will not return himself.

The topic of man's captivity in a net of impenetrable forces that escalate through all acts finds its crescendo in *I Don't Understand*. Again someone visits someone else in an institution, this time the husband visits his wife in the hospital. She suffers from an undiagnosed illness from which she dies in the end. Helpless and lonely because of her absence anyway, he also loses his job at a factory where he has worked for twenty-three years. Both are in their fifties. The four scenes of this one-act play reveal a marriage full of disappointments, repressed rage, habits and cruelties, but also full of warmth, co-dependency and affection.

> He: I haven't always been nice to you.
> She: Me neither. That's life (pp. 207–208).

They need one another like their two parakeets, who prefer to be together in one cage rather than separated in two, although one of them always tears out the feathers of the other. When the woman dies at the end she has drawn the better lot than he, who is left alone by her and terminated by his employer, and drowns his loneliness and humiliation in alcohol and card games.

Both are helpless in the face of forces they don't understand. She is in the hands of the doctors who do not talk to her about her illness, and he is destroyed in a process which calls itself rationalization measures and which lays off old workers. They are victims; there is no higher power to correct the injustice. "Oh well, there is nothing we can do. We are powerless against those people" (p. 201).

Mitterer's work attempts to enlighten like the conventional *Volksstück*, but it does not utilize shock therapy like Turrini's plays or dialectics and didactics like the plays of Brecht; rather, it employs the representation of reality in artistic form. This depiction of problems and conflicts on the stage "naturally" reveals the shortcomings of social and inter-relational situations. Kroetz's words about the importance of empathy from the audience in his plays are also relevant for Mitterer's plays:

> The insight into the human condition leads to empathy, this expresses itself in compassion—at first ... real compassion is the motor for help.[13]

Also important is the realistic representation of language as a mirror for the conscious and unconscious mechanisms of communication. This is especially apparent in *Female Criminal* where the victim's language abounds in threats and verbal attacks. The husband, who does not understand any-thing anyhow, remains unaware of this connection between verbal and actual violence in his marriage, but the audience understands this connec-tion very well. The husband is linguistically so impoverished that he needs the help of newspaper articles in order to understand the incomprehensible and to make his wife understand what has happened. By being exposed to the communicative short comings of the people on the stage, the audience is led to recognize that the fundamental culprit is the lack of communica-tion. This inadequacy makes these people victims and deprives them of the ability to articulate their problems. It becomes clear that the goal of this *Volksstück* is the appeal for a "linguistic and communicative competence."[14]

Like the traditional *Volksstück*, Mitterer's *Visiting Hours* is theater not intended for the big national stages, the Mecca of the intellectuals and bourgeoisie. In Mitterer's opinion they are the wrong place for his plays, since the audience of these stages is already aware of the problems, but the audience of the small, popular stages needs this kind of enlightenment.[15] When he himself was a student, he avoided the national theater in Inns-bruck and visited instead the small stages that were closer to his own world.[16] What Mitterer learned from his own experience confirms the observation that the popular theater targets a special social class, a "target audience" (Müller). The choice of topics and linguistic means is thereby decisive in order to awaken the interest of this special group. Mitterer finds the material for his *Volksstücke* in most cases from present-day events as they make headlines in regional newspapers. Unfortunately, because of the constant change of social conditions and institutions, this contemporary material makes the plays dated and obsolete very rapidly.[17]

On the whole, critics are well disposed toward Mitterer's plays, espe-cially *Visiting Hours* and *Siberia*, and judge them positively. They praise his ability to identify with the common people's problems and express them clearly, his talent to expose people as they are, and to arouse the audience's empathy with a clear depiction of the conditions. One critic writes that already after only a few minutes "there is so much insight and emotion that other authors could make use of for hours."[18] But the same critic also recognizes the weaknesses of Mitterer's realism: "Accusation without excessive consequences, theater without abstraction, reality without the meta-reality of the world of the stage."[19] Repeatedly we find the demand for a higher degree of aesthetics and greater distancing from reality. Reality itself, it is said, can be comical or tragic but not effective dramatically. One critic feels that Mitterer produces "more pity than artistic form,"[20] with the result that he creates a soap opera on stage. Several critics have noted Mitterer's affinity with the Naturalists.

Mitterer writes for an environment from which he himself comes. His youth has been compared with that of Innenhofer, with the difference that he himself does not see it so negatively.[21] Presumably the author does not write out of feelings of rage and protest, although he would have enough reason to do so. However, Mitterer contradicts this claim of Sigrid Löffler personally in a way which is unusual for this reserved man:

> I have never reacted to an article about me but this time I have to do it ... "Blustering anger about the injustices of life are not his thing." Ms. Löffler, writing is for me a question of survival and of course I have written and I will write because the "injustices of the world" make me angry and hurt me.[22]

Born in 1948 as the thirteenth child of a Tyrolean peasant woman, given up for adoption to farm laborers, he grew up in poverty and hard work. The child who spent his days daydreaming and reading became a day-dreaming official with the Innsbruck customs, an occupation which left him much time to read, to write and all that which the people good-naturedly called *Spinnen* (building castles in the air).[23] Today the busy theater and television author, together with his wife Chryseldis, an artist, is an icon of the Tyrolean cultural scene.

In his film scripts, which Mitterer writes regularly in addition to his *Volksstücke* for film and television, he deals mainly with historical and documentary material, as in *Homeland, Sold Out* (*Verkaufte Heimat*, 1988–89) the story of Southern Tyrol at the time of Fascism, and the films about Egon Schiele and Peter Altenberg. A film adaptation of Petzold's *The Rough Life* (*Das rauhe Leben*) is related in content to the themes of his *Volksstücke*. The very successful television series *Piefke-Saga* (1992) deals with the tourist industry and its problems, and he also intends to continue to write children's books, a genre with which he began his writing career in 1973 with the book *The Super Hen Hanna* (*Die Superhenne Hanna*).

In all of his works Mitterer uncovers social mechanisms that most people do not see through. Instead of helplessness toward institutions he would like solidarity, for this is the only way to change what ails society. However, he obviates the question of whether he is a political author with the qualification: "it is politics, isn't it, if one is interested in social problems and if one wants to improve society and people's attitudes and behavior toward one another."[24]

Notes

1. "Ein neuer Volksstückeschreiber," in *Theater Heute*, Vol. 21 (1980), p. 23.

2. Herbert Herzmann, "The Relevance of the Tradition. The Volksstücks of Felix Mitterer," in *Modern Austrian Literature*, Vol. 24, Nos. 3/4 (1991).

3. "Felix Mitterer im Gespräch mit Ursula Hassel und Deirdre McMahon, 19 November 1988," in *Modern Austrian Literature*, Vol. 25, No. 1 (1992), p. 30.

4. Herzmann, p. 176.

5. Herzmann, p. 180.

6. Elisabeth Senn, "Sprache des Lebens: Mitterers Engagement für die Abgeschobenen und Entmündigten," in *Tiroler Tageszeitung* (Innsbruck: 8 November 1989).

7. Felx Mitterer, Stücke, I (Innsbruck: Haymon Verlag, 1992), p. 170.

8. Thomas Thieringer, "Aus dem Leben ausgemustert," in *Süddeutsche Zeitung* (2 April 1990).

9. Martin Schweighofer, "Ein Triumph für Peymann," in *Wochenpresse*, No. 43 (25 October 1990).

10. M. Mertl, "Ein Lästiger kämpft ums Leben," in *Kultur* (22 October 1990), p. 14.

11. Duglore Pizzini, "Der Menschen ganzer Jammer," in *Die Presse* (Wien: 22 October 1990).

12. H. Lehmann, "Genauso wie im richtigen Leben," in *Salzburger Nachrichten* (Salzburg: 17 June 1988).

13. Susan Cocalis, "Mitleid und Engagement," in *Colloquia Germanica* (1981), p. 203.

14. Gerd Müller, Das Volksstück von Raimund bis Kroetz (München: Oldenbourg, 1979), p. 148.

15. "Felix Mitterer im Gespräch ...," p. 20.

16. "Felix Mitterer im Gespräch ...," p. 20.

17. Müller, p. 146.

18. Frido Hütter, "Mantel and Pyjama," in *Kleine Zeitung* (Klagenfurt: 5 April 1990), p. 60.

19. Ibid.

20. Otto Hochreiter, "Wie das Leben spielt," in *Die Presse* (Wien: 18 April 1985), p. 6.

21. Sigrid Löffler, "Ein Experte für die Nichtversicherten," in *Theater Heute*, Vol. 9 (1985), p. 52.

22. Felix Mitterer, "A netts Büable," in *Profil*, No. 8 (Wien: 19 February 1990), pp. 9-10.

23. "Felix Mitterer im Gespräch ...," p. 27.

24. "Felix Mitterer im Gespräch ...," p. 23.

Onward or Downward? The Eternal-Feminine in Felix Mitterer's Play *Die Wilde Frau*

Gerlinde Ulm Sanford

At the outset, a word about the possible translations of the play's title. The German is beautifully ambiguous here. Translations coming to mind most readily are "the savage, the wild, the non-domesticated woman." The woman in the play could be considered savage or crude because she indiscriminately goes to bed with almost all—except for Wendl the youngest—of the loggers. A closer look, however, shows that such an assessment of her character is superficial. The loggers Jogg, Much, and also Lex might generally see her that way, yet there are at least some instances when the woman inspires them to a kind of politeness, to a state beyond their own crude lifestyle. Both Lex and Much propose to her. Lex is most smitten by passion and even love for the woman. This prompts him, on the one hand, to act more brutally, cruelly, and jealously toward the woman than the others. In this sense, one might say that she draws him downward. On the other hand, he takes risks to please her and would like to start a new life with her, which might be considered a striving onward. For Hias, the eldest, sex is not so important any more. Thus the woman arouses in him not so much mere sexual drive, but also memories of the beauty of youth and love. Finally, for Wendl she represents a mother figure, someone who consoles him and lifts his spirits. She is very much like the Virgin Mary whom he worships in the little forest chapel. He does not wish to sleep with her; however, he too is physically attracted to her.

Because of explanatory stage comments, it is normal that the reader—and to some degree also the spectator—has greater insight into the actions than has the protagonist. Mitterer's stage comments are not only very rich

131

and detailed, but sometimes they even give information that is too subtle to be expressed by an actor.[1] Therefore, it is the reader of this play who has the deepest insights into the action in general and into the nature of the female protagonist.

The above translations of the attribute 'wild' could seem already ambiguous enough, yet the German ambiguity goes much further. A Wilde Frau can also be a mythical being, as portrayed in numerous German myths and legends. Mitterer specifically mentions in his introduction to the play: "I had been inspired to the film and the play by so-called Wild Women, called also Salige, or Wood Ladies."[2] The capitalization of 'wild' in the German title is an indication that Wilde Frau is meant to allude to such a mythical being. Wendl and certainly also an observant spectator perceive her mythical traits. There is her strange appearance and later disappearance, her strange singing, her quiet loftiness, and the author's stage remarks—mentioned above—stressing her knowledge *"that in reality, nothing, nothing at all can happen to her."*[3] Also, the sudden impotency Lex is stricken with and his calling her a witch (scene 2) can be interpreted as her possibly having supernatural traits.

Finally, it is of interest for the interpretation of the play that the German word *Wild* can also mean 'game', because such a mythical *Wilde Frau* functions in some accounts as protectress of nature and its gentle creatures in general—as opposed to beasts of prey—and frequently specifically of deer or other wild animals that are at the mercy of the game hunter. One might ponder, therefore, that the woman in the play does not eat from the deer which Lex brings home. She is indeed a protectress of game, of innocent creatures. Wendl, after all, is also such an innocent creature.

The purpose of this brief introduction was to draw attention to these various associations invoked by the play's title. When analyzing the play in more detail, it becomes fully clear that the meaning of *Wild* in "The Wild Woman" is indeed not simple, but rather complex.

The title of this article is, of course, an allusion to the last two lines of Goethe's *Faust*: "The Eternal-Feminine/Draws us onward." I will try to show in the following pages that this "Eternal-Feminine" principle as manifested in the woman of Felix Mitterer's play draws the men onward, yet also downward. Certainly Wendl, but also Hias to some degree, and in several instances even Lex are drawn "onward." In Much and Jogg, the woman arouses only little more than base sexual desires. Lex's relationship to her, however, is more intricate. His passion leads him, on the one hand, to extreme cruelty toward her, in other words, "downward"; yet he also has thoughts and plans for a new and less primitive life, in other words, he strives "onward."

I shall first examine the relationship between the woman and Wendl. Beginning with his very first glance at her, Wendl worships the woman.

When she enters the cabin, he *"respectfully stands back for her and stares at her with big eyes"* (p. 268).[4] He is eager to be at her service by grasping her cape and hanging it up to dry (p. 269). Shortly thereafter, he is crudely teased and insulted by Lex and Much. The woman is a dark-haired, southern-looking type; therefore, Much suspects she is a gypsy (p. 270). Since she does not talk to defend herself, the suspicion of her being a gypsy and all the negative associations related to it linger on throughout the play. In jest, Much suggests that she might even be a relative of Wendl's, because Wendl's father too had been a gypsy: "such a cart pusher! A knife grinder!"[5] Lex takes up this idea and turns to Wendl with a coarse sexual joke: "Then most likely your mother ground his knife, hu?"[6] Much aggravates the insult by speaking in a very primitive and derogatory way about Wendl's mother's pregnancy and Wendl's birth:

> He threw her out, the farmer, when she was so big you could stomp her! And the black devil [the gypsy father] of course over the hills and far away! We caught her then whelping in our stable! Two weeks later, she went into the water, together with her whelp (pup)! Wendl, however, they fished out again.[7]

After this crude account, Wendl begins to cry, yet tries to hold back his sobs and leaves the room. The woman has observed the entire scene and follows the boy. Lex feels pity and goes after them. Through the opened door, he sees the woman comforting Wendl in a very tender way: *"she has her hand holding his cheek, he hides his face in it and sobs."*[8] Another subtle indication of Wendl's instant attachment to the woman is his looking back to her before retiring for the night in the hayloft (p. 271).

During the following evenings, we see Wendl carving on a piece of wood which more and more takes on the shape of the Virgin Mary (pp. 276 and 281). In scene 12 then, we become aware that the Virgin Mary and the woman have merged for Wendl. He describes a small forest shrine with a blackened statue of the Virgin named "Our Lady of the Forest" and its soothing and calming influence on him:

> She is all black. Because some time ago lightening struck there, and she began to burn. When I'm at wit's end, I go to her and talk to her. First I talk to her, then I don't talk anymore and only look at her. And all of a sudden I feel a sweet pain. A very sweet pain. And I forget everything. Everything. It feels each time like dying. So beautiful is that. So beautiful.[9]

After some silence, Wendl himself makes the connection between the Virgin Mary and the woman. He says softly: "She looks like you."[10] These are the last words spoken in this scene. Then the very precise stage comments make clear that the Virgin Mary and the woman have a strikingly similar effect on Wendl. As the Virgin, the woman too soothes and relieves his pain and his tension. The wordless action showing the woman's effect on Wendl almost mirrors his account of the Virgin Mary's effect on him:

Wendl begins to weep softly, starts to sob, he is overcome, his sobbing becomes louder, he tries to suppress it, yet is unable to, he is shaken by it, he
covers his face with his hands, the woman gets up, steps to him, draws his
head onto her shoulder, embraces him, his weeping turns into a release.
Black out.[11]

In both instances the language suggests Wendl's strong attraction to
the Virgin Mary, respect for the women, and relief from emotional, possibly sexual tensions.

All through the play, Wendl is portrayed as being gentle and innocent,
yet also helpless and powerless. When he himself is being abused, he remains passive. When he witnesses the woman's maltreatment, he courageously strives to come to her rescue. In scene 10, Wendl is the only one
who physically attempts to impede Lex when he proceeds to put the
woman in chains (p. 289). This is the more remarkable since he is, of course,
no match for Lex, while Much or Jogg could very well have hindered Lex.
Wendl is also the only one who later, in scene 12, makes an active attempt
to free her (p. 291 f.). Yet he is as helpless and powerless as the deer, except
that he has tears to express his feelings. Thus we find him in tears at the
end of scenes 1, 10, and 12. In the end, scene 18, he is the only survivor,
albeit in tears again.

Next I shall examine the woman's effect on Lex. He seems to be the
most passionate of the loggers. His passion draws him down, on the one
hand, to verbal and physical abuse of the woman and lifts him onward, on
the other hand, to courage and plans for a new and maybe more humane
life with the woman. In my opinion, Wendl and Lex are most deeply
touched by the woman. They are in love with her. Yet while Wendl is too
gentle, too weak, moreover too young for the consequences of love, Lex is
too passionate and resorts to violence as soon as his passion finds resistance.

The woman's reaction to Lex is somewhat puzzling. He is the first to
attempt intercourse with her (p. 272). Why does she not "let" him in scene
2, while she seems to let Jogg, Much, and Hias in scenes 4, 6 and 8? Why
does she seem to let Lex in scene 7? In his introduction to the play, Mitterer
gives the answer. He says that all Wild Women—in the above-explained
mythical sense—impose certain taboos. If the taboo is broken, misfortune
befalls the offender. Then Mitterer continues:

It is difficult to interpret the taboo stipulations, I at any rate have interpreted them in my play such that the man may not possess the woman
and may not take away her freedom.[12]

Mitterer uses the word *besitzen*, which in English can mean 'to own' as well
as 'to dominate' in a sexual sense. The Wild Woman in Mitterer's play
seems to agree to intercourse when it is requested rather than forcefully
demanded.

To answer the above questions one might argue that Lex is brutally forceful and crude in scene 2, while he is considerably more pleading in scene 7. When the woman silently resists his first approaches (p. 272), he becomes angry immediately, wrestles with her, and finally strikes her a heavy blow. His ensuing impotency can be interpreted either as inflicted by the Wild Woman through supernatural powers, or as caused by a kind of scare about his brutal behavior, albeit rather unrecognized by himself. When he returns to the hayloft and Jogg addresses him, the stage comments state that he answers in a scared fashion (p. 273).[13]

Despite Lex's boastful and crude account about his—in reality failed—intercourse with the woman (p. 273), we must assume that she has caused a kind of catharsis in him and that possibly he regrets his coarse behavior. The next morning, he is the one who first suggests that she stay on in the cabin because of the snow. When Jogg speaks of her as a floozy, Lex gets angry. At the end of scene 4, when it seems that the woman agrees to intercourse with Jogg, Lex of course is jealous and calls her a sow (p. 275). Yet in scene 5, he arrives in the cabin with a deer that he has caught specifically to please her.[14] Doing that, he has put his life at risk since the result of poaching might be a bullet in the head. In scene 6, he gets into a fight with Much who claims it is his turn to sleep with the woman. In scene 7, he has secretly returned home from work in order to be with the woman. First he reproaches her in extremely crude terms for being so promiscuous (p. 278), yet clearly his crudeness is caused by aggravated jealousy. He admits to the woman that he never felt as attracted to any other woman as he feels attracted to her, yet she does not react. He almost resorts once more to violence and reminds her that she must not refuse him while she "lets" the others. She continues to ignore his demands. But he then promises not to hit her ever again. He excuses his former violence by saying that it was caused by his extreme passion and pleads with her to understand and not to waste the precious time he has stolen off work. The woman thereupon proceeds voluntarily into her sleeping compartment, and Lex follows. Then "*Black out*," and we must assume that she consents to intercourse. At the end of scene 8, Lex very reluctantly agrees that it is Hias's turn to sleep with the woman.

In scene 9, Lex feels hurt and insulted that the woman refuses to eat from the deer. These feelings continue when she also refuses to permit him to help her carry in water for her bath. If the woman is considered to be a Wild Woman in the mythical sense discussed before, it might follow that she does not wish to eat from the deer. In addition—or so it would seem—she senses that Lex is always on the brink of violence, and she is therefore hesitant to accept any favor from him. Indeed, Lex once more cannot suppress his violent reaction to her apparent indifference toward him. When she takes her bath hidden behind a provisory curtain of clothes, he seemingly accepts that she is not his but rather belongs to everybody: "Why do you hide? Really, you don't need to hide from your bed mates!"[15] He then tears down her provisory curtain, and the woman's breasts are exposed. But in reality, this is only a violent consequence of his jealousy, which is confirmed by the stage comments: *"Lex is jealous, tries to hide it, however."*[16]

In scene 10, which takes place the evening of the same day, we see Lex getting more and more drunk. (His heavy drinking is mentioned throughout the play and explains also to some degree why he becomes violent so easily.) In this scene, Lex's violence reaches its culmination. He tries to force the woman to drink also. He engages in a wrestling game in which two opponents try to pull each other across the table by inter-locking the right middle fingers. He beats Much in the game, yet loses to Jogg, possibly because he is very drunk. When Hias makes trite remarks about Lex's defeat, Lex knocks him down. Lex then loses once more against Jogg, this time in a floor fight in which Lex cheats, in a desperate attempt to impress the woman at any cost. Lex finally goes out and rolls in the cold snow to sober up. He is embarrassed vis-à-vis the woman because he lost the fights against Jogg. When he comes back from the outside, he appears sober.

Lex now claims the woman for himself alone. The Woman nods affirmingly. It is not quite clear, however, whether she affirms to be Lex's alone, or whether she affirms only that she has understood his claim.

> LEX: From today on, you are mine! mine alone! Understood?
> *The woman looks at him quietly.*
> LEX: Have you understood?
> *The woman nods.*[17]

The woman might indeed show agreement by her nodding to both claim and question, indicating that she is his alone and has understood. Only when Lex—a few lines later—threatens to kill anyone who might touch the woman, then the woman realizes that Lex is again about to resort to violence. Therefore, she prepares to leave.

Lex is increasingly driven into tragic desperation because all of his efforts in this scene to "score" with the woman have been unsuccessful. The very moment when Hias insinuates that Lex is impotent with the woman (p. 288) and Lex proceeds to attack him with the knife, the woman attempts to leave—perhaps because she fears that violence is unavoidable. Lex—in his desperation—chains the woman to the house so that she may not leave, thus applying force to make her stay while at the same time losing her by violating her taboo, that is, applying force and taking away her freedom.

In scene 11, Lex's tragic situation is further aggravated. First, Jogg— speaking also for Much and Hias—forces Lex to retract his claim to have the woman for himself alone. Lex—stifled—retracts. It is his turn to sleep with the woman tonight. When he has entered her sleeping compartment, he tries to explain his tragic situation to the woman as follows: He cannot let her leave because he is smitten by passion; he cannot have her for himself alone because the others do not permit it and are too many against him. Yet if the woman were to consent to live with him, he would be willing to set her free now, and she could hide in a cabin until he'd have the job finished and could join her. He promises her never to apply violence again. The woman, however, does not seem to react to his plans. Lex strikes her a blow and forces her. Whether he is again stricken by impotence or whether he succeeds in having intercourse with her is left open by *"Black out."*

One might ask why the woman does not agree with Lex's plan to set her free and to join her later. In scene 12, after he has caught Wendl attempting to free the woman, Lex even repeats his offer to set her free under the condition that she go with him (p. 291). The woman shakes her head refusingly. She most probably senses his ever-ready latent violence, his predatory spirit which takes by force whatever offers resistance. In scene 18, indeed, the stage comments compare him to a predatory animal, to a beast of prey (p. 298). However, that predatory spirit—most drastically shown in Lex, but typical for man in general—is in contrast to the woman, to the Eternal-Feminine she represents, to that aspect of the divine that creates and maintains life.

No doubt the woman is attracted to him more than to the others. The stage comments make that clear a number of times, and the following are two very obvious examples: In scene 17, after Lex has asked her *"almost affectionately"*[18] to dance, she looks at him and then does as he has requested. At the end, in scene 18, when Much, Jogg, and also Lex lie dead on the stage, she kneels down and strokes his hair caressingly, even though his last words before dying were calling her a "damned whore."[19] Lex attracts and repulses the woman more than the others because he embodies "man" at his best and his worst; his best meaning having a strong capacity for love and also compassion, his worst meaning that any obstacle in his pursuits will unavoidably induce him to violence.

Already in his play *Dragon Thirst,*[20] Mitterer portrays a similar magic attraction between the opposite powers of good and evil, love and hatred, prey and hunter. In our play, the conflict is between nature and man. Nature is represented by the woman, Wendl, Hias, the deer, the forest; they seem non-violent and yielding. Man—with positive yet also strongly negative traits—is represented by Lex and to a lesser degree by Jogg and Much. These three men show at times some politeness and/or consideration for the woman; however, more often than not, they appear to be aggressive and violent. Lex is a man who is capable at the same time of love, tenderness, compassion and, whenever he finds resistance, of the opposite— hatred, coarseness and cruelty. His attraction to the woman brings out his best and his worst.

Jogg and Much are in a way comparable to Lex, except that they are portrayed less dramatically. Both their good and also their bad traits are less pronounced than Lex's; correspondingly, the woman has a lesser—

though still great—effect on them. Jogg seems to be the boss of the logging crew. Accordingly, he wants to be the most righteous and law abiding. But being under the spell of physical attraction to the woman, he forgoes his usual moral standards and has intercourse with her even though he is married. In scene 4, when it is his turn to sleep with her, he explains his situation to the woman, thus finding a kind of excuse for sleeping with her. His wife at home is a good woman, yet burnt out and not attractive anymore; therefore, it would be "sweet" (p. 275) to sleep with a young body for a change. His arguments are coarse, but they nonetheless incite some feelings of compassion in the spectator and obviously also in the woman. He concludes his plea with: "Indeed, woman, I'd be grateful if you'd have me!"[21] Thereupon, the woman appears to agree to intercourse with him.

Nevertheless, the next evening—scene 5—when Lex brings into the hut an illegally trapped deer, Jogg wants to set a moral standard again and threatens to fire Lex because of his poaching. Lex, however, counters by threatening that he will make public Jogg's adultery. Therefore, Jogg does not fire Lex. Later—scene 9—when the deer has been cooked for the Sunday meal, Jogg's moral resistance has been reduced to his not eating from the meat. Normally, Jogg goes home to his wife on Sundays. This Sunday, he stays in the cabin, and Lex, Much, and Hias make clear that they are well aware that the woman is the reason for his changed behavior. Still, Jogg tries to keep up a certain orderly standard among the loggers. He is the one who says a prayer before and at the end of a meal. Or, when Lex on that Sunday tears down the clothes behind which the woman is taking her bath and thus exposes her breasts to all the men, it is Jogg who hangs the clothes back up so that she has her privacy again. Nonetheless, he raves about the woman: "Never before have I had such a woman" (p. 282). When he then tries to express the sensations felt with the woman, he finds almost poetic words: "That cushion of moss ... madness ... (*pause*). In the mouth she tastes like raspberries" (p. 282).[22] Still, despite his excitement he maintains some responsibility either toward the woman and/or toward his wife. When the question comes up what might happen if the woman becomes pregnant, Jogg asks: "Well, aren't you careful?" Lex thereupon replies loudly: "Anything else! Do you think I'll jump off in the middle of the most beautiful ride?" Jogg then once again, even though regretfully, acknowledges responsibilities: "That's easy for you to say! If one is married, as I am, then one learns to be careful" (p. 283).[23]

Later that Sunday, scene 10, Lex gets very drunk because he is jealous and angry that the woman does not seem to appreciate his attempts to please her. She does not eat from the deer that he brought as a gift for her. She doesn't want him to carry water for her bath and doesn't want to drink from his brandy. When Lex, in his drunkenness, forces the bottle into her mouth, it is Jogg who finally pushes Lex away from the woman. And a little later, it is again Jogg who defends Hias from Lex's violent attacks (p.

286). Thereupon, when Lex and Jogg engage in a fight, Jogg abides by standard fighting rules, while Lex—desperately wishing to impress the woman—has totally lost his composure and fights unfairly.

During the progress of scene 10—as discussed earlier—Lex is more and more driven to extremes and violence and finally puts the woman in chains so that she cannot run off. Jogg, although at first somewhat undecided, helps Lex by holding Wendl in an iron grip, while Lex hammers the one end of the woman's chain with an iron clamp onto the wall.

The woman is now totally at the men's mercy; even during the night the chain is not removed. Jogg's moral standard does not seem to be offended by the woman's situation. In scene 13, when it is again his turn to sleep with her, he only asks Lex whether the woman is difficult now. When Lex answers affirmatively and suggests that Jogg could make her comply by a box on the ear, Jogg nods in accord. Then, in the woman's sleeping compartment, he says to her that he would prefer if she gave in without him having to hit her. Feelings of moral compunction once more turn up even though rather indirectly: "... I don't like to hit a woman. I don't even hit the horses. I've never done that! ... (p. 293)."[24] Upon that indirect threat and the ensuing plea, the woman seems to agree to intercourse.

Yet in the final scene it becomes clear that the desire to keep the woman in her sexually enslaved condition has reduced Lex, Much and also the righteous Jogg to violent beasts fighting for dominance at any cost. When Lex's attempt to leave with the woman is discovered because the woman refuses to go with Lex, it is Jogg who first reaches for a weapon and who first starts aggressive actions. Much joins in right away, and one act of violence precipitates the next. Jogg has abandoned any former fairness, and he and Much attack Lex brutally with weapons and insulting words. After Lex breaks down and faints, Jogg kicks him with his foot to awaken him and finally shoves the stick of a logging tool into his coat sleeves, thus fixing Lex's arms into the position of a crucifixion. While earlier, in scene 9, Jogg had hung back up the clothes which Lex had torn down and thereby had exposed the breasts of the woman to the view of all, now in the final scene, it is Jogg who tears open her dress so that Lex should be aroused and able to overcome his impotency, as Jogg remarks maliciously. Much joins in with merciless comments: "Well, what's the matter, Lexy? You are a wild stud indeed! Show us how you can perform! Come on, I'll open the stall to your pants!"[25] Shortly later, the stage comments say: *"Lex is being pressed by Jogg onto the* [bare breasted] *woman, she does not move back, she stands eye to eye with Lex"*(p. 299).[26] Her not moving back and standing eye to eye with Lex might be interpreted as a sign of her being attracted to Lex or else as a sign of the same seeming coldness and indifference toward violence demonstrated several times before.[27] However, since the woman caresses Lex's hair before disappearing from the final slaughter, one can interpret these stage comments as confirming again that not only Lex is most passionately attracted to the woman, but also that the woman's relationship to Lex is more complex than that to the other loggers.

Analyzing the character of Jogg, we can once more see the ambiguous effect of the woman. She brings out in Jogg politeness and consideration, even if to a rather limited extent. In the end, however, she is the reason for an already smoldering power struggle between the men becoming a deadly fight when it combines with the men's competition for the woman.

A few words about Much. In the hierarchy of the loggers, he ranks right below Jogg, who is the boss. Much is also a farmer, as he proudly points out vis-à-vis Lex, who was a convict at some time in the past. He too shows positive traits under the influence of the woman. When Jogg first does not consider it right that a woman should spend the night in the cabin, it is not only Lex but also Much who points out that she might freeze to death in the bad weather (p. 269). If morality is at times a problem for Jogg, it is hardly a problem for Much. When Jogg suggests that the woman is a cheap whore and therefore should leave (p. 274), Lex gets angry at Jogg because he is already smitten. Much however says: "Well and what if [she is a cheap whore]? I mean, that would not be bad! Would it?"(p. 274)[28] These words already suggest the routine to be established, namely that all the loggers take turns in having intercourse with the woman. In scene 6, Lex tries to keep Much from taking his turn with the woman. Much defends his rights and uses a tool to attack Lex. It is not so much passion, but rather sudden temper that prompts him to violence. Before he enters the woman's sleeping compartment, he considerately puts his hair in order and then asks whether he may enter. In contrast to Lex, Much has a practical mind. As discussed earlier, Lex proposes to the woman in scene 11. Lex requests her consent only and has no further conditions. In scene 14 then, Much proposes to the woman, but with the reservation that she does not yet have "a loaf in the oven" (p. 293);[29] that is, that she is not yet pregnant.

The woman does not seem to accept Much's proposal, whereupon he gets angry. However, while in scene 11 Lex resorts to violence again when his proposal is turned down, Much evidently also has to force the woman, yet gets his way without striking her, just as was the case when Jogg wanted to sleep with her in scene 13. This seeming incongruence in the woman's reaction can be explained if one assumes not only that Lex feels more strongly attracted to the woman than the others, but also that the woman is more deeply affected by Lex's extreme passion than by the other men's attraction to her. Since the woman is not indifferent to Lex, she might also be more hurt by violence and coarseness coming from him than coming from the others. In addition, we must not forget that Lex is responsible for her being in chains.

The eldest of the loggers is Hias, who distinguishes himself in several respects. Perhaps because of his age, he shows more wisdom than the others, yet also wit and sarcasm, which is mostly expressed in proverbial sayings and rhymes. Lex has very little sense of humor and therefore very often feels rubbed the wrong way by Hias's needling verses. Hias is physically the weakest. Nonetheless, he too feels sexually attracted to the woman. Yet sex is no longer a dominant factor in Hias's life. When Hias for the first time takes his turn to sleep with the woman (scene 8), he drinks up the necessary courage by stealing brandy from Lex's rucksack. He is aware of his age and fears that he might no longer be sexually attractive to a woman. Then, as older people typically tend to do, he reminisces about his younger years, thereby alternating between speaking in drastic prose and almost romantic verses or metaphors. Out of consideration for the woman, he chews a piece of sap so that he might not stink from the mouth before entering her sleeping compartment.

Hias is not a violent man. When it is for the second time his turn to sleep with the woman (scene 15), we may conclude from his words that she refuses to have intercourse with him—maybe because she has in the meantime been chained by Lex. However, Hias does not resort to violence; rather, he is grateful to be able to just lie with her. He feels with her as a child lying next to the mother (p. 294). In this scene, he also indirectly apologizes to her for her being in chains, for his not being able to take active steps to free her, and he promises to try to get the key to the chain by ruse.

On the day following the night with the woman, Hias dies while the woman holds his hand. His last words express compassion for the woman and a prophetic foreboding of the catastrophe. If we consider the woman as being a mythical figure, then Hias's death might be seen as being caused through her influence in order to spare him from the final slaughter. His peaceful death might be seen as being granted by the woman, either because he never turns to physical violence, or because the woman feels pity for his age.

Wendl too is spared the final catastrophe. Both Hias and Wendl are of gentle character. Hias is gentle—not so much in his sometimes rather harsh words, but more because of physical weakness due to old age. Wendl is gentle, perhaps because he is still young and innocent. We cannot tell whether he will be able to maintain his gentleness in his adult years. Both Hias and Wendl, however, are in need of protection, which the woman—if seen as a mythical figure as elaborated at the beginning of this paper—seems to grant them.

In conclusion then, we see that potentially the woman is able to draw the men "onward." We can observe such a positive influence on all the loggers, although to varying degrees. However, competition for power in general and for power over the woman specifically lead to the final downfall of Jogg, Much and Lex—those loggers who are in full possession of their manhood. Hias, the oldest, hardly participates in that power struggle, and his death does not have to be seen as a downfall. Either his death has been effected by the woman, or it is a consequence of old age. In both cases, it might be seen as a benevolent release from the difficulties of life. Wendl, the youngest, is lifted "onward"—and solely onward—through the influence of the woman. As indicated, she represents for him a figure comparable to the Virgin Mary, a figure worthy of worship. At the end of the play, the woman smiles softly at Wendl before she leaves. True, Wendl is left in tears, and he asks her in vain to stay. Her strange singing slowly fades in the distance. Yet he keeps his life, and it stands to reason that he might have learned from the downfall of the other loggers.

At the beginning of the play, Mitterer quotes the famous Homer passage where Circe gives Odysseus instructions how he can hear the bright song of the Sirens without being brought to ruin. Circe advises Odysseus to have himself tied to the mast of the ship. Should he ask to be untied, then his shipmates are to tie him even more firmly. Odysseus, by permitting himself to be tied, purposely has his power restricted and thus is able to hear the song of the Sirens without adverse consequences. Jogg, Much and Lex are brought to their ruin through their uncontrolled pursuit of power in general and of power over the woman specifically. Not the "strong" men in the play survive, but Wendl, the seemingly weakest and most powerless of the loggers, is the only survivor. Wendl is at the same time the one whose attraction to the woman goes far beyond mere physical attraction, since for Wendl she represents a figure of worship. Like the Virgin Mary, she represents an aspect of the divine. Wendl is drawn "onward" through her, just as Faust is drawn onward by Gretchen, by the Mater Gloriosa, by the Eternal-Feminine. This Eternal-Feminine represents the divine in its aspect as origin of life. Mitterer seems to tell us that the relentless pursuit of power leads to destruction, that we do not need men of ruthless action such as Faust. He seems to imply that in the long run more gentle men like Wendl have a better chance to survive because they do not threaten but rather respect the woman per se and worship the principle of life she might represent.

We should probably not try to find in Mitterer's play correspondences to all details of the Homer passage, but we cannot ignore that there are at least several striking parallels as well as several striking contrasts. The Sirens know everything that happens, yet they lure man to his downfall by their enchanting singing; Odysseus enables himself to enjoy their singing by voluntarily having himself restrained by fetters so that he will not attempt to get closer to the Sirens; the woman sings before coming and after leaving mysteriously; the woman is being restrained by chains so that she will not attempt to leave the men; the woman is the image of a mother or the Virgin Mary and not of a Siren.

The Eternal-Feminine in Mitterer's play draws in two directions: onward and downward. Its downward drawing power proves in the end much stronger and cancels out the onward movement. Even though the woman is not purposely behaving in a luring manner and is not dangerous like the Sirens, she has on the one hand a Siren-like effect on Jogg, Much and Lex, and on the other hand, a soothing, comforting and saving effect as a mother or the Virgin Mary on Hias and Wendl. Jogg, Much and also Lex experience that Siren-like effect very strongly, but sense the mother or Virgin Mary effect to a very limited degree only. Unlike Odysseus who has himself tied in order to not give in to the luring of the Sirens, Jogg, Much and Lex do not restrain themselves in any significant way. They recklessly give in to the sexual desire aroused by the mere presence of the woman. Not only do they almost unrestrainedly give in to their passions and emotions, but they also attempt to control the woman by putting her in chains. Unlike the Sirens, the woman is not a dangerous monster. She does not sing to lure the men. In fact, her singing ceases while she is in the presence of the men. She does not intentionally tempt them at all. When she takes a bath, she puts up a curtain. True, her dance at the end of scene 17 is a wild dance and most likely does entice the men. However, she only dances after having been asked "almost affectionately" (p. 296) by Lex, and perhaps she does so in the hope of regaining her freedom.

Why does she prepare to leave in scene 10 and leave indeed at the end of the play? Precisely because of the men's inability to overcome their competition and hunger for power and because of their very limited ability to perceive of the woman as more than just a sex object. The woman knows that her presence contributes—even though unintentionally—to the downfall of the men. And indeed, the woman's presence brings about a precipitous rise of the men's inherent desire to exert power, thus rapidly leading to the final catastrophe. In mythical times, the Sirens function as dangerous monsters. In Mitterer's play, as well as in reality, men slaughter themselves. The woman—as representing the Eternal-Feminine, or the aspect of the divine that creates and maintains life—is "leaving" wherever men slaughter each other. Men, however, are used only as examples; not only men are meant, but mankind in general. At the end of the play, Wendl is left behind by the woman because he has yet to prove himself, and has to try not to follow in the footsteps of the men who have slaughtered each other.

As indicated above, the men in this play are not completely insensitive to the "onward" drawing power exerted by the Eternal-Feminine, yet its downward drawing power is much stronger. Wendl, the one who is the most sensitive to that "onward" drawing power and for whom the feminine does not have a Siren aspect at all, is at the same time the youngest and weakest. Goethe's claim that "The Eternal-Feminine /Draws us onward" does not prove true because of these circumstances. Rather, the woman representing the Eternal-Feminine becomes involuntarily the cause for the final catastrophe.

The play clearly gives the message that men and all human beings need to be more considerate of each other, of all creatures, and of nature in general. It ends in a bloody slaughter, though not without leaving some hope. Wendl, after all, does not die; the woman leaves him with a smile, the storm abates, and the singing is heard again. Maybe in the future it will be heard by gentle men like Wendl and will not be perceived as the luring singing of the Sirens, but rather as the singing of nature.

Notes

1. The German quotes here and in the following footnotes are taken from Felix Mitterer, *Stücke I* (Innsbruck: Haymon, 1992).
Two examples might illustrate this. In scene 12, when Wendl unsuccessfully tries to free the woman from the chains, the stage comments say about her: "*Die Frau ... lächelt ihn an, als ob nichts geschehen wäre, als ob sie wüßte, daß ihr in Wahrheit nichts, gar nichts passieren kann*" (291). ("*The woman ... smiles, as if nothing had happened, as if she knew that in reality nothing, nothing at all can happen to her.*") And later in the scene: "*Sie ist da und gleichzeitig weit weg*" (292). ("*She is present yet at the same time far away.*") In both instances, the stage comments give to the reader information that is important for the interpretation of the woman's nature. However, these comments cannot easily be conveyed by an actor to the spectator.

2. Mitterer, p. 259: "Angeregt zu Film und Stück hatten mich Sagen über sogenannte 'Wilde Frauen,' auch Salige oder Waldfräulein genannt."

3. Mitterer, p. 291: "*Daß ihr in Wahrheit nichts, gar nichts passieren kann.*"

4. "*Wendl weicht respektvoll vor ihr zurück und starrt sie mit großen Augen an*" (268).

5. "A so a Karrenziacher! A Messerschleifer!" (270).

6. "Da hat wohl dei Muatter ihm des Messer gschliffen, ha?" (270).

7. "Außighaut hat er sie, der Bauer, wia sie stampfdick gwesen is! Und der schwarze Teufel natürlich über alle Berg! Bei uns im Stall hamma sie dann beim Werfen derwischt! Zwoa Wochen spater is sie ins Wasser, samt'n Gschrappen! Aber den Wendl ham's wieder außagfischt" (271).

8. "*Sie hat die Hand an seine Wange gelegt, er verbirgt sein Gesicht darin und schluchzt*" (271).

9. "Sie is ganz schwarz. Weil da hat amal der Blitz eingschlagen, und sie hat angfangt zu brennen. Wenn i nimmer ein und aus woaß, geh i hin und red mit ihr. Zerst red i mit ihr, dann red i nix mehr und schau sie nur an. Und aufoamal spür i an süaßen Weh. Ganz an süaßen Weh. Und i vergiß alles. Alles. I kannt jedsmal sterbm. So schön is des. So schön" (292).

10. "Sie schaut aus wia du" (292).

11. "*Wendl beginnt leise zu weinen, fängt an zu schluchzen, es überrollt ihn, er wird immer lauter, er versucht es zu unterdrücken, kann es nicht, es schüttelt ihn, er schlägt die Hände vors Gesicht, die Frau steht auf, geht zu ihm, zieht seinen Kopf an ihre Schulter, umarmt ihn, seinWeinen wird zur Befreiung*" (293).

12. "Es ist schwierig, die Tabuvorschriften auszulegen, ich jedenfalls habe sie in meinem Stück dahingehend interpretiert, daß der Mann die Frau nicht besitzen und ihr nicht die Freiheit nehmen darf" (259).

13. "Erschreckt" (273).

14. In scene 5, he says: "Des is dei Einstandsessen!" (276) ("That is your welcome meal!") and later, in scene 9, when she refuses to eat from the deer, he says to her,

annoyed: "Des is dei Wild! Des hab i dir gschenkt!" (280) ("That is your deer! I gave it to you as a present!").

15. "Was versteckst di denn? Brauchst di doch vor deine Lötter nit verstecken!" (282).

16. "*Lex ist eifersüchtig, versucht es aber zu verbergen*" (282).

17. "LEX: 'Ab heut ghörst du mir! Mir alloan! Verstanden?' *Die Frau schaut ihn ruhig an.* LEX: 'Ob du mich verstanden hast?' *Die Frau nickt*" (287).

18. "*Fast zärtlich*" (296).

19. "Verfluachte Hur" (299).

20. Felix Mitterer, *Drachendurst, Stücke I* (Innsbruck: Haymon, 1992).

21. "Ja, Frau, wär dir halt dankbar, wennst mi a drüberlassatst!" (275).

22. "So oane hab i no nia ghabt." "Der Moospolster ... Wahnsinn ... (*pause*). Im Maul schmeckt sie nach Himbeeren" (282).

23. "Jogg: 'Ja, paßts ihr nit auf?' Lex: (*laut*) 'Sonst no was! Glabst , i spring ab, mitten in der schönsten Fahrt?' Jogg: 'Ihr habts leicht reden! Wenn ma verheirat is, wia i, dann lernt ma's Aufpassen!'" (283).

24. "I schlag nit gern a Frau. I schlag nit amal die Rösser. Hab i nia gmacht!" (293).

25. Much: "No, was is, Lexl? Bist decht so a wilder Hengst! Zoag uns, was du kannst! Kimm, i mach dir den Hosenstall auf!" (298).

26. "*Lex wird von Jogg auf die Frau gedrückt, sie weicht nicht zurück, steht Aug in Aug mit Lex*" (299).

27. For example, when Lex tears down the curtain behind which she takes her bath (282), when Lex puts her in chains (289), when Jogg tears open her dress (298), etc.

28. "Na und? I moan, war ja nit schlecht! Oder?" (274).

29. "A Brot im Ofen" (293).

Violence and Sexual Politics in Felix Mitterer's Plays *Verbrecherin, Heim* und *Die Wilde Frau*

Helga Schreckenberger

Felix Mitterer's dramatic work has been viewed as a continuation of the critical modern *Volksstück*, which was written and performed during the late sixties and early seventies following the rediscovery of the plays of Ödön von Horváth and Marie Luise Fleißer. These two authors of the Weimar Republic are credited with the successful renewal and politicizing of the traditional *Volksstück*.[1] Following their example, authors like Franz Xaver Kroetz, Martin Sperr, Rainer Werner Fassbinder, Peter Turrini and Wolfgang Bauer turned to the genre of the *Volksstück* as a forum for their artistic and political intentions.[2] Like Horváth and Fleißer, they use the formal and structural conventions of the *Volksstück* (the provincial setting, dialect, and stock figures) only to invert or subvert their traditional functions. Thus, unlike the traditional *Volksstück*, their plays do not confirm the existing social order, but rather criticize or at least question it. Although Mitterer concedes to writing "*Volkstheater*,"[3] he denies the direct influence of these modern, critical variants of the *Volksstück* on his development as a writer. Rather, he points to the popular peasant farces he witnessed during his youth in Tyrol.[4] Nevertheless, the themes, structure and didactic orientation of his plays point to the critical *Volksstück* rather than to its traditional model. Like the authors of the modern *Volksstück*, Mitterer uses the genre because of his audience's familiarity with it. But instead of offering light entertainment, Mitterer confronts them with current conflicts and social issues. In his plays, the conflicts very often result from the confrontation of (predominantly) provincial social groups with an outsider or social deviant, a theme which also reoccurs in the critical *Volksstück* of the sixties and seventies.[5] The reaction of the majority is usually a violent one, the violence either being directed towards the outsider or erupting within the group. As many of Mitterer's outsiders are women, violence becomes a gender issue.

The purpose of this essay is to analyze the connection between violence and male-female relationships in Mitterer's plays *The Female Criminal* (*Verbrecherin*), *Going Home* (*Heim*) and *The Wild Woman* (*Die Wilde Frau*). Such a study suggests that for Mitterer, the roles imposed upon men and women by society determine their personalities and are responsible for the violence they inflict upon one another. However, there is a major difference in women's use of violence in comparison with men's. Violence for women is a last resort, a defense mechanism against their oppression by men. Men, on the other hand, use violence to dominate women and to punish any deviant behavior. In addition, the paper examines the play's effectiveness with regard to Mitterer's didactic intentions. He seeks to raise the awareness of his audience concerning gender relations and points to the need for fundamental change. Mitterer considers this his primary goal: "I describe reality as it is and sometimes even choose extreme examples in order to lead people to ask themselves whether the relationship between the sexes should not at long last change, should not become more just and more a true partnership."[6]

Brutality and violence are characteristic thematic elements of the critical modern *Volksstück*. Both Horváth and Fleißer expose the brutality underlying petit-bourgeois existence, often using the relationship between men and women as a paradigm for social relations. While Fleißer and Horváth depict emotional rather than physical brutality, the authors of the new critical *Volksstück* focus on a very explicit portrayal of violence. Murder, maiming, suicide, and violent sexual acts not only provide plot material but are also acted out on stage with the intention of shocking the audience out of its complacency.[7] In doing so, the principal goal of the authors is to show the link between these acts of violence and the given social structures. Franz Xaver Kroetz states:

> People do not realize how violence builds and is released. Violence is an anonymous force. For this reason many contemporary dramatists wish to depict how it is that people seek out violence as their last means of escape. In so doing, I do not seek to defend acts of violence, but rather criticize society.[8]

This statement also reflects Mitterer's intentions. He is less interested in shocking his audience with explicit violence (most of the violent acts happen off stage or are at least concealed from the direct view of the audience) than in confronting them with situations that mirror their own behavior: "The spectators understand that it is not so much my intention to beat them over the head as it is to demonstrate for them just how we all are; this is sometimes painful."[9] By forcing the audience to recognize the destructiveness and wrongness of the players on stage, Mitterer hopes to initiate a new level of consciousness in the audience, and even a change in individual behavior. For this reason, Mitterer—like Kroetz—aims to show the social mechanisms that are the real cause for the misery and unhappiness of his protagonists, which can be overcome not by violent acts, but only by a fundamental change in perception and behavior. Both the illumination of the social context of violence and the urge to change such behavior by showing its destructiveness constitute the political dimension of Mitterer's plays: "It is certainly politics if one is interested in societal connections, and if one changes society and people's treatment of each other for the better."[10]

The one-act play *Female Criminal* attests to Mitterer's intention to promote understanding between men and women by showing the injustice of the traditional gender roles and their ultimate destructiveness for the relationship. The play consists of a dialogue between a married couple. The wife is imprisoned for the attempted murder of her husband, who visits her to find out why she attacked him. The dialogue reveals how deeply imprisoned they both are by traditional gender roles. The husband has exhausted himself by trying to get ahead, surviving the hardship of his demanding job, working overtime and swallowing the injustices of his superiors. While he finds an outlet in mindless entertainment and in taking out his frustrations on his wife, she has no such relief:

> First I make breakfast for all of you, then I get the kids off to school, then rush to work, back at noon to cook and take care of the kids; clean, wash, buy groceries; make dinner, clean up—serving everybody right and left; evenings it's soccer on TV, then into bed with you. Or else you go down to the pub and come home drunk at 12:30, and then you wake me up.[11]

This statement clearly pinpoints the conflict in the domestic and sexual exploitation of the wife. Emotionally and physically exhausted by the demands of her family, her husband, and work, the woman turns to violence. When the husband criticizes her cooking, she stabs him with a kitchen knife. The audience learns about the details of her crime through a newspaper article that the visiting husband reads to her:

> An argument about Saturday night's dinner led to a bloody and brutal act of violence in an apartment in Eggenberg. The 42-year-old Bettina Demel shoved an 11-centimeter-long knife into the stomach of her husband. While the husband sat on the floor in a pool of blood screaming for help, the wife calmly cleaned off the dinner table.[12]

The newspaper article concentrates on the seemingly minor incident that provoked the stabbing, on sensationalist details and on the woman's apparent indifference, thus placing the blame solely on the woman. Like the newspaper article, which reflects public perception, the man only focuses on the action of the woman, not what led to it. When his wife attempts to explain her physical and mental exhaustion, he only reacts with recriminations and self-pity: He also has to work hard, she has made him the laughing stock of the neighborhood, she has destroyed his life. Neither protagonist has the power to see the roots of their misery. While the woman considers herself unstable and shoulders the full responsibility for her crime, the man has located another source to vent his anger on: feminists. They are responsible for his wife's attempt to escape from his domestic tyranny and his daughter's disregard for his wishes. His anonymous letter to a feminist columnist at a major newspaper, filled with assertions of male dominance over women, echoes Fascist ideology and irrational hate. Aside from personal insults, the letter physically threatens the journalist by emphasizing the physical superiority of men, which its author equates with intellectual superiority:

> We'd like to pay you a visit sometime in order to demonstrate for you the power of a real man, since you apparently are ignorant on this point. If you should persist in feeding our women and girls this emancipation crap, you are going to come up against the strength of a man (the weak will always be weak and for this reason silent) and then, dear lady, we'll remove you like a troublesome parasite that is sucking the blood of a pure human being.[13]

In this letter, violence is associated with male supremacy and with the goal of destroying the women who contest it. The blind hatred for the columnist reveals the highly charged emotionality of the topic of emancipation. The demand by women for more equality is perceived as threatening and ignites a wish to strike back at them, to keep them in their place. Mitterer suggests that the man's aggression expressed in this letter is more dangerous than the woman's act of violence because it strives to oppress and destroy. He points to the criminality expressed in the letter and to the emotional sickness that it reveals. The audience learns that the man's attitude toward women, as revealed in his letter, is ultimately the cause for his wife's violent act.

Mitterer aims his criticism not only at individuals, but also at the social structures that ignore and thus prolong the domestic exploitation of women. The legal system condemns the woman as a cold-blooded murderess without taking into account what led her to her desperate deed. The psychiatrist attests to her complete mental fitness: "No sign of mental imbalance," her act is judged as "a cold-blooded act of attempted murder."[14] The medical system is also at fault, not only by discounting the emotional anguish of the woman, but for never providing her with real help. The woman reveals to her husband that in the past years she was only functioning by taking sleeping pills and amphetamines, provided by "compassionate doctors."[15] But if these doctors realize and sympathize with the plight of women, they never challenge the injustice of these women's situations. Indeed, they are only concerned with the capability of women to endure.

The lack of support and understanding for her problems causes the woman to see her only escape as committing violence against her immediate oppressor. Like her husband, she is not able to recognize the social mechanism responsible for their situation and thus feels helpless and abandoned. Mitterer purposefully depicts a woman still caught in a very traditional role: "I describe women figures so that those in the audience who are similarly imprisoned by tradition will think: 'That's just not right. I'm living that way, too, and I shouldn't be. I'm suffering from this, and I know it'."[16] Although Mitterer clearly places the blame for the woman's violent act on the man's constant disregard for her as a human being, he underscores the husband's confusion rather than his villainy. The end of the play reveals that the man also suffers. His life has changed for the worse without his wife. He cannot control his children and has to put up with the interference of his mother. He reluctantly admits loving and missing his wife, and having made mistakes. Mitterer implies that a more equal partnership would have alleviated the suffering on both sides.

The male hatred for women who deviate from their traditional roles, so vehemently expressed in the husband's letter to the feminist newspaper columnist in *Female Criminal*, is the reason for the eruption of violence in Mitterer's play *Going Home*.[17] Although the main theme of the play is society's intolerance of deviant behavior in general, Mitterer makes clear that it is even less acceptable in a woman. The deviants in the play are a young couple, Mike and Nina, on their way from Berlin to Italy. They stop at a Tyrolean village, where Nina commits a theft in the local grocery store. Two local policemen and the manager of the store confront them on the outskirts of town and the policeman in charge turns out to be Mike's father. Mitterer's version of the prodigal son theme deviates from the Biblical happy homecoming since the father cannot accept the son who has rejected the social norms he himself embraces. When the son rejects his father's values once again, he looks for a way to punish him. With the father's consent, the grocery store manager attempts to brutally rape Nina, while Mike is rendered helpless by handcuffs.

The rape scene is portrayed as a conspiracy by men who represent the social order against two outsiders. Mike as the runaway son is to be punished, but it is the woman who is the object of violence. Her gender and her northern German descent, clearly evident in her language, make Nina even more an outsider than Mike.[18] As a thief and drug addict, she has upset the social order. Moreover, her provoking attitude towards the representatives of law and order as well as her contempt for the manager's sexual interest in her enrage the men; thus, the physical and sexual violence is directed against her. Nina's violation is not the punishment of an individual woman but is meant for women in general. This is clearly indicated by the comments of Hermann, Mike's father: "Women don't understand anything about us men. They come between us and rile us up against each other. (*Pause.*) How should we punish them?"[19] Hermann's hatred of women is rooted in his wife's rejection of him. The daughter of a medical doctor, she married beneath her social status when she accepted Hermann's proposal, a fact that her father will never let her forget. The love that she initially felt for Hermann was not strong enough to withstand the social pressure and Hermann's violent nature. She fails to see that Hermann's brutality is caused by his drinking, which in turn stems from the insecurity of never being able to live up to the expectations of his wife and father-in-law.[20] His wife's dissatisfaction with him as a man causes Herman's hatred for women. Like the couple in *Female Criminal*, both Hermann and his wife are blind to the social conditioning that is at the root of their problems. Instead of rejecting the social prejudices that keep them apart, they blame each other. In the wife's eyes, violence is part of Hermann's social standing, of his being a police officer: "That's because he's simply a brutal human being, a policeman."[21] He, on the other hand, directs his aggression against women in general.

As Nina's degradation is meant as a humiliation for his son, Hermann also reveals his chauvinistic view of women as men's sexual possessions. By allowing the violation of his son's woman, Hermann demonstrates his control over his son and at the same time seeks to humiliate his son's masculinity.

The store manager's rape of Nina clearly represents a form of punishment for women who are perceived as a threat to a male-dominated social order. Nina has committed a crime against the store: "Whoever steals from me is my enemy, understand? Whoever makes fun of my canned goods is my enemy. My supermarket is the world, understand?"[22] The supermarket is the arena in which the manager can display power and control. Thus, Nina's theft is a direct challenge to his authority. In addition, the supermarket gives the store manager the opportunity to uphold the hallowed values of the middle class: order, cleanliness and subservient behavior:

> Whenever a can is taken from the shelves, its replacement is there within five minutes. There are no gaps. If a can sticks out two centimeters too far, I go crazy. My co-workers know that. I write the signs for the specials myself, in my wonderful handwriting. The floor is clean and it shines, none of the shopping carts squeaks. The customer is always right.[23]

Because the store manager derives his security from a world that is neat, orderly and controllable, Nina poses a threat. She refuses to adhere to such a strict order and flaunts her contempt until the last minute. Only the combination of physical violence and rape brings her under control. The store manager's rape is clearly not erotically motivated. He seeks to humiliate and hurt Nina. Thus, it is an act of hostility that strives for control, dominance and punishment. This combination of violence and sexual assault corresponds to what A. Nicholas Groth labels as "anger rape."[24] According to Groth, this type of rape is committed by an offender who felt "that he had been wronged, hurt, put down, or treated unjustly in some fashion by some individual, situation or event. Rape served to discharge the resulting anger, resentment and frustration. In this fashion, the anger rapist revenges himself for what he perceives to be wrongs done him by others, especially women."[25] For Groth, the reason for combining violence with sex lies in the perception of rape as the ultimate offense that can be committed against another person.[26] This assessment concurs with that of Susan Brownmiller, who calls rape "man's basic weapon of force against woman, the principal agent of his will and her fear."[27]

In Mitterer's play, the cruel rape attempt not only leaves Nina seriously hurt, it also breaks her psychologically. The assault reduces Nina to a frightened child calling for her mother. In light of the men's brutality, Nina's offenses seem trivial, and Mitterer clearly directs the audience's compassion toward her.

Although Mitterer tries to uncover the deeper reasons for the violence that is unleashed against Nina and Mike, the danger exists that the play will appeal more to the emotions of the audience than to their critical thinking. In his effort to condemn violent behavior against women, Mitterer makes the store manager too despicable. Because the grocer is such a villain, the sexual violence committed against Nina is diminished in that it is perceived as sick behavior, not done by a "normal person." Since he is the only perpetrator of the brutal assault, the roles of the other men are lessened. Moreover, the manager's punishment at the end—his rich fiancée leaves him and the two policemen disassociate themselves from him— might be misconstrued as setting things right, which would preempt any motivation for change.

Another problem is that Nina accepts the blame for what has happened. Her apology, "I'm sorry, Mike, please forgive me. I know that I provoked all of this,"[28] exonerates the men to some extent. Since her self-blame is not contradicted in the play, the audience might agree with this assessment and blame her for the fact that now a reconciliation between Mike and his father is impossible, instead of attributing it to Hermann's unbending demand for his son's conformity.

Violence as a result of male rivalry and profound disregard for human rights and the dignity of women is the subject of the play *The Wild Woman*. In writing this play, Mitterer was influenced by local legends of women who come out of the forest to be among people. The man who falls in love with one of them is warned not to break a certain taboo, for example not to ask her name or not to touch her hair while she is asleep. As long as he keeps his promise he has a wonderful experience with the woman. Invariably, the man always breaks the taboo. The woman disappears, and the man is struck by tragedy.[29] Mitterer rewrites the old legends in order to demonstrate the destructiveness of a male who needs to control and possess weaker members of society—women.

His *Wild Woman* is staged during deep winter in a loggers' camp where five men live together in close quarters, cut off from the rest of the world. A woman appears mysteriously. She does not speak and at first willingly submits to the demands of the men. When one man attempts to claim sole ownership of her, fighting breaks out. The woman tries to leave, but is forcefully retained and chained to the wall. As a result, four of the men die, three violently by killing each other in a fight.

In Mitterer's interpretation of the legend of the Wild Woman, the taboo is "that a man cannot possess a woman and may not deprive her of her freedom."[30] As long as the men assure themselves of the woman's consent and accept her right to refuse them, they are rewarded. But when they take away her freedom she refuses to have sex with them. Their disregard for her wishes is rewarded with violence as they turn on each other and brutally kill each other. The only survivor is the youngest of them, who has refused to join in using the woman or in the struggle to gain control over her.

Mitterer's female protagonist parallels the literary stereotype of the *femme fatale*, a woman of great erotic allure whose overwhelming sexuality seduces and destroys men. In the literature of the turn of the century, she often possesses magical powers and is described as a witch or sorceress.[31] Similarly, all men in Mitterer's play fall under the spell of the Wild Woman. They have never met anyone like her, never desired anyone as much as they desire her. One is even willing to marry her in spite of his father's certain wrath. However, unlike previous creators of *femmes fatales*, Mitterer clearly intends to absolve the woman of any guilt in the men's tragic fate. She neither teases nor seduces the men, nor does she pit them against one another. On the contrary, she tries to leave as soon as she becomes the reason for their fighting. The conflict between the men is not caused by the woman's arrival; they themselves set in motion the events that will cause their destruction. Her presence merely intensifies the conflict, making her a pawn in the men's struggle for power and control.

The play not only denounces violence and disrespect for another person's freedom and autonomy, but also condemns the male chauvinist behavior and thinking patterns that Mitterer holds responsible for the conflict, not only between men and women, but between people in general. He criticizes the constant rivalry and struggle for power among men, their need to assert their superiority, either through physical strength or economic status, their tendency to join ranks against outsiders, to degrade and exploit weaker members of the group, and finally, their deep-seated disrespect for women as human beings.

The group dynamics of the men mirrors that of society. The hierarchy is structured according to authority, physical strength, material possession, age and origin. Young Wendl, the lowest in rank, is an outsider by virtue of his origin (his father was a gypsy), his social status as an illegitimate child, and his age and strength. Within the group, Wendl is assigned the role of the "female." He cooks, sews and keeps the place tidy. But he is also an outsider because of his refusal to adopt what is considered appropriate behavior for a man. He does not join in the sexual exploitation of the woman despite his obvious interest; his distaste for alcohol and violence earn him the disdain of the other men. But his survival illustrates Mitterer's affirmation for this type of manhood.

The relationship between the men is characterized by the violence that manifests itself in their language as well as in their actions. The men constantly taunt and provoke each other and settle arguments through physical force. The presence of the woman introduces sexuality into this highly charged situation. Soon sexual innuendoes, bragging about one's virility and questioning that of the other men dominate the conversation. Mitterer emphasizes the thematic relationship to the present: "Their language isn't much different today. All you have to do is listen in on the conversation at a table for regulars in a Tyrolean inn; you'll hear the same conversation as that of the men in the forest. As soon as a woman enters, the same rooster-like conduct: one has to impress and present oneself."[32] In the play, the male rivalry soon turns into sexual rivalry, where even intercourse becomes a key factor in the struggle for superiority.

In the group of men, Lex is given the role of the villain. From the first scene on he is identified as a troublemaker, a law breaker. He resents Jogg's authority, is easily provoked by Hias's love for proverbial wisdom, and is entrenched in a bitter rivalry with Much for his ranking within the group. Much insists on his superiority since his family owns a farm, while Lex is only a hired laborer. Lex is unhappy with his position in life and wants to possess and control all, by force if necessary.[33] He is also the one who initiates the sexual relationship with the woman. When the women refuses, he beats her into submission, only to find himself unable to perform. In front of the others, he brags of his easy conquest. When Hias reveals that he is aware of Lex's impotence, Lex attacks him with a knife, intent on murder. Lex also sets the general violence in motion by trying to claim the woman for himself.

The behavior of all men is defined by characteristics commonly regarded as masculine: aggression, force, power, strength, toughness, dominance and competitiveness. Because of his low social status, Lex in particular tries to live up to that stereotypical notion of masculinity. He constantly tries to win, to prove his superiority, and to control the situation. He tries to assert his worth as a man through sexuality. Diane Russell suggests that the sexual act often is turned into a power struggle, "particularly by men who feel powerless in the rest of their lives and whose masculinity is threatened by this powerlessness."[34] Lex's sexual violence is not motivated by hatred and revenge, but by the need to assert his power. He does not wish to harm or degrade the woman, but rather to possess her sexually. In such a context, sexuality becomes "a means of compensating for underlying feelings of inadequacy and serves to express issues of mastery, strength, control, authority, identity and capability."[35] By foregrounding the inadequacies and insecurities that are the driving force behind Lex's constant desire for power and control, and by demonstrating the devastating result of this desire, Mitterer rejects such notions of masculinity.

The appearance of the woman not only intensifies the conflict between the men, but also reveals their chauvinistic prejudices against women. For Jogg she is simply a potential troublemaker in the camp; he has no regard for her personal safety. Hias affirms this belief with a proverb that points out the unavoidable harm caused by women. This proverb attests to the fact that this prejudice has taken root in common perception. For the men in the group, the use of women is limited to work and sex. In addition, disparaging remarks about the southern descent of the woman reveal national prejudices as well. Her origin already marks her as a fallen woman, not worthy of being married: "You're not one for us to marry, since you're a foreigner with hot blood."[36] Because of her low value as a "foreigner" she is expected to consent to a sexual relationship. The arguments used by the men to excuse themselves for forcing the woman to have sex with them mirror traditional male chauvinist attitudes. Lex thinks the woman owes him sex because she has had sex with the others. After the woman is forcefully retained at the cabin and now refuses the sexual advances of the men, she is told by Jogg: "There's no more running away now, woman. You came of your own free will and now you're staying for as long as we're working in the forest."[37] The men plainly act out their own desires with no regard for the wishes of the woman. They believe they are entitled to domestic and sexual services from women as a class. Such an attitude reduces the woman to an object that men can use at their will. When Lex attempts to deprive the others of the woman's services they turn against each other like animals, subsequently slaying each other.

The emphasis on the animal-like behavior of the men obscures the influence of social conditioning on their views, attitudes and actions. Thus, Mitterer's play would be misunderstood as a warning against the power of sexual attraction. This is underscored by the motto of the play, Circe's warning to Odysseus about the song of the Sirens. The same danger lies in the fact that the woman obviously possesses mysterious powers. They can be interpreted as a force against which man is powerless. In addition, the play may perpetuate the myth of the uncontrollable sexual instincts of men, which is contained in Jogg's excuse for desiring the woman: "I am a man, after all, and not a boneless fish."[38] As a result, the audience may perceive the events of the play as tragic but unavoidable.

In conclusion, Mitterer explores violence between the sexes in order to initiate social change among individuals. His plays suggest that forcible sexual assault is motivated more by retaliatory and compensatory motives than by sexual ones. However, in portraying men's violence against women, Mitterer inadvertently imputes to women a measure of guilt in provoking male violence, and thus he falls short of his goal.

Notes

1. The term *'Volksstück'* refers to the popular local plays that evolved in the eighteenth and early nineteenth centuries. It includes the *Altwiener Volksstück* as well as peasant farces. Usually written in local dialect, it had a simple, unified plot, drawn from the daily life of common folk, intended to reinforce the just order of the universe (see Jürgen Hein, "Das Volksstück: Entwicklung und Tendenzen," in *Theater und Gesellschaft. Das Volksstück im 19. und 20. Jahrhundert*. Düsseldorf: 1973, pp. 12-14).

2. In addition to Franz Xaver Kroetz, Martin Sperr, Rainer Werner Fassbinder, Wolfgang Bauer, and Peter Turrini, the authors of the critical *Volksstück* of the sixties and seventies include Harald Sommer, Harald Mueller, Franz Buchrieser, Gerald Szyszkowitz and Karl Otto Mühl.

3. Mitterer defines *"Volkstheater"* broadly "als Stücke, die für viele Menschen geschrieben sind, und nicht nur für Intellektuelle." ("Felix Mitterer im Gespräch mit Ursula Hassel und Deirdre McMahon. 19. November 1988" in *Modern Austrian Literature* 25/1, 1992, p. 21).

4. See Hassel and McMahon, "Felix Mitterer im Gespräch," p. 19.

5. For example Horváth's *Bergbahn* (1927-29), Fleißer's *Fegefeuer in Ingolstadt* (1926), Turrini's *Sauschlachten* (1971), Sperr's *Jagdszenen in Niederbayern* (1966) and *Koralle Meier* (1970), and Kroetz's *Stallerhof* (1971). See also Susan L. Cocalis, "The Politics of Brutality: Toward a Definition of the Critical Volksstück" in *Modern Drama* 24/3 (1981), p. 300.

6. "Ich beschreibe ja die Wirklichkeit, wie sie ist, manchmal sogar auf extreme Weise, wie sie seltener ist, um die Menschen anzuregen, darüber nachzudenken, ob sich in diesem Fall die Beziehung zwischen den Geschlechtern nicht endlich ändern sollte, daß sie gerechter wird und partnerschaftlicher." Hassel and McMahon, "Felix Mitterer im Gespräch," p. 26.

7. See Peter Turrini's statement concerning his play *Sauschlachten*: "Theater ist für mich vor allem Sinnlichkeit, Grausamkeit: ich will mich von den Gesetzen einer langweiligen, von Psychologie und Kunstfertigkeit durchsetzten Dramaturgie entfernen, um mich den Abgründen der menschlichen Natur zu nähern. Ich will das Publikum auf diesem Weg mitnehmen: Schock als Ergebnis und nicht als Selbstzweck" (in Ulf Birbaumer, Ed., *Turrini-Lesebuch: Stücke, Pamphlete, Filme, Reaktionen, etc.* Wien: Europaverlag, 1978, p. 126).

8. "Wie Gewalt sich anstaut und entlädt, wissen die Leute nicht. Gewalttätigkeit ist eine anonyme Kraft. Deshalb wollen auch viele zeitgenössische Dramatiker zeigen, wie Menschen dazu kommen, in der Gewalt ihren einzigen Ausweg zu suchen. Mir geht es dabei nicht um die Verteidigung von Gewaltverbrechen, sondern um die Anprangerung der Gesellschaft." Franz Xaver Kroetz and Helmut Walbert, "Die Lust am Lebendigen: Diskussion der Redaktion *kürbiskern*" in Thomas Thieringer, Ed., *Weitere Aussichten ... Ein Lesebuch*. Köln: Kiepenheuer & Witsch, 1976, p. 603.

9. "Die Zuschauer sind darauf gekommen, daß ich sie nicht nur auf den Kopf hauen will, sondern daß ich ihnen zeigen will, wie wir alle sind, was manchmal auch weh tut." Hassel and McMahon, "Felix Mitterer im Gespräch," p. 21.

10. "Es ist ja Politik, wenn man sich für die gesellschaftlichen Zusammenhänge interessiert, und wenn man will, daß sich die Gesellschaft und das Verhalten der Menschen zueinander zum Besseren verändert." Ibid., p. 23.

11. "Zerst Frühstück machen für enk alle, dann die Kinder in die Schual schicken, dann in die Arbeit hetzen, z'Mittag hoam, kochen, die Kinder versorgen; putzen, waschen, einkaufen; Abendessen kochen, abspülen, di hint und vorn bedienen; im Fernsehn Fuaßball, dann ins Bett, mit dir. Oder du gehst zu dein Stammtisch und kimmst bsoffen hoam, um halboans, und weckst mi auf." Mitterer, *Besuchszeit: Verbrecherin* in *Stücke 1*. Innsbruck: Haymon, 1992, p. 178.

12. "Ein heftiger Streit um die Qualität des Abendessens führte am Samstag Abend in einer Wohnung in Eggenberg zu einer brutalen Bluttat. Die 42-jährige Angestellte Bettina Demel stach ein elf Zentimeter langes Küchenmesser in den Bauch ihres Mannes. Während der Mann sich schwer verletzt und um Hilfe flehend in seinem Blut am Boden wälzte, erledigte die Frau seelenruhig ihren Abwasch." Ibid., p. 180.

13. "Wir würden Sie gerne einmal besuchen, um sie [sic!] einmal über die körperliche Gewalt eines wirklichen Mannes aufzuklären, von der Sie anscheinend keine Ahnung haben ... Sollten sie (sic!) weiterhin unsere Frauen und Mädel mit ihrem (sic!) Emanzengewäsch verdummen und versuchen, ihnen einzureden, sie kämen gegen die Kraft eines Mannes ernsthaft an (die Schwachen bleiben eben immer schwach und daher unmündig), dann werden wir Sie, Gnädigste, entfernen wie eine lästige Wanze, die vom Blut des reinen Menschen saugt." Ibid., p. 183. Eva Deissen, the recipient of this letter, is a real-life columnist at an Austrian newspaper with a very high circulation. Letters in reaction to her column mirror very much the tone and implications of Mitterer's fictitious one.

14. "Keine Anzeichen von Geistesstörung" her act is judged as "kaltblütiger Mordversuch." Ibid., p. 180.

15. Ibid., p. 186.

16. "Ich beschreibe halt Frauenfiguren, damit die Zuschauer, die noch so traditionell verhaftet sind, denken: 'So dürfte das mit uns nicht weitergehen. Ja so lebe ich auch, und so sollte ich nicht leben. Ich leide darunter, und ich weiß es'." Hassel and McMahon, "Felix Mitterer im Gespräch," p. 26.

17. *Heim* is an expanded version of the one-act play *Karrnerleut 83*, which is based on the well-known play *Karrnerleut*, written in 1905 by the Tyrolean writer Karl Schönherr. The title refers to the people traveling from village to village at the turn of the century. In Mitterer's modern version, the traveling people are a young couple of runaways.

18. Although they are never explicitly stated, the Austrian/Tyrolean audience is well aware of Austrian national prejudices against northern Germans. These prejudices were satirically treated in Felix Mitterer's four-part television series *Die Piefke-Saga*. "Piefke" connotes the Austrians' derogatory nickname for Germans.

19. "Sie verstehn nix von uns Männern, die Weiber. Sie drängen sich zwischen uns, bringen uns auseinander, hetzen uns gegenseitig auf. (*Pause.*) Wie soll ma sie bestrafen? (*Schaut Nina an.*) Wie soll ma euch bestrafen?" Mitterer, *Heim*, in *Stücke 1*, p. 144.

20. In view of this, Mike's rejection of respectability and material values constitutes an even worse offense since his father had to work so hard for them and never really succeeded in achieving them.

21. "Weil er so ein brutaler Mensch ist! Ein Polizist eben!" Mitterer, *Heim,* p. 156.

22. "Wer bei mir klaut, is mein Feind, verstehst du? Wer sich über meine Sugodosen lustig macht, is mein Feind. Mein Supermarkt is die Welt, verstehst du?" Mitterer, *Heim,* p. 144.

23. "Wenn eine Dose weggenommen wird, steht in fünf Minuten die nächste dort. Es gibt keine Lücken. Wenn eine Dose zwei Zentimeter zwischen den anderen herausschaut, dreh i durch. Meine Mitarbeiter wissen des. Die Plakate für die Sonderangebote schreib i selber; in meiner wunderschönen Handschrift. Der Boden is sauber und glänzt, keiner von den Einkaufswägen quietscht. Der Kunde hat immer recht." Mitterer, *Heim,* p. 144.

24. A. Nicholas Groth and H. Jean Birnbaum, *Men Who Rape: The Psychology of the Offender.* New York: Plenum Press, 1979, p. 14.

25. Ibid.

26. Ibid.

27. Susan Brownmiller, *Against Our Will. Men, Women and Rape.* New York: Simon and Schuster, p. 14.

28. "Tut mir leid, Mike! Entschuldige! Ich weiß, ich hab das alles provoziert!" Mitterer, *Heim,* p. 159.

29. See Mitterer, "Vorwort zu *Die Wilde Frau*" in *Stücke 1,* p. 259.

30. "Daß der Mann die Frau nicht besitzen und ihr nicht die Freiheit nehmen darf." Ibid.

31. See Carola Hilmes, *Die Femme Fatale. Ein Weiblichkeitstypus in der nachromantischen Literatur.* Frankfurt a.M.: Metzler, 1990, p. 28.

32. "Die Sprache, die sie haben, die ist ja heute nicht viel anders. Man braucht sich nur an einen Stammtisch in Tirol zu setzen; da hört man dieselben Gespräche wie von diesen Männern im Wald, wo man meint, das ist ja schon sehr weit weg, und es stimmt gar nicht. Sobald eine Frau eintritt, kommt dieses gockelhafte Gebaren auf: Man muß imponieren und sich präsentieren." Hassel and McMahon, "Felix Mitterer im Gespräch," p. 27.

33. Lex answers Hias's proverbial wisdom: "Die Welt is a Heustock. Wer mehrer owa derfrißt, der hat mehr" with "So ist es! Und ich wer fressen, soviel i kann! Und wenn i mir's mit Gwalt nimm!" (Mitterer, *Die Wilde Frau* in *Stücke 1,* p. 266).

34. Diana E.H. Russell, *Sexual Exploitation. Rape, Child Abuse and Workplace Harassment.* Beverly Hills, London, New Delhi: Sage Publications, 1984, p. 118.

35. A. Nicholas Groth, H. Jean Birnbaum: *Men Who Rape: The Psychology of the Offender.* New York: Plenum Press, 1979, p. 25.

36. "Zum Heiraten bist wohl koane, denk i ma. Landfremd wia d' bist und mit dem hoaßen Bluat." Mitterer, *Die Wilde Frau,* p. 275.

37. "Jetzt gibts koa Davonlaffen mehr, Frau! Du bist freiwillig kommen! Und freiwillig hast di einlassen mit uns! Jetzt bleibst da, solang ma im Wald arbeiten!" Ibid., p. 288.

38. "Ma is halt a Mann und koa Fisch ohne Gräten." Ibid.

The Motif of the Wild Woman in Felix Mitterer, Rahel Hutmacher, and Adalbert Stifter

Dagmar C.G. Lorenz

Supernatural and demonic figures, particularly of women, have often been used in literary texts to signify the uncanny. Romantic literature in particular abounds with such figures. The famous Loreley of Heinrich Heine's and Clemens Brentano's poems, described as a water nymph,[1] resembles the Wild Woman seductress and avenger common in folk tales.

Texts written by men generally depict Wild Women from the male point of view. Heine's Loreley follows this pattern, as do most folk tales and literary texts such as Stifter's novella *Quicksilver* (*Katzensilber*) and, more recently, Mitterer's popular drama *The Wild Woman* (*Die Wilde Frau*). On the other hand, women writers and feminist critics explore mythological woman figures from an intimate, personal perspective. For example, Ingeborg Bachmann's Undine figure in *Undine geht* speaks from a woman's point of view about her suffering and disappointment as a result of her involvement with human men. Also, the Swiss author Rahel Hutmacher empathizes with her supernatural women characters to the point that she actually identifies with them.

According to Julia Kristeva, the fear of death, unbounded instinct, and the female sex as a symbol of the uncanny are related phobias commonly found among men. Klaus Theweleit describes how women—literary characters and historical personalities—are 'neutered' or de-sexualized by male authors, because as the embodiment of Dionysian ecstasy and the realm of *Hades* they pose a threat to the ideological institution of masculinity:

> Particularly the only one, the sensual one, among women has to be de-sexualized because she causes the men capable of arousal to leave the

safety of their life-protecting institutional bodies, to throw themselves into the arms of 'Amor', and offer their hearts to be devoured by a youthful beauty. When ecstasy ends and is transformed into one of the normal states of coldness, the eyes and the brain search for a more stable construct … Woman and her physical beauty are charged with the task to enter into an imitation of God. This is why her most noticeable representatives have to depart into the Beyond … One of the reasons why men have difficulty in dealing with the problems of real women is the following: For every male love, woman is in part the *medicine*—the miracle drug. Woe is her, if she has problems … It still is like a (silent) outcry to heaven to which degree this construct prevents un-celestial women to escape from their confusion, to satisfy just a small part of their own desires and the desires others expect them to satisfy, and to allow others to fulfill their wishes.[2]

Theweleit's observations explain why many women authors choose the figure of the witch or the Wild Woman as the ultimate 'other' to project their alienation onto, while male authors, in their role as guardians and representatives of Western discourse, depict these characters from the outside, preferably as inarticulate or mute.

Kristeva argues that there is a link between the trepidation accompanying the encounter with strangers, a mixture of fascination and rejection, and the 'political' feeling of xenophobia. According to her, both are typical reactions to the 'uncanny' which threatens the adult's identity. The unfathomable in atavistic terms—death, woman or unbridled instinct—as well as the political and cultural 'other' tend to evoke infantile wishes and fears in men.[3]

It seems obvious why women take a different approach to these phenomena: male discourse offers them no opportunity for identification or self-realization, because it reifies female figures and turns them into signifiers of the voiceless and nameless 'other'.[4] Traditionally women have been represented as hybrids of human and animal who inspire desire and contempt, and the realm of the 'unknown', where nature, death, disease, and the demonic reside, has been defined as their sphere. When women address men or the male-dominated public in the language of patriarchy, they cannot but speak and write from a position of otherness. When they speak as women, they speak as residents of Freud's proverbial Dark Continent.

In the framework of Western culture men, by definition, are strangers to the sphere of 'otherness'. The voice of woman may be excluded from the dominant discourse, but it alone speaks with authority about the realm of the unknown, where a male narrator figures at best as an intruder. Orpheus, Odysseus, the diver in Schiller's poem *The Diver* (*Der Taucher*), or the accidental visitor at an orgy in Schnitzler's *Game at Dawn* (*Spiel im Morgengrauen*) specify the position of the male protagonist or speaker vis-à-vis the 'underworld'—the domain of monsters, women, and sexuality. The male protagonist is the representative of the rational universe.

Women authors imbue the familiar images of 'otherness' with their own spirit and speak through them. They de-mystify Wild Women and witches to make them vehicles for their perceptions and, by portraying them as familiar, they assign men and 'humans' the role of the dangerous, inscrutable, and monstrous 'other'. Since the feminist movement of the 1970s, women authors have produced an extensive body of scholarship, fiction, and poetry about wise women and witches—for example Jeanine Blackwell, Barbara Walker, Barbara Frischmuth, Sara Kirsch, and Irmtraud Morgner.

In 1986 Felix Mitterer and Rahel Hutmacher each published literary works about the interaction between Wild Women and human men, *The Wild Woman* and *Wild People* (*Wildleute*) respectively. Both authors are natives of Alpine countries, a geographic area replete with folk legends about Wild People. The fact that both texts were written at the same time invites a comparison and allows us to draw conclusions about the different sensitivities and concerns involved when a male and a female author of the same generation deal with an identical motif. Mitterer's portrayal of the relationship between a Wild Woman and human men corresponds largely with Kristeva's and Theweleit's statements on 'otherness'; however, his play contains additional self-reflective and critical aspects that merit further investigation.

Five male characters are the central figures of Mitterer's drama. The Wild Woman functions as a catalyst to evoke their responses; the reverse is the case in Hutmacher's narrative. The episodes "Breaking Heart" (Herzbrechen), "No More Love" (Keine Liebe mehr), and "To Survive the Winter" (Überwintern) are told from the point of view of Wild Women who have become involved with humans by marriage, as a result of a promise, or to save their lives (*Wild People*, pp. 86-99). Despite these structural differences, both works convey similar views about human nature as basically cruel, selfish, and insensitive. In both cases the Wild Woman represents an alternative to human behavior.

Mitterer characterizes the men through their own words and actions as mercenary, ruthless, despotic, and brutal. Hutmacher uses the same technique to expose the negative traits of her male and female human characters, particularly their thoughtlessness and self-centeredness which cause others unnecessary suffering. In other words, Hutmacher's stories offer comments on human society in general, whereas Mitterer focuses exclusively on the male psyche. However, his male characters are sufficiently complex to provide insights into the organization of social interaction in general.

Wild People—women, men, and children—figure among the demonic figures in folk tales, and best known among them is the witch. For centuries witchcraft was considered "a dark and horrible reality," as Montague Summers observed.[5] Bächtold-Stäubli discusses, among many other mythological figures, that of the Wild Woman, the Wild Man, or Wild People, who play an important role in the folk tradition of the Alpine regions.[6] Wild People roam the mountains and valleys alone, as families, married couples, pairs of brothers, brothers and sisters, or sisters. While the men are ascribed impish and frightening traits, the women, also referred to as "holy women," can assume goddess-like qualities (*Handwörterbuch*, p. 970). Occasionally they have individual names such as Stuze or Muze. It is interesting to note that devil figures occasionally appear, as the Wild People do, dressed in green, and have similarly strange-sounding names.[7] Bächtold-Stäubli points out that the descriptions of the Wild People are ambiguous. They can be helpful, kind, and industrious, but they can also be vengeful and malicious. Occasionally they lure children away from their human homes and the Wild Women seduce human men. These characteristics associate the Wild People with the superstitions about witches.[8] Among the *Salige* there can be "wunderschöne Weibsbilder" (amazingly beautiful women figures) of considerable wisdom and skill. They are noted for their alluring singing and their ability to soar through the skies on clear, moonlit nights (*Handwörterbuch*, pp. 971-973).

Wild People, and similar characters such as Hans Christian Andersen's Little Mermaid, have frequently been depicted in intimate relationships with humans, even as their spouses (*Handwörterbuch*, p. 974). Marriages between them and humans are usually described as extraordinarily happy and advantageous to the human partner. Usually they end because the human husband transgresses against a taboo specified by the woman before the wedding; for example, wife beating, asking about the wife's name or family, touching her in a certain way, or using profane language (*Wilde Frau*, p. 76).

The protagonist of Felix Mitterer's play *The Wild Woman* (which ends in the destruction and self-destruction of the male characters) is a particular variant of the Wild Woman, namely the Wild Cook. Claudia Schmölders maintains that this character plays a more dangerous role in folk tales than the sexually aggressive witch. The Wild Cook performs domestic tasks, including cooking, and achieves considerable power over human males by being in charge of their food and living quarters.[9] In Mitterer's drama, the Wild Woman serves as a catalyst to explore five male characters, lumberjacks who are living in a remote hut in the forest. As is usually the case in folk tradition, the men, with one exception, are unaware of the Wild Woman's true identity and the risk they take by provoking her wrath.

The setting of the play, some undefined past and a place far from civilization, has the earmarks of a test tube. The men represent certain age groups—adolescence (age 17), young adulthood (age 25), mature adulthood (age 30), middle age (age 45), and old age (age 70). They are also defined by their social status and their individual psychological makeup, albeit to a lesser extent. The age and the background of the female character is irrelevant since she is only defined by her effect on the men. As a literary construct she reproduces and questions the concept and function of femininity as established in male discourse since Greek antiquity. Everything about her signals 'otherness'—her silence, her dark complexion and dark hair, her reactions, her appearance, and her gender.

Mitterer's Wild Woman is reminiscent not only of folk tradition, but also of literary models such as the protagonist of Adalbert Stifter's novella *Quicksilver* (1847)—a "brown" girl of obscure origins who becomes friends with the children of a prosperous land owner.[10] Stifter's characters, including the human adults, are more refined than Mitterer's lumberjacks, who, except for the adolescent Wendl, mistreat the stranger physically. Abuse does occur in *Quicksilver* as well, but in a more subtle psychological fashion. Here the humans take the girl's presence for granted during the summer months but forget her as they leave for the city during the winter. They reward her for her spectacular rescue effort by trying to 'tame' her. In Mitterer as well as Stifter, the youngest boy is sensitized by the stranger and his future life presumably continues to be affected by her.

Mitterer's play deals with an attractive woman and five uneducated men living separated from their families and other women. Thus the situation is quite different from *Quicksilver* where sexuality is not an issue. In *The Wild Woman* sexuality is of primary importance both as genuine desire and, even more importantly, as an expression of virility and dominance among the men. The latter relate to the woman to whom they have no social or family obligations primarily in sexual terms by making her their love object. *The Wild Woman* is a literary experiment exploring the behavior of men of different age groups and their socialization in an androcentric environment toward a lonely, seemingly unprotected female. Since the setting of the drama makes it unlikely that the men will be held accountable for their actions, their interaction with the woman conveys paradigms of male desire. For example, the old man approaches the woman gently, merely asking her for physical closeness, the younger men make sexual demands, and the boy admires her from afar, limiting his sexual activity to masturbation (p. 38).

Stifter's nameless and silent Wild Girl, on the other hand, enters a cultivated microcosm shaped by the spirit of enlightened humanism. Yet the carelessness on the part of civilized humans, as well as their attempts to make the girl conform to their way of life, suggest intolerance toward the stranger as an autonomous being. The steward, an unrefined man, reveals the latent brutality that is repressed by civilization when he suggests catching the girl who helped his master to avert catastrophe, while the enlightened father suggests that she be gradually domesticated:

'I'll catch the thing,' said the steward. All three children cried out in fear and protest in response to his remark. 'Don't do that,' the father said. 'The girl rendered my mother and my children the greatest service today. She is not to be treated harshly in general, but now less than ever, as long as she does not cause any harm. We will investigate and when we find her, she must be treated well, so that she learns to trust us. We will find out how we can reward the child and perhaps make her life more productive than she would ever imagine' (p. 297).[11]

In fact, the father and the steward agree that the Wild Girl must be trained and socialized, that is made productive according to their plans; they differ only in the manner in which they want to achieve this goal.

Stifter establishes a connection between his protagonist and the Wild Woman tradition by having the grandmother in his novella recount a tale about a mysterious, industrious girl of dark complexion who works as a farmer's helpmate until a strange messenger informs her about the death of a certain Sture Mure, a name which makes sense only to her. A similar story is recorded in Andrian's collection of folk tales; it involves a Wild Woman who works as a maid until her name is revealed by a voice calling: "Forest Man, Forest Man, tell Girangingele that Hörele has died."[12] In both stories the woman leaves as soon as her ancestry and her name are revealed. Except for the names, which Stifter changed into "Rauhrinde" and "Sture Mure," the folk tale and the grandmother's story in *Quicksilver* are identical.

Stifter's and Mitterer's female protagonists are inspired by Alpine folklore, as the allusions to folk tradition reveal, namely the folk tale in *Quicksilver* and Mitterer's own statements and source material dealing with the motif of the Wild Woman in the appendix of *The Wild Woman*.[13] Both authors emphasize the element of mystery associated with the Wild Girl or Woman by describing her appearance and behavior in detail, without offering any psychological interpretation. Nothing is known about her family or her people. She surfaces seemingly from out of nowhere as a contrast to human conventions and society. Mitterer calls to mind the alluring singing and the ability of the *Salige* to soar through the skies by specifying in his stage directions that "the strange singing of a woman's voice" be heard (*Wild Woman*, p. 10) before the woman manifests herself among wind and snow at the men's door.[14] In the end, she disappears "in the darkness and the drifting snow" and "the strange singing of the woman's voice arises once again" (p. 67).[15]

In both Stifter and Mitterer the Wild Females are self-motivated, reacting in ways that seem almost abnormal, since they are isolated from any larger social or cultural context. Their reason for making contact with humans is unknown, as are their thoughts, feelings, and values, which they express only through actions, body language, crying, or by touching someone. It is obvious to the viewer or reader, but not necessarily to the humans in the text—particularly those blinded by lust—that the Wild People display emotions which are considered normal or even desirable by humans. The girl in *Quicksilver* acts with greater circumspection and concern than the adults who are dominated by materialistic considerations; consider, for example, that during a fire the people save their belongings, but forget one of the children in the burning house.

The Wild Female of both texts is clearly not bound by human conventions. Stifter's girl wears a green 'unisex' costume, and the human family takes great pains to have her change into a conventional dress. Mitterer's Wild Woman apparently has no notion of human morality and attaches little significance to the sexual act. When she objects to Lex's advances it is because he makes demands and beats her rather than asking for her favors. She is altogether unimpressed by Much's and Lex's promises to make a commitment to her and take her away as their wife (pp. 51, 56, 62). Her disinterest in the men's attention and her transgression against human gender roles, which lead the men to consider her a whore (pp. 20, 67), suggest a profound difference between her view of the world and theirs.

Mitterer offers a series of clues about the woman's identity, for example her aversion to the venison that Lex offers to her. Deer or *Rehe* are the sacred animals of the *Salige Frauen* (*Handwörterbuch*, pp. 604, 617). Throughout the play Mitterer places the Wild Woman into a number of mythological and religious contexts. For one thing, she is associated with Circe, the sorceress from Greek antiquity who seduced Odysseus. Before the play opens Much appears alone on stage in the pose of a classical bard, singing verses 37-54 from book twelve of Homer's *Odyssey*. Later, when Lex hangs the slaughtered deer like a crucified man in full view of its patroness, a correlation between the Wild Woman and the Virgin Mary is established (p. 25). Wendl's remarks confirm this impression:

> Down there where two trails intersect there is a wayside shrine. In it stands a Madonna. 'Our Lady of the Forest' they call her ... She is black all over. Because once she was hit by lightning and she started to burn. Whenever I am unhappy and I don't know what to do, I go there and talk to her. First I talk to her, then I stop talking and only look at her. And suddenly I feel a sweet pain. A very sweet pain. And I forget everything. Everything. And every time it happens I feel like dying. It's that beautiful. So beautiful ... She looks like you (p. 54).[16]

Thus, the goddess-like qualities of the Wild Woman mentioned by Bächtold-Stäubli and in a different context by Theweleit are evoked. However, in their attempts to conceptualize the stranger, the men compare her to animals. Hias for example likens her to a cat (p. 49) and a fish (p. 48), Lex insults her as a sow (p. 24) and a cow (p. 42) and calls her a "windige Stuten" (p. 20), an infamous mare. While Sanford attributes to Lex a capacity for genuine tenderness (p. 175), it would appear that his vacillating between sentimentality and brutality indicates the kind of pathology typically ascribed to the authoritarian proto-Fascist personality as described by Adorno and other scholars on whose works Theweleit bases his arguments to a large extent.[17]

Both *Quicksilver* and *The Wild Woman* portray patriarchal discourse critically as a means of domination rather than communication. In both works the insistence of the adult characters on the woman's otherness, and ultimately her inferiority, constitutes a disturbing element. In Stifter it is the grandmother and the children, and in Mitterer it is the adolescent and the old man who approach the stranger with a measure of respect and love; among the men it is only the adolescent Wendl who neither insults her nor supports the other characters' transgressions against her. The Wild Female's inability to speak is irrelevant to the youngsters who have not yet been indoctrinated by patriarchal discourse and who communicate with the strange woman intuitively and directly. Stifter and Mitterer imply that the males who have been exposed to the Wild Female's influence in their formative years will remain outsiders to the patriarchal mainstream. They suggest, in other words, that 'masculinity' is the result of social conditioning and male bonding.

In *The Wild Woman* the gender roles define power positions and are somewhat detached from biological sex. The lumberjacks determine status by who does the 'woman's work' and by their supposed sexual prowess. Much, for example, taunts Lex for being a peasant rather than a farmer and embarrasses him repeatedly by bringing up his past as a convicted poacher (*Wild Woman*, p. 8). Lex in turn ridicules Hias because of his age and presumed sexual impotence: "Heavens! What do you think you can do with your rusty old grave cutter, you old fart!"[18] (p. 31).

The correspondence between biological sex and gender roles becomes immediately evident when the woman enters the scene. Up until that point Wendl had acted as the housewife, but Jogg suggests immediately that he now stop mending his jacket: "Stop doing that, boy! Since there's a woman around, let her do it!"[19] (p. 14). What this suggests, of course, is that any woman's status is lower than that of the least privileged male. When the woman later on refuses to serve the men, Wendl is asked to resume his previous duties: "From now on you are the cook again! But watch out that you don't set her free! Then I'll kill you"[20] (p. 53). The woman's silence and her inexplicably gentle and compliant demeanor in response to the men's brutality baffle and confuse the characters in the play;[21] they also allow the reader or viewer to perceive her as either superior or inferior to human beings.

In contrast to Stifter's and Mitterer's treatment of the Wild Woman, Rahel Hutmacher's novel *Wild People* (1986) transcends the boundaries between the familiar and the 'other' by juxtaposing the point of view of the humans with that of the Wild People, a perspective similar to the one Ingeborg Bachmann assumed in *Undine Goes* or Barbara Frischmuth in *The Mystifications of Sophie Silber* (*Die Mystifikationen der Sophie Silber*). Unlike the male authors, Hutmacher makes the sphere of the Wild People transparent and thus opens it up to scrutiny. She reveals that beyond certain physical and cultural qualities, the emotional and spiritual difference between both groups is negligible. If there is any difference at all, it is that the Wild People possess a greater degree of sensitivity, partly as a result of their precarious situation. They are apparently physically weaker than humans and cannot ward off the inequities they suffer because of the humans' superstition and prejudice. Hence there are obvious causes for their reticence and circumspection, since they have every reason to fear the humans as persecutors.

Hutmacher also introduces a host of themes from popular legends and fairy tales involving Wild People in order to construct individual characters and their cultural background. She integrates motifs such as the Wild People's singing, their role as helpers and destroyers, their love relationships with humans, and their desire to communicate with human children. Hutmacher explains the latter propensity as emanating from the Wild People's desire to bring about a change of heart in the human race which would lead to a peaceful co-existence (*Wild People*, pp. 162-164).

Hutmacher's Wild People have voices, individuality, and cohesive thoughts. Throughout her novel she reveals the xenophobia, sexism, and paranoia inherent in traditional folk narratives about Wild People or, for that matter, in popular views about any group placed into the role of "other." Hutmacher's individual narratives convincingly portray in psychological terms the plight of those suffering from human injustice. One of these episodes involves a Wild Woman who chooses to marry a human man rather than a tree, as her father had wished (*Wild People*, p. 86). Despite her conjugal happiness, she faces an untenable situation: she cannot return to her people, because her father mourned her as if she had died,[22] but neither can she live in human society where people mock and torment her. She finds it increasingly difficult not to become resentful and prejudiced. Her husband, although in love with his exotic wife, seems to defend and excuse his peers' behavior, maintaining that the humans do not act out of maliciousness. The Wild Woman did not foresee these difficulties before her marriage, and her options are to cancel her commitment to her husband and live without his love, or to stay with him and become bitter as a result of the continuing persecution:

> If I leave I lose the kisses of my human husband. If I stay, it will eat away at my bones, my arteries, and my heart: It would eat away even at a heart made of iron ... When that happens I become so that the 'come, please come' of every human male gets stuck in his throat. As soon as he wants to embrace me, kiss me, and give me hearts made of sugar I only have to look in his face and he becomes completely alienated. His hands fall off, and his tongue rests in his mouth like a stick (*Wildleute*, p. 87).[23]

Since the Wild Woman in Mitterer's play is the only female character and is juxtaposed by five males, she is not only significant as an extra-human figure but as woman in an archetypal sense; as a creature of nature, as Sanford argues (p. 178), or as a cipher for the essence of womanhood, *"das Ewig-Weibliche"* (the Eternal-Feminine). In Hutmacher this is not the case. Because of the multitude of characters and situations in *Wild People*, the figure of the Wild Woman eludes the gender specificity she is assigned in *The Wild Woman*. She is a member of a foreign group, the *Wild People*, rather than Woman confronted by Man. Hutmacher's speaker clearly does not represent the archetypal female, but read in context, the episode *Breaking Heart* is a comment on intimate encounters between members of clearly defined, perhaps even hostile groups. Hutmacher's three episodes describing the plight of Wild Women among humans thematize the fate of outsiders and members of oppressed groups living in a foreign dominant culture. While Mitterer prioritizes the problem of male-female relationships using ethnic and cultural differences to amplify his major theme, in Hutmacher's text the effect is the opposite: the problem of gender is subordinate to the problem of cultural and ethnic prejudice. In this respect her work resembles Stifter's *Quicksilver* more closely than does Mitterer's.

The topics of Mitterer's other works shed light on the context in which *The Wild Woman* is to be read. Plays such as *The Children of the Devil (Die Kinder des Teufels)*, *Stigma, Eine Passion, Homeland, Sold Out (Verkaufte Heimat)*, *There's No Finer Country (Kein schöner Land)* and the short stories in *At the Edge of the Village (An den Rand des Dorfes)* attest to the author's awareness of the interconnectedness of misogyny, xenophobia, anti-Semitism, National Socialism and Fascism as symptoms of mass hysteria and irrationalism. For example Mitterer's historical drama on the witch trials in seventeenth-century Salzburg, *The Children of the Devil*, is written with a view of Austria's recent past.[24]

There are also parallels between *The Children of the Devil* and *The Wild Woman*. It is an historical fact that in the Salzburg trials approximately one-third of the accused were female, but Mitterer reduces this percentage even more by showing eight male and two female youths suspected and executed as witches. As in *The Wild Woman*, Mitterer often uses female figures to expose the corruption of patriarchal systems, for example Magdalena Pichlerin in *The Children of the Devil*, a strong female figure who survives the male characters and is the last one to be executed. This pattern is repeated in the drama *Stigma* as well as in the short story *Christine's Womb (Christines Schoß)*, a narrative about a woman who is crippled by doctors and the male-dominated medical establishment.[25] Without overemphasizing cause and effect, Mitterer allows the non-traditional behavior of these women to be interpreted as a result of abuse experienced at the hands of men. Christine, for example, lives with a woman friend after her divorce, while the young beggars of *The Children of the Devil*, abandoned and abused children, turn to a cult figure for salvation.[26] Finally, the Wild Woman uses her supernatural or suggestive powers to destroy the men who have mistreated her.

In addition to neutral or negative women figures, who have been co-opted by oppressive systems, strong women figures emerge in Mitterer's works as an alternative force to patriarchal and Fascist society, and often as society's best—albeit repressed—potential. Hutmacher's works, on the other hand, focus on the content of alternative, oppressed, and occult cultures whose methods of processing and utilizing information differ markedly from those of contemporary Western civilization. Her intuitive and sensual language reproduces archaic or childlike ways to relate to reality and undermines rational and scientific discourse. Hutmacher's language, like that of other German-Jewish authors such as Gertrud Kolmar or Ilse Aichinger, is associative and possesses musical and poetic qualities. She composes anti-worlds replete with images of organic communal lifestyles in natural settings. All of her central characters are female.[27] In contrast to most of the female figures in Mitterer, their identity is not constructed in opposition to a male character or group, nor is a male required to lend them form and profile. On the contrary, Hutmacher's fluid characters are defined in speech processes. In her texts, identity is established through predominantly cerebral and emotional processes; hence the dream-like quality of her work.

A first glance at Hutmacher's texts reveals subjectivity as the most important characteristic of her prose, in contrast to Mitterer's historical and social critical approach. As a psychotherapist, Hutmacher derives her most poignant images from the study of dreams as well as occult or psychological literature, such as the works of C.G. Jung or Sigmund Freud. She subverts the androcentric discourse of mainstream psychotherapy or psychology and lends it a cultural critical slant. Rather than relying on the traditional binary opposition of male–female, Hutmacher represents the 'human' discourse as unified. From the perspective of extra-human creatures the difference between male and female humans is negligible. In *Wild People* the intolerance of human males *and* females determines the status of the Wild Woman, as it does that of all Wild People. The relationship between the Wild Woman and her human husband is de-emphasized, and the episode leaves little room for the discussion of gender problems. In *Daughter*, published one year later, the male-female dichotomy is entirely irrelevant, as the author reveals the interaction between women in an archetypal setting with a focus on the development of the young protagonist.

This matrix already defines *Wild People*. Not man and woman, but majority and minority, the dominant group and the oppressed group, face each other. Even on an individual level, the difference between human females and Wild Women is highlighted, and neither is relegated to the role of 'other'. Each party's concerns are explored in the text, and emotions and thoughts are given equal time. From the reader's perspective it is obvious that the mutual maligning on either side is the result of profound misunderstandings and conflicts of interest which arise from the desire of the humans to dominate the other group (ostensibly the Wild People, but by implication any other group as well), expand their sphere of influence, and create a world of conformity. For the most part, Hutmacher indicts the humans, both men and women, for the disharmony and suffering on both sides.

Hutmacher's perspective is informed not only by her professional interests, but also her background. As a Jewish woman in a German-speaking Christian country, she is familiar with the phenomenon of marginality in more than one sense. This awareness is reflected in *Wild People*. In "Breaking Heart," the personal relationship between the man and the woman plays a relatively minor role. There is clearly love and desire on the part of the Wild Woman and her human husband despite their ethnic and cultural differences. The suggestion of a tree as another, possibly more compatible mate for the Wild Woman suggests, in a humorous if not grotesque way, that it is not the individual differences, but the group identity that poses the problem. The lovers may think that they are compatible, but their communities do not.

In the absence of love, difference emerges as a problem. In 1986 the horrors of the Holocaust once again made headlines after Ronald Reagan's visit at a *Wehrmacht* and SS cemetery in West Germany, and also during the election campaign of Kurt Waldheim, a former Nazi, who successfully ran for the office of president in Austria. Hutmacher's awareness of the rise of anti-Semitism and hate crimes in Europe is indirectly reflected in *Wild People*. In this historical context, her *Wild People* are justified in luring human children away from parents who refuse to learn from history, in order to give them playful, life- and pleasure-oriented education, and to teach them respect for others and love of peace. Encapsulated in their values is perhaps the only viable option for the future of mankind. As humans destroy one another in the form of groups perceived as alien, and as they proceed to plunder the natural habitat of the Wild People (the environment), they work toward the devastation of all life.

The fate of the Wild Woman who married a human shows that human adults are too set in their ways to change. Unable to accept difference, they hate and destroy. The Wild Woman, cut off from her environment while among the humans, senses that further exposure to human society poisons her mind and causes her to hate herself and others. This aspect of the story can be read as a parallel to the fate of post-emancipation German-speaking Jews. Jews were the targets of hatred and persecution from the outside, but they also suffered from internalized hatred, as both Theodor Lessing and Sander Gilman have argued.[28] While *Wild People* is an open enough text to be applied to any situation where a powerful and an oppressed group live in immediate vicinity to one another, one of its subtexts addresses the failed symbiosis of Christians and Jews and, more specifically, the Holocaust.

Mitterer has displayed an interest in these topics in a variety of works, and allusions to ethnic conflicts are made in *The Wild Woman* as well. Much surmises that the woman is a gypsy and links Wendl to her because of his illegitimate background:

> Perhaps she is one of your relatives, Wendl! ... His father is also one of those wagon people! A knife grinder ... The farmer kicked her out when she was fat like a mortar! And the black devil was gone, of course! We found her giving birth in our stable! Two weeks later she went into the water together with the bastard! But they pulled Wendl back out[29] (pp. 14-15).

Uncanny powers on the part of Mitterer's Wild Woman figure are suggested by the fact that Lex is incapable of consummating the sex act with her, despite the fact that she does not resist him physically.[30] The final brawl can also be interpreted as caused by the woman's supernatural power. At the same time, there seems to be a limit to what she can do. Like Hutmacher's Wild Woman in "No More Love," Mitterer's protagonist apparently cannot leave unless certain conditions are met; she disappears when justice is done and the perpetrators are permanently eliminated. Because the women characters in both works are shown to possess an obvious capacity for tenderness and love, they appear justified in using their special powers. From this perspective, the dark woman endowed with supernatural powers could be interpreted as an avenger of Wendl's humiliated and persecuted mother, as the guardian angel of her humiliated son, and thus as a manifestation of his mother's spirit. On the other hand, one might also argue that the killing is caused by the males' own destructive potential which the woman unleashes, since by her mere presence she inspires cruelty, jealousy, possessiveness, and competitiveness in the adult men.

Despite the obvious difference in emphasis and approach, Mitterer's and Hutmacher's works display striking similarities. Both texts portray the point of view of the outsiders or oppressed as justified, and each denounces patriarchal society with its built-in ethnocentrism and misogyny. Hutmacher's readers gain direct insight into the Wild Woman's psyche, whereas Mitterer suggests to his audience conclusions about the character and motives of the Wild Woman based on character interaction and textual signals.

As is the case in the Swiss and Austrian folk tradition, and in literary works such as Stifter's *Quicksilver*, the figure of the Wild Woman is a powerful symbol revealing, not as Bächtold-Stäubli claims, the ambivalent character of demonic forces, but rather the ambiguity of the human mind and civilization. Hutmacher uses the characters of Wild People to show the effects of human activities on non-human beings as well as the impact of a dominant culture on the oppressed. Mitterer, more specifically, exposes misogyny, the hatred of women and the female body on the part of men, and the mechanisms by which men control female sexuality—physical force, confinement, rhetoric, and superstition, for example: "Because it is a fact that poisonous gasses emanate from women, you understand? They ruin the hay!"[31] The dynamics he uncovers during the encounter between the men and the Wild Woman are the same that generate ethnocentrism, discrimination and oppression in general, as well as the exploitation of the animals and the vegetation of the earth—the realm of the Wild People. Neither Hutmacher nor Mitterer discusses these phenomena in the context of a specific historical area, or of a political or social system. Their texts are deliberately ahistorical and are intended as an indictment of the human race as a whole. Hutmacher shows that all humans are implicated in crimes against nature and other living beings, while Mitterer explicitly highlights human males as the major perpetrators.

Notes

1. Ludwig Bechstein, *Märchen und Sagen* (Berlin: Knaur, 1940), p. 207. "A mermaid or Rhine-nymph."

2. Klaus Theweleit, *Orpheus und Euridike* (Basel: Stroemfeld/Roter Stern, 1988), p. 907. "Gerade diejenigen unter Frauen, gerade die sinnlich-Einzige, die Erregbaren unter den Männern dazu veranlaßt, den Schutz der bisherigen lebensbewahrenden institutionellen Körper zu verlassen, sich in die Arme 'Amors' zu stürzen und ihr Herz einer blutjungen Schönen zur Verspeisung anzubieten, muß entsinnlicht werden. Wo der Rausch endet und übergeht in eine der normalen Kälten, hält das Auge plus Hirn Ausschau nach haltbareren Konstruktionen ... Der Frau fällt die Bürde zu, eine Gottesnachfolge antreten zu müssen mit der Schönheit ihres Leibs; daher müssen ihre auffälligsten Exemplare ins Jenseits ... Einer der Gründe, warum Männer sich so schwer auf die Probleme wirklicher Frauen einlassen können, kommt von hier. In jeder männlichen Liebe ist die Frau zur Hälfte *Medizin*—die Wunderdroge. Wehe, sie hat Probleme ... Wie sehr ... nichtgöttliche Frauen durch diese Konstruktion um die Chance gebracht werden, einen Teil der (an sie und durch sie) umlaufenden Wünsche tatsächlich zu befriedigen, selber der Zerrissenheit zu entkommen und eigene Wünsche befriedigen zu lassen, schreit weiter (stumm) zu den Himmeln." All translations from the German texts are my own.

3. Julia Kristeva, *Fremde sind wir uns selbst*. Trans. Xenia Rajewsky (Frankfurt: Suhrkamp, 1990), p. 208.

4. As Simone de Beauvoir in *Das andere Geschlecht* (Hamburg: Rowohlt, 1951), p. 12, observes: "Die Gattin darf also am Mana des Gatten nicht teilhaben, sie muß eine Fremde sein, fremd also auch dem Klan." (The wife is thus barred from sharing her husband's *manna*; she must be a stranger, even to her clan.)

5. Montague Summers, "Introduction." *Malleus Maleficarum of Henrik Kramer and Johann Sprenger* (1486-87), transl. Montague Summers (New York: Dover, 1971), p. v-xi. Here, p. vii.

6. Hanns Bächtold-Stäubli, *Handwörterbuch des deutschen Aberglaubens* (Berlin and Leipzig: Walter de Gruyter, 1935/36), pp. 967-969.

7. Emil König. *Hexenprozesse* (Berlin: Bock, o.J), pp. 55-56. A boy said to have been abducted by Wild Women in a German tale was observed by lumberjacks who noticed his green costume. Claudia Schmölders, Ed. *Die wilde Frau.* "Die wilden Frauen im Untersberge," (Köln: Diederichs, 1984), pp. 96-97.

8. Felix Mitterer, Die wilde Frau (München: Friedl Brehm Vlg., 1986), p. 76. [Excerpt from Deutsche Volkssagen, Ed. Leander Petzold (München: C. H. Beck, 1978)]. One of the most frequently mentioned crimes of witches concerns a man's sexual potency, (Malleus, p. 4) and another one involves the stealing of children (p. 99). There were supposedly more female than male witches (p. 6).

9. *Die wilde Frau*, Ed. Claudia Schmölders (Köln, Eugen Diederichs, 1983), p. 67. "Die 'wilde Köchin' ist eine weit gefährlichere Figur als die sexuell aggressive Hexe, denn sie ist existenziell mächtiger."

10. Adalbert Stifter, *Sämmtliche Werke* V. 1, Ed. Franz Egerer, Adolf Raschner (Prag: Calve, 1908), pp. 263-342.

11. "'Ich fange das Ding,' sagte ein Knecht. Alle drei Kinder taten auf die Äußerung hin einen Angstschrei der Abwehrung. 'Lasse das,' sagte der Vater. 'Das Mädchen hat meiner Mutter und meinen Kindern heute den größten Dienst erwiesen. Darf man es überhaupt nicht rauh behandeln, so darf man jetzt umso weniger, so lange es sich nicht schädlich erweist. Wir werden es schon auskundschaften und zu finden wissen, dann muß es gut behandelt werden, daß es Zutrauen gewinnt, und wir werden die Art schon finden, wie wir das Kind belohnen und ihm sein Leben vielleicht nützlicher machen können als es jetzt ahnt."

12. "Waldmann, Waldmann, sag' zum Giragingele, das Hörele sei gestorben" (*Wilde Frau*, p. 73).

13. Gerlinde Ulm Sanford, "Brutalität und Zärtlichkeit in Felix Mitterers Volksstück *Die Wilde Frau*," *Modern Austrian Literature* 26, 3/4 (1993), p. 169.

14. "[D]er merkwürdige Gesang einer Frauenstimme."

15. "[V]erschwindet in der Dunkelheit und im Schneetreiben." "Der merkwürdige Gesang der Frauenstimme kommt wieder auf, entfernt sich, verstummt."

16. "Da weiter unten, da wo sich zwoa Weg kreuzen, da is a Bildstöckl. Da drin steht a Muattergottes. 'Unsere Frau im Walde' hoaßt ma sie ... Sie is ganz schwarz. Weil da hat amal der Blitz eingeschlagen,und sie hat angfangt zu brennen. Wenn i nimmer ein und aus woaß, geh i hin und red mit ihr. Zerst red i mit ihr, dann red i nix mehr und schau sie nur an. Und aufoamal spür i a süaßen Weh. Ganz an süaßen Weh. Und i vergiß alles. Alles. I kannt jedsmal sterm. So schön is des. So schön ... Sie schaut aus wia du."

17. Theodor W. Adorno, Else Frenkel-Brunswick, Daniel J. Levinson, Newitt R. Sanford, Ed. *The Authoritarian Personality* (New York: Harper, 1950). Cf. also Eugen Kogon, *Der SS-Staat* (Frankfurt: Verlag der Frankfurter Hefte), p. 632. Kogon defines "romanticized brutality" as the basis of the Nazi regime. Also the depiction of Nazis in the works of Holocaust survivors and intended Nazi victims such as Jakob Lind, Erich Fried, and Edgar Hilsenrath emphasizes the combination of sentimentality and brutality.

18. "Geh! Was willst denn du no ausrichten! Alter Schneebrunzer! Mit dei'm rostigen Grabstichel!"

19. "Laß des, Bua! Wenn schon a Frau da is, soll die des machen!"

20. "Ab jetzt bist du wieder die Köchin! Aber wehe, du laßt sie frei! Dann schlag i di ab!"

21. "Brutalität, besonders häufig verbunden mit Gewalttätigkeit, mit unverhüllt zur Sprache gebrachten privatesten Sexualerlebnissen oder Sexualproblemen ist meines Erachtens überhaupt ein Zentralthema oder jedenfalls immer wieder aufgegriffenes Stilmittel unserer modernen Literatur," observes Ulm Sanford in "Brutalität und Zärtlichkeit", p. 167.

22. This element suggests the Jewish custom according to which the parents mourn a child who abandons the community as if he or she had died.

23. "Gehe ich weg, verliere ich die Küsse meines Menschenmanns. Bleibe ich hier, zernagts mir die Knochen, die Herzadern und das Herz: es würde selbst ein eisernes Herz zerfressen ... Aber dann bin ich so, daß jedem Menschenmann sein Komm doch komm im Halse steckenbleibt. Kaum will er mich umarmen, mich küssen und mir Zuckerherzen schenken, muß ich ihm nur ins Gesicht sehen, und er wird sich ganz und gar fremd. Seine Hände fallen ihm ab, und seine Zunge liegt wie ein Stock im Mund."

24. Felix Mitterer, *Die Kinder des Teufels. Ein Theaterstück und sein historischer Hintergrund*. Mit Beiträgen von Heinz Nagl, Norbert Schindler, Meinrad Pizzinini (Innsbruck: Haymon, 1989).

25. Felix Mitterer, "Christines Schoß." In: *An den Rand des Dorfes* (Wien, München: Jugend und Volk, 1981), p. 115-122 .

26. Norbert Schindler, "Die Entstehung der Unbarmherzigkeit. Zur Kultur und Lebensweise der Salzburger Bettler am Ende des 17. Jahrhunderts," *Kinder des Teufels*, pp. 134-145. The victims of the Zauberer-Jackl-Prozesse (1675-90) were "nahezu ausschließlich Bettler und Vaganten."

27. Rahel Hutmacher, *Dona/Wettergarten: Geschichten* (Frankfurt/M: Fischer, 1984); *Tochter* (Darmstadt: Luchterhand, 1987).

28. Theodor Lessing, *Der jüdische Selbsthaß* (Berlin: Jüdischer Verlag, 1930); Sander Gilman, *Jewish Self-Hatred. Anti-Semitism and the Hidden Language of the Jews* (Baltimore and London: The Johns Hopkins Press, 1986).

29. "Vielleicht a Verwandte von dir, Wendl! ... Sei Vater is aa so a Karrenziacher! A Messerschleifer ... Aussighaut hat er sie, der Bauer, wia sie stampfdick gwesen is! Und der schwarze Teufel natürlich über alle Berge! Bei uns im Stall hamma sie dann beim Werfen derwischt! Zwoa Wochen spater is sie ins Wasser, samt'n Gschrappen! Aber den Wendl hams wieder aussagfischt."

30. This is another instance where the Wild Woman and the witch are closely associated. According to the *Malleus Maleficarum* (p. 99), witches produce impotence and can "keep silent under torture."

31. Hias claims: "Weil des is nämlich so, daß von die Fraun giftige Dämpf ausgehen, verstehst? Dadurch werds Heu hin!" (p. 13).

"You Women Don't Have It Easy."[1]
The Dramatization of Gender Issues
In the Plays by Felix Mitterer

Ursula Hassel

With the statement quoted in the title of this essay the husband in Mitterer's one-act play *We Don't Understand Anything* (*Man versteht nichts*), who feels helpless and frustrated, expresses his sympathy and compassion for his wife who is in the hospital and seriously ill, but is left in the dark about the real state of her health. We as the audience must assume from several allusions within the play that she suffers from cancer. The husband's words might serve as a heading for the author's own treatment of his female characters, as they describe quite well the underlying emotion that accompanies Mitterer's portrayal of female figures and the dramatization of female problems and concerns in his plays. Quite a few of Mitterer's plays focus on the plight of women in a society in which they are disadvantaged in many ways and his work reflects great sensitivity and understanding for their situation. Thus Beth Bjorklund's thesis that the contemporary *Volksstück* does not seriously deal with the interests and concerns of women and with gender problems, which she puts forward in an interesting essay on the *Volksstück* as a "gender-linked genre," would have to be modified for Felix Mitterer.[2] Mitterer himself explains in an interview in 1988 that he has always been quite repelled by macho behavior and that he has always felt much closer to women than to men.[3] He also declares that the effort to make the audience aware of conflicts in male-female relations and to demonstrate the necessity for a change toward more equality and partnership is one of the major intentions of his plays.[4] This essay will have a closer look at how the author's interest in and concern for female issues and problems in the relationship between the sexes is reflected in his plays, which facets of male and female experience he selects for depiction on stage, and how he tries to realize his emancipatory effect on the audience.[5]

In many of his plays Mitterer focuses on people whose attitudes and behavior do not conform to the norms and expectations of mainstream society. They represent "the others" who by being different, no matter in what respect, arouse aggression from the establishment. This interest in outsiders and outcasts of society and the process of being stigmatized has been identified as a typical feature of the new critical *Volksstück* in the succession of Ödön von Horváth and Marieluise Fleißer.[6] In his notes on *There's No Finer Country (Kein schöner Land)*, Mitterer says about this specific theme:

> The victims are 'the others.' And these 'others'—the outsiders, the outcasts—are a continuous theme in my literary work. A great majority of people live in constant fear of 'the others,' they have aggressions against them all the time, no matter in what respect they are different (and in the beginning it is quite harmless): different haircut, different clothing, different behavior, different inclinations, different attitudes, different language, different color, different religion, different customs and traditions.[7]

In his enumeration of qualities that make people different, Mitterer might also have added "sex," as the fact of being female in many cases—both in reality and in literature—is enough to cause one's exploitation and victimization. Methlagl in his short interpretation of *The Wild Woman (Die Wilde Frau)* talks about "the aggression against the feminine as the absolutely other."[8] Thus not only the old, the handicapped, and foreigners have the status of being underprivileged, but also women.

In the Passion Play *Stigma*, which is set in the early nineteenth century, the sufferings of the protagonist Moid (dialect form of Maria) parallel the stations of Christ's Passion. The play starts off by illustrating that the farmhand Moid is at the bottom of the social hierarchy; within the farming household her place is even below the lowest male farm laborer.[9] She is denied the right of self-determination and is put under pressure by the male members of the household. She defends herself against the sexual harassment by Ruepp, the farmer's son, and against Bast, the senior farmhand who urges her to marry him, by withdrawing into a very intense relationship with Jesus Christ. This love of Christ also saves her from her own sexual temptation (which according to the moral code of the Catholic Church would lead to sin) and can thus be seen as a compensation for unfulfilled latent sexual desires. Her identification with Jesus Christ culminates in her developing the stigmata of Christ's suffering and in experiencing the Passion. Her suffering, however, does not make her invulnerable to further human exploitation. When her employers, the farmer and his wife, realize that her experience of the Passion is a marketable event that attracts big crowds of country and town folk, they take the opportunity to make money out of her suffering by selling drinks to the visitors. The farmer's wife would even like to ban poor people from visiting because they do not promote the business. She frankly admits: "Just like farmhands! How's a person supposed to make a living? If I had my way, they wouldn't be allowed in here at all, but the Priest ..."[10] For the farmer the profit he can make out of Moid is the only reason to keep her after her value as cheap labor has decreased.

Moid's suffering of "heavenly" wounds does not make her unassailable to the sexual abuse by humans, but rather provokes their urge to possess her even more. Ruepp, disguised as the devil, finally beats her unconscious and rapes her. After this humiliation, which is perceived by Moid as a bad dream, a new step in her Passion is initiated. She now has to confront two high-ranking official representatives of state and church who have come to examine her "case." That Moid cannot win in this encounter is self-evident. The Professor and the Monsignor have soon passed their judgment on her: The representative of science and the state finds out that Moid is pregnant and "diagnoses" that she is a hysterical epileptic whose wounds are self-inflicted and who has thus deceived everybody. The Monsignor's version is that Moid is possessed by demons who have to be exorcised.

These two interpretations of Moid's state are indicative of the way in which women have been assessed by anti-feminist theories for the past few centuries. Women were seen as being much closer to nature, primarily moved by instincts, and equipped with a destructive sensuality. Their nature and especially their sexuality were demonized, which culminated in the witch-hunts and witch trials of the sixteenth and seventeenth centuries.[11] Later on, women who did not conform to the role that patriarchal society envisaged for them were regarded as hysterics by science and medicine. Their "witchcraft" was now reinterpreted as a product of their distorted psyche. In *Stigma* Mitterer makes use of these male projections of female nature and illustrates their degrading and humiliating effect on the individual and how these spiteful notions serve to maintain the status quo of the social, clerical, and political system. In Moid's case, for the Professor and the Monsignor, the fact of her pregnancy is proof of her unrestrained sexuality which by state and church is perceived as a threat that has to be banned. The Monsignor's statement that Moid is possessed by the devil reveals its closeness to the accusation of witchcraft and is an expression of the church's rejection and fear of female sensuality and sexuality in general.

For the audience witnessing this process of humiliation and suffering, Moid's degradation becomes almost unbearable during the ensuing exorcism. The Monsignor, who is preoccupied with Moid's sin of voluptuousness, finds her possessed by three demons representing lechery, blasphemy, and rebellion. A release of tension is brought about when the demons decide to leave Moid and turn to a much more interesting object, namely the Monsignor himself. Especially "Schnalljuza," the demon of lechery, finds it much more appropriate to move over into the Monsignor, who is now shaken by fits and seizures. Like Seppele, the audience feels relieved and satisfied when the demons indict the Monsignor for having committed the sins of lechery, blasphemy, and opposition against the authorities of the church hierarchy. They also reveal the sins of the farmer, his son, and the senior farm-hand, which leads to Bast killing Ruepp for raping Moid. Even though it is now evident that Moid has been forced into sexual intercourse against her will, she is by no means considered innocent. Bast looks at her "with deep loathing and bitterness"[12] and the Monsignor still calls her the root of all disaster. He crudely states that "everything bad comes from women!"[13] Thus their notion of Moid oscillates between a lustful creature with demonic powers and the perception of the parish priest for whom she is still an "innocent child of God" and "a saint."[14] But being an outsider himself the parish priest does not have the power to protect Moid from the strict verdict of the official church hierarchy. While all the others (except Ruepp) go unpunished out of the exorcism—above all of course the Monsignor himself—even though this cruel procedure has brought to the light their own desires and drives hidden beneath their consciousness and the façade of respectability, Moid as a female and the weakest member within the social structure is the only one to be actually found guilty. Mitterer here illustrates how she is made a scapegoat by her fellow beings and how they have her atone for the urges and sins which they cannot accept within their own personalities. The result is that Moid is excommunicated. The parish priest looks through this mechanism and he serves as the author's mouthpiece when he says to Moid:

> And as far as the demons are concerned, they don't prove anything at all. Every one of us, every human being is possessed by demons. They only have to be awakened! And sometimes, I think to myself, there's nothing satanic, nothing bad at all with these demons, they're only an expression of longing for freedom. The good Monsignor Pfötscher should realize this best of all. But he doesn't want to admit to this. And it's because of this that you are excommunicated, Little Moid.[15]

Being considered a threat to the public by both church and state, Moid is then prosecuted to be put into jail. She is killed by the police during the arrest when she tries to save Seppele, who urges her to escape, from being shot. Thus the play ends by her martyrdom.

Despite the humiliations Moid has to suffer, which finally lead to her death, Mitterer also portrays her as a woman who shows signs of strength and power. Her stigmata are not only outward signs of her sufferings and her position as a helpless victim, but they also make her special.[16] As the parish priest puts it, she has been chosen by God to edify the believers, strengthen their faith, and show them the right track (p. 36). This is seen as a distinction and an honor and Moid is suddenly recognized as an authority, at least by the poor village folk. People now consult her about their physical, psychological, and social problems and they believe in her power to help them. In the beginning the only consolation Moid is able to give is the affirmation that she will pray for them (p. 42), but then she turns into a rebellious fighter for the rights of the poor and disadvantaged. In a radical interpretation of the Sermon of the Mount she expresses her despair about the injustice of the social structures that keep the farm laborers in poverty and dependency. Her speech culminates in a plea for more justice on earth: "I want justice to prevail in this world, not just in heaven!"[17] She thus unmasks the reference to a better life in heaven as inappropriate, an empty promise that has often been used by church officials to keep the poor people down and prevent them from revolting against their lot. This rebellious attitude constitutes the second reason why Moid is perceived as a threat to the public and has to be done away with: She not only threatens the tight morality of the Catholic Church, but she also calls into question the power structures of state and church and their alliance. Like Jesus himself, she sides with the poor against the representatives of the establishment. The image of Moid as a female Christ figure becomes visual when after her death she rests in Seppele's lap and they thus form a pietà. But in Mitterer's play the male-female roles are reversed.[18] That Moid's message has had a great impact on the poor farm laborers and maids is revealed at the end of the play: They all come together to demonstrate their solidarity with Moid and the very last words are spoken by an old servant woman who develops her vision of the Last Judgment (p. 97). But in contrast to the Book of Apocalypse, the envisaged savior here is a woman. She is seen as the one who will sit in judgment upon the rich and privileged, who will do justice and ultimately save the world. Mitterer here stresses the emancipatory power of women who stand for the principle of justice and who are set against a world of power struggles represented by the male-dominated state and the official church hierarchy.

The mysterious woman in Mitterer's play *The Wild Woman* (*Die Wilde Frau*) is another example of a female figure who is on the one hand humiliated and abused, but on the other hand shows strength and power. This strange woman arrives at a lumberjacks' hut one night in winter seeking shelter from the snowstorm outside. She is unknown to all of the five men in the hut and she does not say a single word during the whole play. Mitterer keeps it unclear if she cannot speak or if she just does not want to. The play now focuses on the dynamics within this group of people, five men and one woman—a constellation similar to that in his later play *Munde*. Like in *Munde* these people are in an extraordinary situation, being isolated and cut off from the surrounding civilization, and thus all of their energy concentrates on what is going on in the hut. Even before the woman arrives out of the dark, the tensions and latent conflicts between the members of the group become perceptible. These people are together for practical reasons and not out of friendship. The woman stays with the men for several days and during that period all their aggressive and possessive instincts that have been festering beneath the surface are projected onto her and ultimately break through. During the first night she is sexually abused by Lex; when she silently tries to defend herself against him, he beats and rapes her. But Lex fails sexually which annoys and provokes him even more. After this all the other men except for the youngest, Wendl, sleep with her, taking turns each night. On the second day the foreman Jogg tells the woman that she can stay for a few days until the weather has changed, but that she has to do the housework for them. The role the men have chosen to impose on her can easily be described: She is their sexual object and their housewife.

As mentioned above, Lex is the one who takes the initiative with respect to their dealings with the woman. From the beginning Mitterer stresses Lex's discontent with his work and situation as a poor and dependent lumberjack and his barely restrained aggressiveness. The fact that he has been in jail for poaching also indicates his competitive and hunting instinct. With the arrival of a female creature these drives are turned into a new direction. The woman now becomes the central focus of his competitive, aggressive, and possessive urges and ultimately that of all the men. Having failed sexually Lex now tries to impress the woman by what he considers proofs of his virility and male domination, all of which have a touch of violence. He goes out poaching, bringing back a deer which he proudly presents as her "Einstandsessen" (a welcoming meal) (p. 26). But the woman refuses to accept this gift, thus demonstrating her rejection of the brutal and domineering side of his character. After her sexual abuse has been initiated, the woman also becomes the object of a male power struggle. The first real fight between the men occurs when Lex tries to prevent Much from going to the woman on the third night thus claiming her for himself. Much wins against Lex, having all the others on his side (Jogg comments: "By rights it's his [Much's] turn today!").[19] At this early stage of events, however, they are both shocked that they have actually used violence against each other and Lex warns Much not to attack him again, thus alluding to the further course of events.

While Lex's attitude toward the woman from the beginning is marked by brutality and vacillates between fascination and overt contempt when he feels his sexuality and his dominance are threatened, the others at first defend her against his violent outbreaks. Jogg prevents Lex from disturbing her privacy while she takes a bath (p. 37) and when he tries to force liquor down her throat (p. 42). But the rivalry with Lex arouses their possessive instincts and soon the woman becomes the target of their aggressions, as well. When the woman tries to escape after Lex has again claimed her as his property, Jogg does not want to let her go and after a short moment of indecision he even helps Lex to chain her to prevent her from running away. He rectifies the question of property rights by bluntly declaring:

"You are not his property alone, but you belong to all of us!"[20] To Jogg's mind the fact that she has got involved with them deprives her of the right of self-determination. Having become the object of their power struggle she has to stay until this fight has somehow been decided. The new stage in the relationship between the men and the woman is manifested by the chains around her ankles: She is no longer their guest, but their captive.

In his dramatization of the distorted relationship between the men and the woman, Mitterer shows how closely sex and violence can be intertwined. Since the male attitude toward the female is purely egotistical and the desire to dominate and possess is the men's prime motivation for the relationship, violence and brutality become the overriding feelings which ultimately lead to destruction. But with two of the five men the relationship is different. Both Wendl and Hias, the youngest and the oldest, do not have a purely sexual and egotistical interest in the woman. Hias does sleep with her, but he does not use force and when he goes to her for the second time, he is not primarily looking for sexual fulfillment but is more interested in mutuality and understanding:

> If you don't want to, woman, we'll just leave it. We don't have to ... It's good enough that I can lie close to you. You are so warm, woman! So nice and warm! When I lie close to you, my old bones don't hurt any more and I feel like a babe lying close to its mother. Had not thought that I would be able to experience something like that again. I'm grateful to you for that, woman.[21]

Being with the woman does not arouse the urge to dominate and subjugate her, but brings out the tender side in him. With her he experiences moments of pleasure and he enjoys her presence; she makes him feel warm and good and he is grateful to her. In contrast to Lex and Much who both offer to free the woman from her chains only if she leaves the hut with them, Hias, who did not agree to her imprisonment in the first place, would like to set her free if he could, but he does not feel strong enough. After his second encounter with the woman Hias dies with the woman holding his hand (pp. 58-59), but he is in a peaceful and tranquil state of mind. His last words concern the woman: He asks his fellows for her release because he has a presentiment of coming disaster.

Wendl's feelings toward the woman are devoid of any possessive or violent aspects. He is the youngest and weakest of the group of men and he is not taken seriously by them because of his age, his sensitivity, and the fact that he is the illegitimate child of a woman who got involved with a gypsy. Wendl is shocked when he sees the woman being humiliated by the other men and he tries to free her from the chains several times even though Lex intimidates him (pp. 53-54). But he does not succeed. Wendl feels a deep veneration for the woman and he, who barely speaks in the presence of the other men, opens up to her in a moment of closeness (p. 54). For him she is a personification of the Mother of God and he compares her to a small statue, blackened by lightning, which he consults when he is desperate and looking for consolation. Like the statue of the Virgin Mary, the woman gives him the feeling of belonging and security and with her he experiences moments of devotion, passion, and love. In her presence he has the courage to express his emotions and at last his pent-up feelings of loneliness and anxiety break through in a crying fit which has a relieving effect on him. Thus Mitterer does not only portray the inability of his male characters to express their desire for union with a woman in other than violent ways, but he also gives us glimpses of the possibility of understanding and tenderness in male-female relationships.

The play, however, inevitably moves toward the final catastrophe. Once the power struggle between the men has started, it cannot be stopped again. Lex provokes the ultimate outbreak of aggression and violence by going down to the woman at night and trying to persuade her to leave the hut with him alone. When Much and Jogg wake up and realize what he is planning to do, a brutal fight starts in which the three men finally kill each other. While Wendl is horrified at what has happened, the woman leaves the hut calmly and well composed.

In *The Wild Woman* Mitterer draws on ancient legends that are still alive in the Alpine regions. They all deal with the sudden appearance of one or several mysterious female creatures—often called "wilde Frauen" (wild women)—who come out of the woods and get into contact with the "ordinary" humans. The men are attracted to them because of their beauty and in many stories a marriage between one of these wild women and a man follows. But this union is always connected to a certain condition stipulated by the woman which must not be violated by the man, for example that nobody may know her real name or that the husband must never beat her.[22] As long as this condition is accepted they live in harmony and happiness. But in the majority of the stories the man breaks the taboo mostly out of curiosity or because he cannot restrain his feelings and the woman leaves him never to return. By doing harm to the woman the man thus also damages himself and destroys his personal happiness.

Like the wild women in the folk legends, the woman in Mitterer's play is surrounded by the aura of mystery which gives her power and strength. Even more so than in *Stigma*, Mitterer stresses the ambivalence between weakness and power, victimization and self-determination in this female character. One factor that contributes to her mystery is the fact that she does not speak. On one level this speechlessness might be seen as a handicap. But then, as Mike Rogers points out with respect to the retarded boy in the play *No Place for Idiots*, this deficiency is compensated by other means of communication.[23] Like the boy Wastl, the woman does find ways to express herself and her body language is probably much more honest and genuine than the violent and sometimes abusive language of the men or the borrowed language of Hias who constantly quotes set phrases and proverbs. The woman's speechlessness also signifies the lack of a meaningful language and real understanding between the sexes. Even if the woman did talk, she would probably not be able to change the course of events and prevent the men from victimizing and humiliating her. On another level her dumbness is a sign of her power and superiority. Like the wild women she tries to protect herself, to preserve a certain amount of independence by making part of her personality inaccessible to the men and this annoys and provokes them.

Up to the point when the men chain her, the woman actually has a certain amount of freedom. She has come of her own free will and she is also free to leave. In two instances within the play she contemplates leaving but then decides against it (pp. 17 and 22). Another expression of her relative independence and power is the fact that she does not get emotionally involved with any of the men and that she rejects any efforts of each of the men to impress her and claim her for himself. She does not seem to be affected by their actions, but rather stays indifferent. In contrast to the men, who get entirely worked up and are preoccupied with their emotions, the woman remains cold blooded and even reacts calmly to their acts of violence. When Wendl vainly tries to free her from the chains, she almost comforts him in his desperation (p. 52). It is this air of imperturbability and tranquillity that makes her superior to the men and gives her power. Mitterer underscores this impression by stating in the stage directions that the woman behaves *"as if she knew that in reality absolutely nothing can happen to her."*[24] When the men address her tenderly and with respect or show positive feelings, however, she also reacts emotionally and with understanding. So she comforts Wendl when he is jeered at by the other men because of his lineage (p. 16) and she reacts tenderly in the scenes with Wendl and Hias referred to above. But even with the other men there are moments in which she fulfills their wishes and does not reject them. So she does the housework for them until she is chained and in the scene after Hias' death she also dances for them when Lex *"fast zärtlich"* (almost tenderly) (p. 60) asks her to do so in order to cheer them up. The ultimate proof of the woman's superiority is the fact that like in the ancient myths she leaves the scene alive, while the aggressions the men have directed against her are turned against each other and in the end cause their own destruction.

In both plays, *Stigma* and *The Wild Woman*, Mitterer portrays the female protagonists to a certain extent as victims. They are humiliated and abused by men and cannot defend themselves against attacks from men or male-centered society. The position of female characters as victims is a dramatic conception that has a long tradition in German drama.[25] Beginning with the rise of the *bürgerliches Trauerspiel* in the eighteenth century, women often had to play the role of loving and suffering victims on stage. According to the concept of this genre the women had to be sacrificed or sacrifice

themselves in order to defend the order of the newly established patriarchal nuclear family with its specific morality against the claims and the dominance of the aristocracy. In the social drama of the nineteenth century, the
critical emphasis was on the social conditions within society and the morality of the patriarchal family which caused the victimization of the women.
Mitterer now not only questions and denounces the social, political, and
religious conditions which all contribute to the female status as victim, but
like the representatives of the critical *Volksstück* in the 1920s and 1930s,
Horváth and Fleißer, he scrutinizes the problem of victimization and
exploitation as a gender-linked issue and he challenges the portrayal of the
stereotyped female victim. It is true that Moid in *Stigma* is sacrificed, but as
demonstrated above she is not only a victim and a martyr, but also a rebellious revolutionary. The woman in *The Wild Woman* is humiliated and
abused by the men, but she is the one who walks out of the lumberjacks'
hut in the end, alive and well composed as if nothing had happened, leaving behind her tormentors who have killed each other.

The woman in the latter play incorporates many features which are
commonly attributed to the female character or which make up the myth of
what is feminine in cultural history. She is seductress, whore, and Virgin
Mary, she is housewife and mother, a witch with supernatural powers and
an idol, she is victim and tormentor. It is striking, however, that the woman
represents all of these antagonizing features simultaneously, as well as
some that do not fit the image, for example that she is both weak and
strong, passive and active, cold and gentle. Thus Mitterer questions the
feminine stereotype, as the woman cannot clearly be identified as one of
these by the five men or by the audience; she represents all of these characteristics and none at the same time. Moreover, the play illustrates that all of
the qualities that make up the myth of the feminine are male projections
imposed on the woman. It is not she who seduces the men, but they force
her to get sexually involved with them, calling her a whore afterwards.
They project their own desires and drives onto her, making her the cause of
their own shortcomings and aggressive actions. Thus the title of the play
may also be understood ironically: Not the woman is the wild one, but as
Lex admits himself, the men are wild and cannot control their urges (pp. 29
and 51). When Lex fails sexually after having raped her, he of course
blames her for it, calling her a "Hex" (witch) (p. 19). The ambivalent qualities they see in her are projections of their own ambivalent feelings of
admiration and contempt. Even Wendl's image of her as the Mother of God
is a projection of his own imagination and is entirely unfounded by anything the woman does. When Wendl at the end of the play cries out for the
Mother of God to help him and then begs the woman to stay, she leaves,
mildly smiling at him, demonstrating the discrepancy between Wendl's
fantasies and the reality of the play. Thus, by dramatizing the making of a
myth, Mitterer reveals its inadequacy and takes it apart. The message of the

play can also be expressed in wider terms: As long as women are deprived of the right to develop their own vision of what they are and what they want to be and do, there will not be any real understanding and partnership between the sexes.

Although the two plays *Stigma* and *The Wild Woman* are set in situations which at first seem to be archaic and quite far away from our contemporary reality, they nonetheless analyze social structures and patterns of behavior and interpersonal relationships that are highly relevant to the contemporary audience. In *The Female Criminal (Die Verbrecherin)*, one of Mitterer's four one-act plays in the collection *Visiting Hours (Besuchszeit)*, he focuses on a couple of our time. The wife tries to kill her husband by stabbing him with a kitchen knife in cold blood. This act of violence is the only way for her to free herself from the role of being housewife, mother, and employee that is imposed on her by her husband and the traditional gender-specific role expectations, a burden that she is not able to carry anymore. This is not a crime of passion, but the inevitable release of pent-up aggressions and frustrations that have been festering in her subconscious for a long time. The woman is so much alienated from her own inner feelings, however, that she cannot understand her deed (for example pp. 20 and 23).

The husband and the wife come together when he visits her in jail. In the conversation they have during this encounter, the wife's motivation for her deed is brought to the surface and becomes understandable to the audience, but not to the characters in the play. This is probably the first really meaningful conversation they have had in a long time. Thus the deed has brought them together in some way, but it also seals their ultimate separation. As the woman says herself: "There's no hope for us, Kurt. We'll never come together again. The knife will always be between us."[26] The fact that she had to resort to an act of violence, which they both do not accept but condemn completely, prevents them from coming together again. But it also reflects how much they have been alienated from each other during their marriage. The woman gives a vivid description of her monotonous and oppressive life that had become meaningless to her (pp. 21-25). Her love for her husband had slowly faded away as family life had only meant to her the performance of strenuous duties as housewife and servant of husband and children. Even though she also had a job, it was her task to take care of the children and do all the housework. Moreover, she felt abused by her husband because he took it for granted that she waited on him and he took all his anger and frustrations out on her: "And you always dumped everything onto me. I had to pay for your every aggravation."[27] They did not even spend their leisure time together since he had his own separate social life with his peers bowling, sauna and drinking (p. 24).

While the play clearly indicates that their problem is a gender issue with general social implications and relevancy, the woman and even more so her husband have so deeply internalized the code of the traditional gender roles that they perceive the fact that she was not able or willing anymore to endure such a life (which is considered normal by many people) as her private and individual failure that she alone has to be blamed for. How much the husband is trapped in the specific set of gender-linked norms is revealed by his reaction to his wife's deed. What offends him most is the fact that he is now considered a "softy" by his peers and also by himself (p. 24). The image of a wife almost killing her husband completely contradicts the traditional conception of the gender roles according to which the man is the one who has to show physical strength and must never let the woman get the upper hand in their relationship. Male superiority, which is entirely founded on physical strength, is also his main argument in a letter to the editor in which he threatens and insults the "feminists" ("Emanzen") (p. 27) whom he blames for instigating the women to rebel against the men and patriarchal society. This letter is an outlet for his aggressions, which clearly have a Fascist tendency (pp. 27-28). By directing his anger and rage at the feminists he avoids the painful and shaking confrontation with the causes of his wife's deed which would threaten his own identity and his outlook on life. Toward the end of their encounter, however, it becomes obvious that he also suffers greatly from their alienation. He confesses that despite the events he still likes his wife, that he feels lonely and misses her, and that he cannot cope with his present situation living together with his mother and his children with whom he does not get on well. He even admits that he has also made mistakes: "Often I hate you—and how! And I want you despite everything; I miss you. But I don't understand you. Sure, I made some mistakes, I admit that."[28] But the knife as a symbol of the wounds they have inflicted on each other will forever separate them. By illustrating that life in the patriarchal family with its traditional norms of role behavior does not do justice to either partner and ultimately causes their suffering, Mitterer tries to provoke the theatergoers to change their own situation.

The male type who plays an important part in many of Mitterer's plays is the macho. These men are constantly striving for dominance over females and males and they contribute to the atmosphere of violence and competition not only between men and women, but also among men. Some of these men, like the husband in *The Female Criminal*, suffer from the role they feel they have to play, but they do not have the courage to break out of their behavioral patterns. Most of these men, however, have a special interest in maintaining the traditional gender-specific roles because they derive their feeling of self-assurance and their identity from the privileged and domineering position this traditional pattern guarantees them. Macho behavior in Mitterer's plays can be characterized by the effort to display what these men perceive as virile qualities. They are reckless, boastful, and always seeking opportunities to compete with others, thus trying to prove their physical strength, power, and superiority. Ruepp in *Stigma* is a representative of this type, as is Lex in *The Wild Woman*. Mitterer himself says about these young men:

> I was never a macho first of all because I was such a shy boy from the country who was afraid of other people all the time. Especially in Tyrol we also have these supermen and that mainly refers to mountain climbing and skiing: running up a mountain within two hours when others need six; I have always been utterly disgusted by this. And I also hated these regular drinking sessions.... As soon as a woman enters they start this courting behavior. You have to impress and show off. I always found that highly unpleasant....[29]

In the play *Munde* Mitterer portrays one of these Tyrolean "supermen." Like Lex in *The Wild Woman*, Gerhard creates a tense and aggressive atmosphere which in the end leads to a tragedy. He turns the outing of the five employees of a roofing company, who climb up the mountain "Munde," into a serious competition. Like the group in *The Wild Woman*, these people are isolated on the summit of the mountain, thus being inextricably exposed to each other's attacks. What may have been planned as an enjoyable social activity by the majority of the group is from the beginning perceived by Gerhard as a competitive enterprise. As it turns out later he has tried to impede the others by putting heavy stones into their backpacks. The order in which the five colleagues reach the summit does not primarily reflect their physical fitness, but rather their urge to compete and their need to prove themselves by outdoing the others. Gerhard of course reaches the summit first, having left his girlfriend Petra far behind. He is followed by the apprentice Tommi, who is torn between being put off by Gerhard's behavior and trying to emulate him in order to win his recognition. The third one to arrive is Willi, the oldest and the master craftsman, who is respected by the others—except by Gerhard—because of his position, his human qualities, and his technical skill. The secretary Petra and the Turkish worker Memet reach the summit last. Petra, who had not voted for this strenuous activity in the first place, is totally exhausted and Memet, who has helped her up, had been burdened with the heaviest load by the others, sign of the lowest position in the social pecking order. Mitterer characterizes his figures not only by what they say, but also by their outfit and the kind of liquor they drink, as these are indicative of their attitudes and the image they want to create of themselves. Gerhard, who wears the fanciest outfit and drinks what he considers "hard" liquor, namely whiskey, dismisses Tommi's Bacardi rum as "women's drink" ("Weibergsöff") (p. 239). He provokes the others by silly strong-arm stuff and makes fun of anything that to his mind is a sign of weakness or clumsiness. He does not care at all about the fact that Petra is angry, but expresses his contempt for her by calling her a stupid cow (p. 243). The main target of his jibes is of course

Memet, the foreigner, who as an "intruder" does not have the right to be different: "You have to adapt now that you are here!"[30] When Memet rejects the pork sausages, he forces him to "adapt" by secretly putting them into his soup, which causes Memet to vomit (pp. 253-255).

The "supermen" in Mitterer's plays, with their urge always to dominate, their contempt for "weakness" and anything that deviates from their normality, and with their racist and xenophobic tendencies, show many features that Theodor W. Adorno has described as typical of the authoritarian personality.[31] While these men jibe at others all the time, they are very easily offended once their image is threatened. When Gerhard is criticized not only by his colleagues, but also by his girlfriend, he starts to behave even more aggressively. He has a tense and competitive relationship with each of the men, but as it turns out his main antagonist is Willi. Gerhard envies Willi his job as a master and he challenges his authority. He has successfully ingratiated himself with his boss because he wants to take Willi's place. The argument between the two culminates in Gerhard's disclosure that the boss, another of these "supermen," thinks that Willi is too old, has become unfit for the job, and that he wants to get rid of him. This news completely shatters Willi; it deprives him of his pride as a craftsman and his human dignity and makes his life seem worthless. Even though Petra reveals the motives for the boss's decision, which do not have anything to do with Willi's skills, and Memet shows his great respect for his master, Willi in the course of the evening on the summit disappears in the dark, presumably to commit suicide. This development arouses Memet's aggressions against Gerhard and now that this person, whom he admired and respected, has been destroyed by Gerhard, he finds the courage to challenge him (pp. 266-271). He provokes him by telling him that he has slept with Petra, thus threatening Gerhard's sexuality; this leads to a fight between the two in which Gerhard is defeated. Memet does not kill him, but for once Gerhard is the one who feels fear of death and whose ego is shattered. Thus the power relations have been changed at the end of the play. It is questionable, however, if those who have challenged the power structures will have any impact once they are back in their everyday circumstances.

Like Gerhard in *Munde,* the other supermen in Mitterer's plays are counteracted by anti-types of the macho. These male figures represent—as Methlagl puts it—"das Anders-Männliche" (the other-male)[32] and by being different in their attitudes and their behavior they arouse the aggressions of the "supermen." They do not conform to the image of the strong and boastful male, but overstep the narrow boundaries of what is considered typically male or virile behavior by their antagonists. Often these men are still quite young and have not been entirely initiated into the male community with its specific code of behavior. The junior farm-hand Seppele in *Stigma,* Wendl in *The Wild Woman,* and to a lesser extent Tommi in *Munde* are representatives of this young anti-type. These men are understanding and considerate and they show feelings of gentleness and vulnerability, traits that are contemptuously dismissed as effeminate by the machos. Wendl cries when he is viciously bullied by the other men and even Tommi shows that he has been offended by being excluded from a photograph that was taken of all the other roofers and that will be discovered again in a hundred years' time when the church will be roofed again (p. 260). Especially Seppele and Wendl are sensitive toward their own and other people's feelings and thus they identify with those who are victimized. The plays reveal that in reality these men are much stronger and more courageous than the "supermen" as they are willing to be on the side of the outsiders and underprivileged. Seppele is the only one who protests when Moid is bound to a chair before the exorcism, and in the end he is even willing to sacrifice his life for her. Wendl tries to free the woman from her chains, thus provoking a beating from Lex. As shown above Memet, an outsider himself, is another example of someone who is willing to show solidarity.

The representatives of the "other-male" violate the strict gender-specific roles in yet another way. They take on jobs that in the traditional patriarchal family are allocated to the domain of the women. Wendl does the housework in the lumberjacks' hut and Memet does not mind doing his own laundry, which surprises Petra (pp. 257-258). The old man in *No Place for Idiots* takes care of the retarded boy who has been neglected by his parents, and he supports and promotes him emotionally and intellectually. But an old man successfully trying to replace father and mother threatens the image of the intact patriarchal family and that inevitably brings him into conflict with the authorities. The doctor firmly states that "a child belongs in a family or to a woman."[33]

As we have seen, Mitterer in his plays is very much concerned with the situation of women and the state of gender relationships in our society. Like other authors of the critical *Volksstück*, he calls into question the norms and behavioral patterns that are engendered in the nuclear family and that reflect the structures of patriarchal society with its specific power relations. The circumstances in which most of his characters live are still patriarchal; Mitterer's point of view, however, is clearly anti-patriarchal. More explicitly than other authors of this genre he marks the problems in interpersonal relationships as clearly gender linked, thus challenging the stereotype of male and female behavior and its treatment in literature. As this analysis has illustrated, the gender problem is not at all exclusively seen as a women's, but also as a men's issue.[34] Some of Mitterer's characters, both male and female, try to break out of the "gender trap," to transgress the limitations of the role imposed on them, and thus hint at possible ways of liberation. But in the context of the plays these figures do not really succeed. Lacking in Mitterer's plays is the portrayal of women and men who have successfully freed themselves from the restrictions imposed on them by male-dominated society and who have intruded into those spheres traditionally occupied by members of the other sex. But such alternative role models would be quite removed from the experience of the people Mitterer wants to reach with his plays. Moreover, the presentation of solutions would not comply with the author's dramatic intention. He wants the audience to analyze the relations presented on stage as part of their own reality, or at least to recognize their relevancy to their own situation and turn their anger and rage about the suffering into positive action leading to change.

Notes

1. "Ihr Frauen habts es nit leicht."

2. See Beth Bjorklund, "A Gender-linked Genre? Or Why Women Do Not Write *Volksstücke.*" *Modern Austrian Literature,* 26 (1993), No. 3/4, pp. 129-142.

3. See Ursula Hassel and Deirdre McMahon, "Interview mit Felix Mitterer," in *Das zeitgenössische deutschsprachige Volksstück. Akten des internationalen Symposions, University College Dublin, 28. Februar—2. März 1991,* ed. Ursula Hassel and Herbert Herzmann, Stauffenburg Colloquium, 23 (Tübingen: Stauffenburg, 1992), p. 294. First published as "Felix Mitterer im Gespräch mit Ursula Hassel und Deirdre McMahon. 19. November 1988," *Modern Austrian Literature,* 25 (1992), No. 1, pp. 19-39.

4. See Hassel and McMahon, p. 293: "Ich beschreibe halt diese Frauenfiguren, damit die Zuschauer, die noch so traditionell verhaftet sind, denken: 'So dürfte das mit uns nicht weitergehen. Ja, so lebe ich auch, und so sollte ich nicht leben. Ich leide darunter, und ich weiß es.' Ich beschreibe ja die Wirklichkeit, wie sie ist, manchmal sogar auf extreme Weise, wie sie seltener ist, um die Menschen anzuregen, darüber nachzudenken, ob sich in diesem Fall die Beziehung zwischen den Geschlechtern nicht endlich ändern sollte, daß sie gerechter wird und partnerschaftlicher. Das ist meine Intention."

5. The plays this essay will focus on are the following: *Stigma. Eine Passion* (Feldafing/Obb.: Friedl Brehm, 1983); *Die Wilde Frau. Ein Stück* (München: Friedl Brehm, 1986); *Verbrecherin,* in *Besuchszeit. Vier Einakter* (München: Friedl Brehm, 1985) pp. 17-30; *Munde,* in *Stücke 2* (Innsbruck: Haymon, 1992), pp. 231-273; *Kein Platz für Idioten. Volksstück in drei Akten* (München: Friedl Brehm, 1979). The page references will be integrated into the text and refer to these editions.

6. See Thomas E. Bourke, "'Der muß weg!' Ausgrenzungsmuster in den kritischen Heimatstücken aus dem bayerischen und österreichischen Raum," in *Das zeitgenössische deutschsprachige Volksstück. Akten des internationalen Symposions, University College Dublin, 28. Februar—2. März 1991,* ed. Ursula Hassel and Herbert Herzmann, Stauffenburg Colloquium, 23 (Tübingen: Stauffenburg, 1992), pp. 247-260.

7. "Die Opfer sind 'die Anderen' [sic]. Und diese 'Anderen'—die Außenseiter, die Ausgestoßenen—sind ein durchgehendes Thema meiner literarischen Arbeit. Ein großer Teil der Menschen hat ständig Angst vor 'den Anderen', hegt ständig Aggressionen gegen sie, ganz gleich, auf welche Art sie anders sind (und es beginnt ganz harmlos): andere Frisur, andere Kleidung, anderes Gehabe, andere Neigungen, andere Ansichten, andere Sprache, andere Hautfarbe, andere Religion, andere

Sitten und Gebräuche." *Kein Schöner Land. Ein Theaterstück und sein historischer Hintergrund* (Innsbruck: Haymon, 1987), p. 91.

8. "Die Aggression gegen das Weibliche als das schlechthin andere." Walter Methlagl, "Zu Felix Mitterer: 'Die wilde Frau,'" in *Die Wilde Frau. Ein Stück*, by Felix Mitterer (München: Friedl Brehm, 1986), p. 78.

9. See Hassel and McMahon, p. 293: "Es beginnt damit, daß wir zeigen, sie ist die Allerletzte von allen. Sie steht unter allen. Unter dem letzten Knecht kommt noch sie, die Magd." Moid's low status is also reflected in the payment: She gets even less than Seppele, the somewhat retarded male junior farm-hand (p. 44).

10. "Lauter Dienstboten! Und da soll ma a Gschäft machen! Wenns nach mir gang, dürften die gar nit kommen, aber der Herr Pfarrer ..." (p. 41).

11. See Uta Treder, *Von der Hexe zur Hysterikerin. Zur Verfestigungsgeschichte des 'Ewig Weiblichen,'* Abhandlungen zur Kunst-, Musik- und Literaturwissenschaft, 345 (Bonn: Bouvier, 1984), pp. 3-11. Treder gives a short historical overview of the image and perception of women as witches and hysterics through the centuries and examines their treatment in selected works of prose fiction of the second half of the nineteenth century. Mitterer himself has devoted a play to the topic of witch-hunt. In *Die Kinder des Teufels* he focuses on the biggest witch trial in Europe in the seventeenth century: *Die Kinder des Teufels. Ein Theaterstück und sein historischer Hintergrund* (Innsbruck: Haymon, 1989).

12. *Mit tiefer Verachtung und Bitterkeit* (p. 80).

13. "Omnia mala ex mulieribus! Alles Schlechte kommt von den Weibern!" (p. 82).

14. "Ein unschuldiges Gotteskind" and "eine Heilige" (p. 82).

15. "Und was die Dämonen anbelangt, so beweist des gar nix! Jeder von uns, jeder Mensch hat Dämonen in sich! Man braucht sie nur zu wecken! Und manchmal, denk i ma, is so a Dämon gar nix Teuflisches, gar nix Schlechtes, sondern nur unsere Sehnsucht nach Freiheit! Der Monsignore Pfötscher sollt des am besten wissen. Aber er wills nit wissen, er wills nit wahrhaben! Und deswegen bist du exkommuniziert, Moidele" (pp. 90-93). See also Mitterer's own statement about the Catholic exorcism in the "Programmheft" for *Stigma* for the *Jura Soyfer Theater Linz* and the *Vereinigte Bühnen Graz* 1987 quoted by Deirdre McMahon, "The Resurrection of the Passion Play: Remarks on Felix Mitterer's *Stigma, Verlorene Heimat* and *Kein schöner Land*," in *Das zeitgenössische deutschsprachige Volksstück. Akten des internationalen Symposions, University College Dublin, 28. Februar—2. März 1991*, ed. Ursula Hassel and Herbert Herzmann, Stauffenburg Colloquium, 23 (Tübingen: Stauffenburg, 1992), p. 243.

16. See Mitterer's own statement about Moid: "sie ist eigentlich eine sehr starke Persönlichkeit mit sehr viel Kraft ... Dann wird sie plötzlich dadurch, daß sie die Wunden Christi bekommt, zu etwas ganz Besonderem und wird so zu einer Figur, die vom Volk verehrt wird und die Mut gibt. Sie ist auch die, die die Welt auffordert, dem Wort Christi wirklich zu folgen, Gerechtigkeit zu üben." Hassel and McMahon, p. 293.

17. "Ich will, daß auf dieser Welt Gerechtigkeit herrscht, und nit erst im Himmel!" (p. 43).

18. See also Bourke, p. 260.

19. "Von Rechts wegen is er [Much] heut dran!" (p. 289).

20. "Du ghörst nit ihm! Du ghörst uns alle!" (p. 47).

21. "Wennst nit willst, Frau, nacha laß ma's bleiben. Es muaß ja nit sein ... Is ja schon fein, wenn i bei dir liegen derf. Du bist so warm, Frau! So schön warm! Wenn i bei dir lieg, tuan meine alten Knochen nimmer weh, und i kimm ma vor wia a Kindl, des bei seiner Muatter liegt. Hatt ma nit denkt, daß i so was noamal erleben derf. Dafür dank i dir, Frau" (p. 57).

22. Excerpts from these legends can be found in the edition of *Die Wilde Frau* by Friedl Brehm Verlag, pp. 68-76.

23. See Mike Rogers, "'Nie sah ich einen dummen Jungen geistreicher darge-stellt!' Zur 'Dummheit'-Problematik bei Felix Mitterer," in *Das zeitgenössische deutschsprachige Volksstück. Akten des internationalen Symposions, University College Dublin, 28. Februar—2. März 1991*, ed. Ursula Hassel and Herbert Herzmann, Stauf-fenburg Colloquium, 23 (Tübingen: Stauffenburg, 1992), pp. 262-266.

24. *Als ob sie wüßte, daß ihr in Wahrheit nichts, gar nichts passieren kann* (p. 52).

25. See Angelika Führich, *Aufbrüche des Weiblichen im Drama der Weimarer Republik. Brecht - Fleißer - Horváth - Gmeyner*, Reihe Siegen: Beiträge zur Literatur-, Sprach- und Medienwissenschaft, 109 (Heidelberg: Carl Winter, 1992), pp. 1-12.

26. "Es hilft alles nix, Kurt. Wir kommen nie mehr zamm. Da is immer des Messer zwischen uns" (p. 29).

27. "Und alles abgladen auf mi. Jeden Ärger von dir hab i büßen müssen" (p. 24).

28. "Oft haß i di. Und wia i di haß! Und trotzdem mag i di. Und du gehst mir ab. Aber i versteh di nit. I versteh di nit. Aber sicher hab i a Fehler gmacht. Des gib i schon zua" (p. 29). Mitterer says about this couple: "man merkt eigentlich, wenn dieser Mann und diese Frau miteinander reden, wie beide darunter leiden, nicht nur sie, sondern auch er, daß er der 'Mann' sein muß, das Familienoberhaupt sozusagen, und daß es vielleicht viel schöner wäre, wenn sie gleichberechtigte Partner wären, daß dann das Leiden auf beiden Seiten weniger wäre." Hassel and McMahon, p. 293.

29. "Ich war nie ein Macho, schon deshalb nicht, weil ich so ein schüchterner Bub vom Land war, der also ständig vor allen Menschen Angst gehabt hat. Beson-ders bei uns in Tirol gibt es auch diese Supermänner, und das bezieht sich vor allem auf Bergsteigen und Schifahren: also in zwei Stunden auf den Berg rennen, wo andere sechs brauchen; mich hat das eigentlich immer fürchterlich angekotzt. Und diese ganzen Stammtischrunden waren mir auch zuwider ... Sobald eine Frau eintritt, kommt dieses gockelhafte Gebaren auf: Man muß imponieren und sich präsentieren. Das war mir immer höchst unangenehm...." Hassel and McMahon, pp. 293-294.

30. "Ihr habts euch gefälligst anzupassen, wenn ihr daseids!" (p. 251).

31. See Theodor W. Adorno, *The Authoritarian Personality* (New York: Harper, 1950).

32. Methlagl, p. 78. See also Bourke, pp. 259-260.

33. "A Kind ghört in a Familie oder zu oana Frau" (p. 63).

34. This is an aspect that Bjorklund misses in the contemporary *Volksstück*. See Bjorklund (pp. 137).

Timely Meditations or Not Yet!
Social Criticism in Felix Mitterer's
Siberia

Gerd K. Schneider

> "Alas," said the mouse, "the world is growing smaller every day. At first
> it was so big that I was afraid. I ran on and I was glad when at last I saw
> walls to the left and right of me in the distance, but these walls are closing
> in on each other so fast that I have already reached the end room, and
> there in the corner stands the trap that I am heading for." "You only have
> to change direction," said the cat, and ate it up.[1]

Kafka's *Little Fabel* (*Kleine Fabel*) surely has many interpretations. Personally
I consider this little masterpiece a *Lebenslauf*, or a *curriculum vitae*. The
mouse (or man) is faced in youth with an almost unlimited amount of
space and time; the many possibilities one has are almost frightening. Later
in life, one can see the faint outlines of the two walls which we cannot
escape: space and time. First we run towards them, but then this activity is
reversed—they come toward us, picking up speed and confronting us.
Finally the inevitable happens; man is devoured by the cat or death.

Another story depicts the fate of prisoners in the Middle Ages. One of
the punishments devised by the captors was to put them in a cell which, at
first, provided ample space for their activities. As time went on, the prisoners noticed that the ceiling was lowered somewhat and that the walls had
moved toward them. This reduction of space continued little by little, until
there was only enough room left to crawl, then to sit on the bed; in the end
they were crushed.

In both narratives, one fiction and the other real, man could not change
directions because to do so is not permitted to mortals. Time is spent waiting, waiting for death. Common to the mouse in Kafka's fable and the prisoners in their shrinking cell is that the characters are two dimensional—

they only live in the past and the present. Both have no future. This is exactly the fate of old people or, as they are sometimes called, seniors, the protagonists in Felix Mitterer's *Siberia*.

Siberia is based on a one-act play *Abstellgleis* (*Siding*) which was performed together with three other one-act plays under the title *Besuchszeit* (*Visiting Hours*) in Vienna in 1985. Another source for *Siberia* is the documentary report by Magdalena Stöckler who worked as a nurse in an Austrian Senior Citizen's Home. This report is contained in *Arbeit mit alten Menschen* (*Work with Old People*), which mentions the following:

> It is démodé to speak about the dignity of old age. This is a concept which is about to disappear, just like so much else. This seems to be superfluous, young people think, who do not know or realize that dignity is something precious for people who are getting old and have, as a consequence, painfully given up so much. These young people do not realize that they themselves will desperately need this dignity when they are old. Otherwise the young would not deny this dignity to the old.[2]

In addition to this generational conflict based on a misunderstanding between old and young, there seems to be a basic fear of old age in the young. "The old man in a crib," this report continues, "covered with excrement, confused, slobbering, is looked upon as a disfiguration of human life. He is the apparition of one's own potential future, releasing so much anxiety that it mobilizes archaic forms of defense and conquest from the earliest childhood: *the destruction of the threatening*."[3] This destruction of the threatening can take on many forms, and euthanasia as it was practiced in the Third Reich is probably the most radical of them. One is afraid of becoming old, and the old person is just like a mirror in which one recognizes oneself with all the physical and psychological shortcomings old age brings. Norbert Elias states that our feelings of self-control (*Selbstkontrollen*) "are experienced like a real existing wall"[4] and Günter Hennecke, in his review of the Zurich performance, suggests we erect "seelische Gummiwände" or "emotional rubber walls"[5] to separate us from the seniors we don't want to see.

The senior in Mitterer's monologue play *Siberia* spends the last days of his life in an old-age home. This old-age home is a waiting chamber for death, a chamber whose ceiling and walls are closing in on him, more every day. This old man is not an easy person; he tends to be querulous and he complains a lot. He knows that he is a bother to those around him when he admits:

> I know I'm hopeless.
> I'm just pig headed.
> A pig-headed sonofabitch.
> It happens at my age.
> We all get that way here.
> It's frightening.[6]

To call him a 'man' or 'person' actually is a misnomer because he is not treated as one; in this place (ironically called home) he is a dehumanized object, an object which has been shelved and forgotten.

The dramatic monologue is divided into five stages which show the increasing disintegration of the old man. First we see him on his crutches which enable him to get across the space still allotted to him. Then he literally hangs in a walking scaffolding which allows him still a little mobility in his rapidly deteriorating condition. After that his bed becomes his living space; he is still permitted to sit on top of his bed and is still able to swing his legs. Even this mobility is lost in the fourth stage where he is shown *in* bed—hardly able to turn over. In the final scene he is shown immobile, covered up in the bed from which he will never get up. In all these phases he speaks with imaginary persons; three of these dramatic monologues are directed to his daughter-in-law, one to his son, and the last one to the President of the Republic who has "come" because the old man had written an urgent letter. He speaks, probably not so much because he hopes for an improvement of his present condition, but because speaking is proof of his existence, an act of self-preservation. As he explains to his son: "I'm more outspoken [than you]. Otherwise I'd rot" (p. 43).

As the title *Siberia* suggests, the old man is surrounded by cold, chill and indifference. However, Siberia also means to him something that happened in his past. He was deported to this region as a prisoner of war. He now compares these "two" Siberias:

My second deportation.
The second deportation in my life.
The first was to Siberia.
As a prisoner of war.
The second was here, to this "home"!
Just like Siberia! (p. 30)

The second "deportation" was done at the wish of his daughter-in-law who feels that she is incapable of looking after him after he has broken his hip. Both Siberias differ in one important aspect, however; in the first Siberia there was hope to get out, now there is no such hope. In the first deportation he could still envision a future and plan for it by learning, for example, Russian; now there is no future and therefore no need to prepare for it. Things do not get better now—they only get worse as the diminution of powers progresses and the physical shortcomings multiply at an ever-increasing rate.

There are many shortcomings in old age. One of them is that the seniors have to wear diapers because of deteriorating body functions. This is the case with his neighbor, whose dignity suffers as a result:

That one over there
doesn't open his mouth anymore.
Won't say a word.
When the nurse went to feed him

he'd only open his mouth a little.
So she hit him with a spoon.
No luck.
So she hit him again!
It didn't help.
He was so humiliated
when they have to wash him
and put a diaper on him, too.
It's not like that with me.
. . . .
I [still can][7] go to the can by myself,
I don't crap in my diapers. (p. 40)

This "still," however, is indicative of the time to come, when he, too, will be treated like the person he just described. Toward the end, when the president and his wife "visit" him, he has reached this stage:

I must appear pretty helpless to you
right?
It isn't easy.
I crap in my diapers
which, I hope, doesn't bother you.
Just hold your nose,
Madame. (p. 61)

There is another passage in the text which also suggests that with the passing of time things get worse. It is a black humor joke circulating in the nursing home which Mitterer found in the documentary report written by the nurse Stöckler; he inserted this piece into his play as follows:

I'll tell you a joke;
you hear it around here all the time.
A clown performs at an old folks' home.
He looks through the curtain and says:
Is everybody here?
Yes,
scream the patients.
But not for long,
screams the clown. (p. 51)

The old man tries to keep this "but not for long" away as long as possible. He has a strong will to live and he uses it to fight against the conditions existing in this place. This fight Mitterer sometimes indicates through carefully chosen words, as for instance with the word *durchbeißen* which literally means "to bite through" but has the idiomatic meaning of "to fight one's way through." In the following passage Mitterer moves very quickly from the abstract to the concrete in combining these two levels; this, unfortunately, is not shown in the English translation. The German text reads:

Aber ich beiß mich schon durch.
Schau, ich hab noch meine Zähne! (p. 51)

The rendering into English is:
> But I'm hanging in.
> I still have my own teeth! (p. 39)

"Hanging in" is too passive a state for this struggling old man, and probably "I am fighting it out" would be a better description of his character. This passage informs us further that this old man is still allowed to retain his dentures overnight, whereby the most important word again is "still":
> They took everybody's teeth away.
> That way they don't have to clean them.
> More work.
> Overtime.
> Think about it:
> cleaning sixty dentures.
> No, double that, uppers and lowers.
> A hundred and twenty dentures to clean!
> It's not possible, you can see that.
> But I still have mine, you see.
> The successful outcome of my bribery.
> But for how much longer?
> I don't have any more money.
> You've got it now. (pp. 39-40)

Briberies are customary in this senior citizens' home. The nurses do everything for money. They let the old men retain their dentures or they expose their breasts for them; for a little more the inmates are even allowed to touch the breasts. Once the savings of the old people are used up, the strip show is over, and this is what the old man is afraid of. Then the dehumanizing process accelerates; the troublemakers are isolated in a special section from which they do not emerge again until after their death— sometimes two in a cheap coffin which saves labor and capital. That the old discarded people become associated with old discarded furniture is indicated when the old man is told that his son has no time to visit him. The reason: he has to work so that he can pay off the newly acquired furniture. The response of the old man is:
> New furniture? New furniture?
> Why new furniture? Is the old furniture broken?
> So what if it's old!
> It's my furniture
> and it's good furniture!
> Solid wood! (p. 22)

A society which throws still-functional furniture away also throws people away even if they are useful and functional. The reasons and attitudes underlying both actions are the same.

Only one being is left which makes his life worth living—his dog who is dearer to him than any other living being:

> God forgive me, but this dog
> was the most important thing in my life, next to my wife.
> The most important, really.
> Complete love.
> Complete trust.
> Complete fidelity.
> Without conditions.
> [That you don't find in man.] (p. 14)[8]

The love between the man and his dog is mutual; he loves this animal just as much as the animal cares for him. Unfortunately, the old man is not allowed to see his dog because regulations do not permit the inmates to have animals, a regulation the man does not understand:

> Why can't you bring your pets
> to a "home" like this?
> I'd take care of him,
> with pleasure!
> Then I'd have something to do. (p. 14)

Later on he urges his family to treat his dog well, an animal which is kind and understanding and which never did harm to people. However, something has happened now because he wants the dog to attack the "white coats" or nurses. This change of mind follows his realization that he has no funds left to pay the nurses for exposing their breasts (p. 41). The only love he now has is that between him and his little dog. In addition, the dog is the only being who would fight for him since his family refuses to do so:

> I'm warning you, you better treat my dog well!
> He doesn't know the meaning of the word "Attack."
> Nope.
> My dog doesn't know what "Attack" means,
> absolutely not!
> But now I'm ready!
> I'm ready and I could teach him:
> Attack!
> Attack the white uniforms!
> I've written
> to the Bundespresident. (p. 41)

This passage is commented on by Leopold Rosenmayr as follows:

> One can see very clearly how his love for the dog surfaces out of the frustrating realization that he will no longer be able to view the breasts. However, his wish to turn to his dog will not be fulfilled because he is not allowed to return home. This results in aggression. Until now he never had the idea to make the dog attack, but "now I'm ready!" He wants this animal, dear to him, to revenge him, the helpless old man, on the authorities of this hospital or "home," the "white coats." And just as he protests with the help of the dog, he appeals to the only reasonable authority for him, the President of the Republic.[9]

He writes him an (imaginary) letter in which he informs the highest authority of the country of the inhuman conditions existing in this place:

Please, more respect for the aged!
The residents are being
neglected,
drugged,
humiliated,
and beaten!
Locked in their cribs!
Stripped of their honor!
Severe shortages of staff!
Resulting in lack of care!
Stench clouds over the entire home!
Stench of the plague!
Stench of corpses!
Stench of the grave!
Come here and
see for yourself, Herr Bundespresident!
This is an S.O.S. call!! (p. 42)

When the old man finds out that his old dog was put to death, his will to live is broken. The fate of the dog and his own fate run parallel; they are both old (p. 13) and the old man also calls himself a "stubborn old dog" (p. 50). Because the dog was too old, did not eat anything and lost his hair, his usefulness was greatly reduced, and he was put to sleep.

To die peacefully is also desired by the old man when he speaks to his daughter-in-law:

Do you know what I want?
Help.
Help!
At least help me with this!
Help me to die!
Help me to die!
. . . .
What's left to do?
An exit!
A half-way decent exit. (p. 49)

This passage reminds us that in the Third Reich euthanasia, or geriatric cleansing, was practiced in old-age homes. The old man refers to this practice when he talks about his neighbor, a former SS man, who is now afraid that the same thing may happen to him that he had advocated as a young man:

Now I tell him about euthanasia!
I've convinced him
it's coming back.
For old folks!

Now he's afraid.
Now he's shitting in his pants.
. . . .
He was in favor of euthanasia!
As a young man.
As a handsome young soldier
with a death-skull on his cap.
You don't work, you don't have the right to exist!
No exceptions! (p. 45)

While the old man also sided with the young in their revolution against the old, he drew the line when his old father was concerned. He did not participate in the railing against the old, even if it meant trouble with the authorities. He was against "authority from nightsticks, authority at gun point" (p. 47). This included the order for racial segregation and racial annihilation, to consider the Jewish race inferior to the non-Jews. His wife Agnes was also Jewish, but when the order came to divorce her because of her race, he refused by reassuring her:

You're crazy,
I said.
I'll never divorce you
because of those goose-stepping bastards.
Absolutely not! (p. 45)

He not only refused to separate himself from his beloved Agnes, he also showed his acceptance of other people, regardless of race:

The German people!
What do I care about "the German people"?
People are people!
The Jewish tailor
who always gave us credit,
why does he suddenly become a criminal?
My dear Agnes,
why should she be worth any less
because of her heritage? (p. 47)

This attitude, more prominent in age than in his youth, leads him to regret having fought for the National Socialists:

It was for these pigs,
I'm ashamed to say,
that I went to war! (pp. 47-48)

At the end the old man takes leave of life with words directed to the president and his wife; these words are probably the most intimate, touching, and poetic words of the whole play:

You know, Mr. President,
Madame.
I used to sing every day

to keep
my body from shrinking.
But now I have to admit
the battle's over.
It's not death,
but the long, drawn-out process of dying
that frightens me.
Dying like this,
here,
and now.
If you don't mind
I'd like to be left alone now. (pp. 63-64)

Rosenmayr offers the following comment on this passage:

> With these words the play closes and with it the circle of disappointed
> hope and love. The man who became isolated after the death of his wife
> was unable to cope with his own descendants. He landed in a typical
> social institution, in an old-age home, under conditions which finally
> make him want his own lonely death instead of love.[10]

At the end of the Kafka parable quoted in the beginning, the cat said to
the mouse: "You only have to change directions." That the mouse cannot
do, just as the old man in Mitterer's play cannot turn the clock back. But it
may be said that at the end of Mitterer's play these words force themselves
upon the listener or the reader: You only have to change the direction of
your thinking. This can be done because we can all help to make the situation of the old people in the nursing homes a little more bearable than described in this play. That Mitterer's play is not too far from reality is quite
evident in the tragedy of the old-age home in Lainz where mercy killing of
old people took place after *Siberia* had been written. What is needed is to
change our attitude toward old age, to accept old people the way they are
even if they are as stubborn and pig-headed as shown in the old man. This
man also had these attributes in his youth; in his own way he was outspoken in his rejection of the Third Reich ideology at a time when it took
courage to do this. Now this desirable trait becomes a liability because
authorities of the nursing home demand total submission from the people
whom they should care for.

What we can do, so Mitterer seems to suggest, is to make it a little easi-
er on these old people so that their self-esteem, which is undermined by the
diminution of powers, does not suffer more because of rejection or human
indifference. Finally, a change of attitude toward old age will ultimately
benefit all of us, since the "you" in the following quote directed to the old
man's daughter-in-law could well be any one of us:

> Why are you crying?
> You don't have to cry.
> Stop it, you know I can't stand that,

or I'll wind up feeling sorry for you!
And that wouldn't be right, would it?
You don't have to die.
Not yet! (p. 50)

Notes

1. Franz Kafka, *Shorter Works*. Vol. I. Translated and edited by Malcolm Pasley (London: Secker & Warburg, 1973), p. 142.

2. Hilarion Petzold, Ed., "Die Verletzung der Alterswürde—zu den Hintergründen der Mißhandlung alter Menschen und zu den Belastungen des Pflegepersonals." In: *Mit alten Menschen arbeiten. Bildungsarbeit, Psychotherapie, Soziotherapie* (München: J. Pfeiffer, 1985), p. 553. The translation is mine. The original passage reads: "Von der 'Würde des Alters' zu sprechen ist eine demodierte Sache. Es ist dies ein Begriff, der im Verschwinden begriffen ist wie so vieles. Er scheint überflüssig geworden zu sein, finden die Jungen, die nicht wissen und auch nicht verstehen, daß bei den vielfältigen schmerzlichen Verlusten und Einbußen, die das Alter bringt, die Würde etwas Kostbares ist. Sie wissen nicht darum, daß auch sie im Alter die Würde einmal notwendig brauchen könnten. Sonst würden die Jungen den Alten die Würde nicht verweigern."

3. Hilarion Petzold, Ed., p. 558. The translation is mine. The original passage reads: "Der alte Mensch im Gitterbett, eingekotet, verwirrt, sabbernd, wird als Disfiguration des Menschlichen gesehen. Er ist das Gespenst eigener möglicher Zukunft, das so angstauslösend ist, daß es archaische Formen der Abwehr und Bewältigung aus der frühesten Kindheit mobilisiert, die *Vernichtung des Bedrohlichen*."

4. Norbert Elias, *Über die Einsamkeit der Sterbenden in unseren Tagen* (Frankfurt am Main: Suhrkamp, 1982), p. 86. The translation is mine. The original passage reads: "[Die Selbstkontrollen werden in diesen Gesellschaften häufig derart in die heranwachsenden Menschen eingebaut, daß] sie wie eine tatsächlich existierende Mauer erlebt werden."

5. Günther Hennecke, "Sprengkraft der Vergangenheit," *Neue Zürcher Zeitung*, 16 November 1989, Fernausgabe Nr. 266: 37.

6. Felix Mitterer, *Siberia and Other Plays. A Monologue*. Translated by Margit Kleinman and Louis Fantasia (Riverside: Ariadne: 1994), p. 25. All other quotes referring to the English translation of *Siberia* have been taken from this edition.

7. The translation omits the important *still* or the German *noch* ("Ich geh ja noch selber auf's Klo") of the German version, p. 52.

8. The translators did not translate the line supplied in square parentheses. The German version reads: "Das gibt es doch alles nicht beim Menschen" (Felix Mitterer, *Sibirien. Ein Monolog* (Innsbruck: Haymon-Verlag, 1989), p. 22.

9. Leopold Rosenmayr, *Die Kräfte des Alters* (Wien: Wiener Journal Zeitschriftenverlag Ges. m.b.H., Edition Atelier, 1990), p. 123. The translation is mine. The original passage reads: "Man sieht deutlich, wie aus der frustierten Lebenssituation, wonach es mit dem 'Busenschauen' nunmehr 'leider auch vorbei sei', die Liebe zum Hund zur Sprache kommt. Aber dieser Wunsch, sich dem Hund zuwenden zu können, wird dem Alten nicht erfüllt, weil man ihm verwehrt, nach Hause zurückzukehren. Daraus resultiert bei dem Alten Aggression. Noch nie sei er auf die Idee

gekommen, den Hund zum Angriff zu veranlassen: `Aber jetzt bin ich soweit!' Er will, daß dieses ihm nahestehende Tier ihn, den hilflosen alten Mann, gegenüber dem Spital- bzw. Heimsystem, `den weißen Kitteln' räche. Und so wie er mit Hilfe des Hundes aufbegehren will, so rekurriert er auch auf die oberste ihm noch einsehbare Macht, den Bundespräsidenten."

10. Rosenmayr, p. 124. The translation is mine. The original passage reads: "Damit endet das Stück, und so schließt sich der Kreislauf der enttäuschten Hoffnung und Liebe. Der nach dem Tod seiner Frau Vereinsamte konnte mit der eigenen Nachkommenschaftsfamilie nicht zu Rande kommen. Er landete in der typischen Institution der Gesellschaft, im Altenheim, unter Bedingungen, die ihn schließlich dazu bringen, sich statt Liebe einen einsamem Tod zu wünschen."

About the Contributors

Dr. **Gudrun Brokoph-Mauch is** Harriet Lewis Professor of German at St. Lawrence University, Canton, New York.

Dr. **Bernd Fischer** is Associate Professor of German at The Ohio State University, Columbus.

Dr. **Todd C. Hanlin** is Professor of German at the University of Arkansas, Fayetteville.

Ursula Hassel is a Lecturer in The Teaching Methodology of German As a Foreign Language at the University of Bonn, Germany.

Dr. **Herbert Herzmann** is Senior Lecturer in German at University College, Dublin, Ireland.

Dr. **Jutta Landa** is a Lecturer in German at the University of California at Los Angeles.

Dr. **Dagmar C. G. Lorenz** is Professor of German and a member of the Executive Board of the Melton Center for Jewish Studies at The Ohio State University, Columbus.

Dr. **Nicholas J. Meyerhofer** is Professor of German and Chair in the Department of Modern Languages at Northern Arizona University, Flagstaff.

Dr. **Jennifer E. Michaels** is Professor of German at Grinnell College, Grinnell, Iowa.

Dr. **Gerlinde Ulm Sanford** is Associate Professor of German Languages and Literatures at Syracuse University, Syracuse, New York.

Dr. **Gerd K. Schneider** is Professor of German Languages and Literatures at Syracuse University, Syracuse , New York.

Dr. **Helga Schreckenberger** is Associate Professor of German at the University of Vermont, Burlington.

Dr. **Karl E. Webb** is Professor of German and Humanities at Northern Arizona University, Flagstaff.

Index

ARIADNE PRESS
Studies in Austrian Literature, Culture and Thought

ARIADNE PRESS
Translation Series

February Shadows
By Elisabeth Reichart
Translated by Donna L. Hoffmeister
Afterword by Christa Wolf

Night Over Vienna
By Lili Körber
Translated by Viktoria Hertling
and Kay M. Stone

The Cool Million
By Erich Wolfgang Skwara
Translated by Harvey I. Dunkle
Preface by Martin Walser
Afterword by Richard Exner

*Farewell to Love and Other
Misunderstandings*
By Herbert Eisenreich
Translation and Afterword
by Renate Latimer

Professor Bernhardi and Other Plays
By Arthur Schnitzler
Translated by G.J. Weinberger

Negatives of My Father
By Peter Henisch
Translated by Anne C. Ulmer

On the Other Side
By Gerald Szyszkowitz
Translated by Todd C. Hanlin
Afterword by Jürgen Koppensteiner

*I Want to Speak
The Tragedy and Banality
of Survival in
Terezin and Auschwitz*
By Margareta Glas-Larsson
Edited and with a Commentary
by Gerhard Botz
Translated by Lowell A. Bangerter

The Works of Solitude
By György Sebestyén
Translated by Michael Mitchell

Remembering Gardens
By Kurt Klinger
Translated by Harvey I. Dunkle

Deserter
By Anton Fuchs
Translated by Todd C. Hanlin

From Here to There
By Peter Rosei
Translated and with an Afterword
by Kathleen Thorpe

The Angel of the West Window
By Gustav Meyrink
Translated by Michael Mitchell

*Relationships
An Anthology of Contemporary
Austrian Literature*
Selected by Adolf Opel

ARIADNE PRESS
Translation Series

ARIADNE PRESS
Translation Series

The Bengal Tiger
By Jeannie Ebner
Translation and Afterword
by Lowell A. Bangerter

The Condemned Judge
By Janko Ferk
Translation and Afterword
by Lowell A. Bangerter

Night Train
By Elfriede Mayröcker
Translation and Afterword
by Beth Bjorklund

Three Late Plays
By Arthur Schnitzler
Translated by G.J. Weinberger

The Slackers and Other Plays
By Peter Turrini
Translated by Richard S. Dixon

Five Plays
By Gerald Szyszkowitz

A Man Too White
By György Sebestyén
Translated by Michael Mitchell

The Baron and the Fish
By Peter Marginter
Translated by Lowell A. Bangerter

Krystyna
By Simon Wiesenthal
Translated by Eva Dukes

On the Wrong Track
By Milo Dor
Translation and Afterword
by Jerry Glenn

Unsentimental Journey
By Albert Drach
Translated by Harvey I. Dunkle

Reunion in Vienna
By Edith Foster
Afterword by H. von Weizsäcker

Return to the Center
By Otto von Habsburg
Translated by Carvel de Bussy

When Allah Reigns Supreme
By Susi Schalit

*Thomas Bernhard and His
Grandfather Johannes Freumbichler:
"Our Grandfathers Are Our
Teachers"*
By Caroline Markolin

*1938...and the Consequences
Questions and Responses*
By Elfriede Schmidt

ARIADNE PRESS
Autobiography, Biography, Memoirs Series